I0760114

OPERATION DESERT STORM

OPERATION DESERT STORM

HOW TWO YOUNG INTELLIGENCE ANALYSTS AND AN INFANTRY BATTALION CHANGED THE WAR IN IRAQ

FRANK HANCOCK

Pen & Sword
MILITARY
AN IMPRINT OF PEN & SWORD BOOKS LTD.
YORKSHIRE – PHILADELPHIA

First published in Great Britain in 2025 and reprinted in 2026 by
PEN AND SWORD MILITARY
An imprint of
Pen & Sword Books Limited
Yorkshire – Philadelphia

ISBN 978 1 03613 043 5

A CIP catalogue record for this book is available from the British Library.

Typeset in Times New Roman 10/13 by SJmagic DESIGN SERVICES, India.
Printed and bound in the UK by CPI Group (UK) Ltd, Croydon, CR0 4YY.

The Publisher's authorised representative in the EU for product safety is Authorised Rep Compliance Ltd., Ground Floor, 71 Lower Baggot Street, Dublin D02 P593, Ireland | www.arccompliance.com

For a complete list of Pen & Sword titles please contact

PEN & SWORD BOOKS LIMITED
George House, Units 12 & 13, Beevor Street, Off Pontefract Road,
Barnsley, South Yorkshire, S71 1HN, England
E-mail: enquiries@pen-and-sword.co.uk
Website: www.pen-and-sword.co.uk

or

PEN AND SWORD BOOKS
1950 Lawrence Rd, Havertown, PA 19083, USA
E-mail: uspen-and-sword@casematepublishers.com
Website: www.penandswordbooks.com

CONTENTS

Preface		vi
Glossary		viii
Contributors		xii
Prologue		xiv
Chapter 1	A Renaissance and Smashmouth Army	1
Chapter 2	The 101st Airborne Division (Air Assault)	11
Chapter 3	1st Battalion, 327th Infantry	16
Chapter 4	Deployment	32
Chapter 5	Operation DESERT SHIELD	48
Chapter 6	Covering Force	61
Chapter 7	Air Assault – The Plan	75
Chapter 8	Operation DESERT STORM	81
Chapter 9	Tactical Assembly Area CAMPBELL	89
Chapter 10	God Bless Thinking Soldiers	111
Chapter 11	G-2 to G-1	121
Chapter 12	G-Day	129
Chapter 13	FOB COBRA	145
Chapter 14	Surrender	162
Chapter 15	Task Force CITADEL	178
Chapter 16	G+1 to G+3 and Ceasefire	186
Chapter 17	Going Home	197
Chapter 18	Joint Readiness Training Center	205
Chapter 19	"All's Well That Ends Well"	210
Works Cited		216

PREFACE

On 2 August 1990, Iraq invaded its neighboring country Kuwait. The reason for the invasion was Iraq's debt to Kuwait. Kuwait had loaned money to Iraq during the 1980–88 Iran-Iraq War and, in 1990, Kuwait demanded its money back. Iraq invaded Kuwait instead. Iraq then moved its army to threaten an invasion of Saudi Arabia. A coalition of thirty-nine nations sent forces to protect Saudi Arabia from further aggression by Iraq.

DESERT SHIELD was the name given to the operation that protected Saudi Arabia. Its timeframe was 10 August 1990 to 17 January 1991. DESERT STORM was the name of the operation that would expel Iraqi forces from Kuwait and its time frame was 17 January to 28 February 1991. This book tells the story of 1-327 Infantry, a battalion of the 101st Airborne Division (Air Assault), and its participation in Operation DESERT SHIELD/DESERT STORM (DS/DS).

The genesis of this book dates from 1992/93. At the time, I was a student at the US Army War College and wrote my mandatory Strategic Research Paper on my experience as the commander of 1-327 Infantry in DS/DS. The paper was titled "North to the Euphrates, Part I: The Taking of FOB COBRA." In my paper, I explained the experience of the battalion and the lessons learned from that experience. The paper was used by several authors in their research and writing about the first day of DS/DS. 1-327 Infantry participated in the defense of Saudi Arabia but received notoriety on the first day of the ground war. 1-327 Infantry was the lead element of the ground invasion and participated in a consequential battle deep inside Iraq, for which it would be awarded the Valorous Unit Award.

To write the book, I asked several members of my battalion to assist me. The reader will see narratives from numerous contributors who added their perspectives to the 1-327 Infantry's story. The contributors range from privates to a retired 4-star general. The contributors were either members of the battalion or were associated with, or worked with, the battalion in DS/DS. The narratives are the contributors' own stories. I asked the contributors to do two things: "Tell **your** story of what happened" and "Tell the truth … warts and all." Each narrative is identified with the contributor's name and the position he held at the time of the battle.

There are also "Observations" throughout the book. These are distilled insights concerning what happened and why it happened. Contributors were asked to reflect on what happened and relate any lessons learned that they felt could be useful to future soldiers.

To assist in understanding the book a glossary of rank, unit sizes, staff positions and responsibilities, acronyms, and contributors are listed.

GLOSSARY

Enlisted Ranks

Private – PVT – enlisted soldier
Private First Class – PFC – enlisted soldier, outranks a private
Specialist – SPC – Outranks PVT and PFC – has been in the army three years or more
Sergeant – SGT – Section or Team Leader – Leads three to five soldiers
Staff Sergeant – SSG – Squad Leader – Leads nine to eleven soldiers
Sergeant First Class – SFC – Platoon Sergeant – Assists Platoon Leader in running a platoon (thirty soldiers)
Master Sergeant – MSG – Senior Staff Non-Commissioned Officer
First Sergeant – 1SG – Senior enlisted soldier in a Company (130 soldiers)
Command Sergeant Major – CSM – Senior enlisted soldier in battalion (700 soldiers), a Brigade (2,200 soldiers), or a Division (18,000 soldiers)

Officer Ranks

Warrant Officers – WO – Pilots or other specialty positions
2d Lieutenant – 2LT – Platoon Leader
1st Lieutenant – 1LT – Specialty Platoon Leader or Company Executive Officer
Captain – CPT – Company Commander or a staff officer
Major – MAJ – Staff officer
Lieutenant Colonel – LTC – Battalion Commander or staff officer
Colonel – COL – Brigade Commander or senior staff officer
Brigadier General – BG – One Star – Assistant Division Commander
Major General – MG – Two Stars – Division Commander
Lieutenant General – LTG – Three Stars – Corps Commander
General – GEN – Four Stars – Commander of Central Command

Battalion Staff Responsibilities

Executive Officer/XO – Responsible for coordinating the staff
S1 – Personnel matters – pay, promotions, transfers
S2 – Intelligence and Security
S3 – Operations and Plans
S4 – Logistics/Supply
Commo/Signal Officer
Chemical Officer
Chaplain
Maintenance

Unit Designations

Squad – 9 soldiers
Platoon – 35–40 soldiers
Company – 130 soldiers
Battalion – 700 soldiers
Brigade – 2,200 soldiers
Division – 18,000 soldiers
Corps – 50–60,000 soldiers
Army – 150,000 soldiers

Army Acronyms and Nicknames

AA – Assembly Area
AASLT – Air Assault
ABU – Nickname for A Company, 1-327 Infantry
AD – Armored Division
ADA – Air Defense Artillery
ADC (O) – Assistant Division Commander for Operations
ADC (S) – Assistant Division Commander for Support
AH1 – Attack Helicopter (Cobra)
AH64 – Attack Helicopter (Apache)
AO – Area of Operations
ARTEP – Army Training and Evaluation Program
Bastogne Bulldogs – Nickname of 1-327 Infantry
BCTP – Battle Command Training Program

BDE – Brigade
BN – Battalion
CAS – Close Air Support
CE II – Camp Eagle II
CENTCOM – United States Central Command (General Schwarzkopf's command)
CFA – Covering Force Area
CG – Commanding General
CH47 – Cargo Helicopter (Chinook)
CIB – Combat Infantryman Badge
CINC – Commander in Chief
C2 – Command and Control
CMTC – Combat Maneuver Training Center
CO – Commanding Officer
CONEX – Container Express
CONUS – Continental United States
CP – Command Post
CPX – Command Post Exercise
CTC – Combat Training Center
DISCOM – Division Support Command
DRB – Division Ready Brigade
DRF – Division Ready Force
DS – Direct Support
EA – Engagement Area
EDRE – Emergency Deployment Readiness Exercise
EIB – Expert Infantryman Badge
EPW – Enemy Prisoner of War
FA – Field Artillery
FAARP – Forward Area Arming and Refueling Point
FDC – Fire Direction Center
FIST – Fire Support Team
FLIR – Forward Looking Infrared Radar
FLOT – Forward Line of Troops
FM – Field Manual
FOB – Forward Operating Base
FORSCOM – US Army Forces Command
FRAGO – Fragmentary Order
FSO – Fire Support Officer
FTX – Field Training Exercise
HMMWV – High Mobility, Multipurpose, Wheeled Vehicle
ID – Infantry Division
JAG – Judge Advocate General

JCS – Joint Chiefs of Staff
JOTC – Jungle Operations Training Center
JRTC – Joint Readiness Training Center
KKMC – King Khalid Military City in Saudi Arabia
LZ – Landing Zone
MILES – Multiple Integrated Laser Engagement System
MLRS – Multiple Launch Rocket System
MRE – Meal, Ready to Eat
MSR – Main Supply Route
NBC – Nuclear, Biological, Chemical
NOE – Nap of the Earth
NOD – Night Observation Device
NTC – National Training Center
NVG – Night Vision Goggles
OH58 – Observation Helicopter (Kiowa)
OP – Observation Post
OPCON – Operational Control
OPFOR – Opposing Force
PB – Pyridostigmine Bromide (nerve agent pretreatment pill)
POW – Prisoner of War
PX – Post Exchange
PZ – Pickup Zone
RGFC – Republican Guard Forces Corps
RPG – Rocket Propelled Grenade
SAMS – School of Advanced Military Studies
Screaming Eagles – Nickname given to the 101st Airborne Division (Air Assault)
SITREP – Situation Report
SLGR – Small, Lightweight, GPS Receiver
SOP – Standing Operating Procedure
SWA – Southwest Asia
TAA – Tactical Assembly Area
TF – Task Force
TOW – Tube-launched, Optically-tracked, Wire-guided missile
UH1 – Utility Helicopter (Iroquois but called Huey)
UH60 – Utility Helicopter (Black Hawk)

CONTRIBUTORS

Stan Banach – Private First Class, Headquarters Company, Mortar Platoon, 1-327 Infantry

Frank Bills – Corporal, NBC NCO, 1-327 Infantry

Darcy Brewer – Captain, Commander, C Company, 1-327 Infantry

John Chappell – Major, Battalion Executive Officer, 1-327 Infantry

Dick Cody – Lieutenant Colonel, Battalion Commander, 1-101 Aviation

Jose Delgado – Captain, Battalion S2, 1-327 Infantry

Bruce Dittfield – Private First Class, Driver for Battalion CSM and Battalion Commander, 1-327 Infantry

Dave Esposito – 2d Lieutenant, 1st Platoon Leader, A Company, 1-327 Infantry

Tom Evans – 2d Lieutenant, Battalion NBC Officer, 1-327 Infantry

Patty George – 1st Lieutenant, Intelligence Officer 311 Military Intelligence Battalion

Al Gill – Captain, Commander, D Company, 1-327 Infantry

George Glaze – 1st Lieutenant, Support Platoon Leader, 1-327 Infantry

Jesus Gonzalez – Sergeant, Battalion S2 Intelligence Analyst, 1-327 Infantry

Tom Guleff – Captain, Battalion S1, 1-327 Infantry

Rich Hagedorn – Private First Class, Mortar Platoon, 1-327 Infantry

Frank Hancock – Lieutenant Colonel, Battalion Commander, 1-327 Infantry

Jeff Hawk – Sergeant, Truck Driver with VII Corps, Historian

CONTRIBUTORS

Jesse Hernandez – Private First Class, 3d Platoon, A Company, 1-327 infantry

Mike Huebner – 2d Lieutenant, 3d Platoon Leader, A Company, 1-327 Infantry

Matt Karres – 2d Lieutenant, 2d Platoon Leader, C Company, 1-327 Infantry

Mike Kloppenburg – Private First Class, 3d Platoon, A Company, 1-327 Infantry

Sung Lee – Captain, Battalion Signal Officer, 1-327 Infantry

Steve McFarland – Specialist, Driver for Battalion S3, 1-327 Infantry

Jim McGarity – Lieutenant Colonel, Executive Officer, 1st Brigade, 101st Airborne Division (Air Assault)

Larry Morato – Private First Class, D Company, 1-327 Infantry

Robert Nichols, Command Sergeant Major, 1st Brigade, 101st Airborne Division (Air Assault)

Jon Nordin – Private First Class, D Company, 1-327 Infantry

Linda Patterson – Civilian, Patriot from San Mateo, California

Chris Reed – Captain, Assistant S4, 1-327 Infantry

Bill Reister – Captain, US Air Force, Battalion Air Liaison Officer, 1-327 Infantry

Johnnie Riley – Command Sergeant Major, 1-327 Infantry

Ken Russell – Captain, Commander, A Company, 1-327 Infantry

John Santini – Captain, Battalion Assistant S1, 1-327 Infantry

Arthur (Butch) Schwoyer – First Sergeant, C Company, 1-327 Infantry

Gerry Tertychny – 1st Lieutenant, Executive Officer, A Company, 1-327 Infantry

PROLOGUE

Major Khadir

Iraqi Army Strong Point 100 miles north of the Saudi Arabian Border
2100 hours
21 February 1991
Three Days Before the Ground War Begins

Major Samir Ali Khadir commanded the 2d Battalion, 843d Brigade of the Iraqi 45th Infantry Division. This infantry battalion was comprised of reservists and was formed in August 1990. The battalion had a veteran cadre. Most of the men had fought in the eight-year Iran-Iraq War and a substantial number were wounded in that war. Major Khadir was one of those veterans and had been wounded twice.[1] Khadir took command of the 2d Battalion in December 1990. To assume command, he drove his personal car from his home to the battalion's position and left it there.[2]

The 2d Battalion had been assigned the mission of occupying a defensive trench line position 100 miles north of the Saudi Arabian border. The rationale for the trench line was the hard-surfaced road just to the north of it that ran east-west. Iraqi intelligence picked up indicators that the French 6th Light Armored Division was in the far western sector of Saudi Arabia. The French 6th Division consisted of motorized and armored vehicles. Iraqi intelligence analysts studied the geography of the area and concluded that the French would use the road north of Major Khadir's position for movement to the east. Iraqi intelligence was absolutely correct—the French planned to use the road as a major avenue to sweep east and flank Iraqi units in Kuwait and southern Iraq. Iraqi intelligence told Major Khadir that, because his position was 100 miles deep in Iraq, it would take the French column four days to get to his position once the expected ground war began. From his trench line position, and with his 344 men and 8 tons of ammunition, Major Khadir was in a very good position to slow down, if not temporarily stop, a French advance.

To make his defensive position more effective, Major Khadir took several measures to "hide" his unit. Despite having a trench line that was nearly a mile long and in an open desert, Major Khadir used deception methods to misdirect

Coalition intelligence analysts. Positioned on top of a large plateau, the Iraqis became miners and dug caves into the backside of the hill. Guns, ammunition, people, beds, TVs, and everything that would give away their position were placed in the caves. During daytime, no Iraqis would be visible and at night only minimum movement took place. Their four ZPU4 anti-aircraft weapons were hidden so as not to give away their position, and even their sanitary actions were restricted. No slit trenches or latrines were built so the trench line appeared to be empty. Indeed, at every echelon, Coalition intelligence analysts labeled this position as "unoccupied."[3] Major Khadir's deception efforts worked. Coalition intelligence analysts who looked at this position believed there was no one there.

As Major Khadir went to sleep that night of 21 February, he had no idea that in three days he would be involved in one of the most consequential, if not *the* most consequential, battles of the first day of Operation DESERT STORM. At approximately 0800 hours on 24 February, Major Khadir and the men of his battalion would be engaged in a three-hour battle for their lives.

That same evening, 100 miles south of Major Khadir's position, two American intelligence soldiers, one a 29-year-old captain and the other a 26-year-old sergeant, were somberly briefing their battalion commander on their new analysis concerning the "unoccupied" trench line. What their analysis revealed, and what their battalion commander did with their findings, would dramatically change the trajectory of the upcoming battle at the trench line. Major Khadir's enemy would not be the French 6th Division. His enemy would be Americans. Americans with an eagle on their left shoulders.

SGT Gonzalez' Conundrum

Northern Saudi Arabia – 3 Miles from the Iraqi Border
2100 Hours
21 February 1991
Three Days Before the Ground War Begins

SGT Jesus Gonzalez was the 26-year-old Intelligence Specialist for the 1st Battalion, 327th Infantry Regiment (1-327 Infantry), a 700-man unit of the 101st Airborne Division (Air Assault). Having been in the Army for eight years, Gonzalez learned his trade as an Intelligence Specialist at Fort Huachuca, Arizona, and had been a soldier in 1-327 Infantry for almost two years. For the last six months, he plotted and templated enemy locations opposite 1-327 Infantry. The templating process was taught to all U.S. Army intelligence analysts during their developmental training to help them systematically estimate where **unreported** enemy units or positions were most likely located. The process is based on historical and doctrinal reports and reduces uncertainty for commanders and staff.

SGT Gonzalez was one of four members in 1-327 Infantry's Intelligence Section. The "Boss" was CPT Jose Delgado, a smart and highly competent intelligence officer who had considerable operational experience. 1LT Bowman, a recently arrived intelligence officer, and MSG Smiley, an infantryman detailed as the group's senior noncommissioned officer, rounded out the section.

1-327 Infantry recently deployed into the far western part of the Saudi Arabian desert as a prelude to the expected ground war. The enemy unit Gonzalez now focused on was the Iraqi 45th Infantry Division. The 45th Division's location had been dropped from most higher-level intelligence reporting because of its status as a reserve unit that had little armored capability. However, it was still a threat to 1-327 Infantry.

Using all the available reported enemy locations, reconnaissance flight information, Iraqi tactical doctrine, and his own estimates, Gonzalez painstakingly plotted and templated the likely locations for the 45th Division's units, based on his experience and analysis. Aside from his boss, Gonzalez was the only Intelligence Analyst in the battalion, so his assessment was critically important and had to be both thorough and precise.

In late February 1991, as the Persian Gulf War ground into its seventh month, the details for the highly secret Coalition ground attack that 1-327 Infantry was to spearhead were released. Gonzalez quickly secured a copy of the operation order and plotted the different locations where his battalion would be inserted. While templating, Gonzalez became alarmed that one insertion location straddled a trench line he deduced as containing significant enemy forces. Unfortunately, his higher headquarters had reached different conclusions and labeled the same position "unoccupied."

Despite his confidence in his estimates and analysis, over the next few hours Gonzalez precisely re-plotted every enemy location—hundreds of different data points. He secretly hoped that his calculations were wrong and that he would not have to do what he knew in his heart he had to do, which was tell his boss. When he was finally through and looked at his analysis, he said one word over and over—"Damn!"—as he deliberately walked over and informed CPT Delgado.

Notes

1. Charles Lane Toomey. "XVIII Airborne Corps in Desert Storm." p.328.
2. Recollections of Captain Al Gill who interrogated Major Khadir.
3. Toomey, p.325

CHAPTER 1

A RENAISSANCE AND SMASHMOUTH ARMY

The 1990 US Army
1973–1990

Time works by measuring periods between the past, present, and future. To grasp the magnitude of the quick and decisive victory that the US Army achieved in DESERT STORM, you must understand the history of that 1990 Army. The 1975 Army, the 1980 Army, and even the 1985 Army did not have the capability of the 1990 Army. The 1990 US Army was developed for battle and for winning the battle quickly. Its creation was a mix of military genius, political vision, and hard work by dedicated, patriotic, and professional soldiers. Its formation is an epic story.

When the US Army deployed to Saudi Arabia in August 1990 for Operation DESERT SHIELD/DESERT STORM, it was arguably the most lethal army the United States ever sent into combat. No American army has ever been as prepared to fight and win the first battle as this 1990 Army. It was a "Renaissance Army" of astute thinkers and elegant war theories. It was also a "Smashmouth Army" that would break your nose and cut out your guts. It had the world's finest equipment, it had excellent leaders and soldiers, and it was trained to exacting standards. 'No More Task Force Smiths,' referring to the defeat of an American infantry battalion in the first battle of the Korean War, and "Fight Outnumbered and Win," referring to defeating the Soviets in Europe, were the rallying cries for this Army.

When the 1990 Army ultimately did battle with the large and modern Iraqi army, reportedly the fourth largest in the world, it went through it, as General Patton once quipped, "Like crap through a goose." But this time the goose had diarrhea. More eloquently, historian Robert Citino would write in his book, *Blitzkrieg to Desert Storm*:

> Desert Storm was the most successful campaign in U.S. military history. It liberated Kuwait in record time and shattered Saddam Hussein's war making capability, although the man himself—as well as his regime—would show surprising staying power.

> Although the Iraqis fought badly and were ineptly led, Desert Storm did manage to evict a huge, mechanized army out of its heavily fortified positions and then destroy it at an almost nonexistent cost.[1]

The story of how the Army became this fearsome organization starts with the 1973 "not-so-good" post-Vietnam Army, travels through the 1980s, and finds its destiny in the sands of Saudi Arabia and Iraq in 1991.

The 1973 US Army

If the 1990 Army was the best Army the United States ever fielded, the 1973 Army might have been the worst, or at least the worst of the twentieth century. The Army had just exited from the Vietnam War and, despite winning almost all battles and engagements in that conflict, was condemned for losing the war and pilloried in public opinion. The ignoble evacuation of Saigon in 1975 would cap off this disastrous era.

In June 1972, I graduated from West Point, chose the infantry branch, and married. In the fall, I went to Fort Benning, Georgia, for schooling: the Infantry Officer Basic Course, Airborne School, and Ranger School. Finished with training, I headed to West Germany. In March 1973, I started my Army career with 1st Platoon, C Company, 2-30 Infantry, 1st Brigade, 3d Infantry Division in Schweinfurt, Germany. Schweinfurt was located about 50 miles north of Nuremburg and had been bombed in World War II because of its ball bearing factory.

My first formation with my platoon in March 1973 went like this: "Good morning, men. I am Second Lieutenant Hancock and I am your new platoon leader." From the platoon came a soft but clearly audible, "Fuck you, motherfucker," etc. Not what I expected but entirely in character with the 1973 Army. I would soon find out that the previous platoon leader had been arrested for smoking hashish with the platoon. I saw that lieutenant only once and he was in leg irons, handcuffs, and under guard.

I learned also a "good soldier" didn't mean the soldier didn't do dope—it just meant that he didn't do dope while on duty. Our company commander was the most hated man in the company, had been threatened with a knife, and had his car vandalized. Company Charge of Quarters (CQs), typically sergeants, were armed with metal "bunk adapters" (steel poles) for protection at night. Company officers were required to make a before and after midnight check of the barracks. There were three officers in my company, so every three days I would drive 15 miles to the barracks at 11 PM, stay for an hour and check after midnight, and then drive 15 miles back home. This was typical of the 1973 Army. As LTC (Ret) Michael

Lee Lanning, author and my next-door-neighbor, said in his book *Battles of Peace,* about his company command tour in Schweinfurt in 1974: "If the Russians could see this they would attack tomorrow." [2]

Beginning of a Renaissance

From this post-Vietnam Army would arise a force that would destroy the Iraqi Army in four days. This turnaround didn't happen overnight. Over the next seventeen years, changes were top-down, bottom-up, and inside-and-out adjustments that fundamentally changed how the Army fought and the culture of the Army itself.

Two events in particular forced the Army to reconsider its dismal posture and look to the future. These events were the Yom Kippur War and Soviet expansion through the 1970s. These two events would drive the Army to take a multitude of thoughtful and concrete steps towards rebuilding its capabilities and reorienting its efforts.

The Yom Kippur War

In October of 1973, Israel was attacked by an Arab coalition on the Jewish holy day of Yom Kippur. The lethality of Soviet equipment and doctrine, the enormous expenditure of ammunition and destruction of vehicles, and the early success the Arab coalition enjoyed against the Israeli Defense Force (IDF) severely jolted the US Army. The Yom Kippur War spotlighted the limitations of American arms, which the Israeli Army used, and the capabilities of Soviet arms, which the Arab armies used.

Soviet Aggression

After the end of the Vietnam War, there was a push in America for a peace dividend and a retrenchment in military spending. In May of 1977, at an address at the University of Notre Dame, President Carter said, "Being confident of our own future, we are now free of that **inordinate fear** of **communism** which once led us to embrace any dictator who joined us in that **fear**." Cancellation of the B1 Bomber, cancellation of the neutron bomb, and a proposed withdrawal of troops from South Korea were some of President Carter's actions aimed at achieving the peace dividend.

President Carter's peace rhetoric, however, did not affect Soviet expansion, which continued in the late 1970s. The 1979 Soviet invasion of Afghanistan sparked the establishment of the Rapid Deployment Joint Task Force (RDJTF). Soviet expansion also had the effect of contributing to the 1980 election of Ronald Reagan as President.

End of the Draft and "Be All You Can Be"

After he took office in January 1969, President Richard M. Nixon established a commission to examine the feasibility of an all-volunteer military force. The recommendations of this commission, headed by Secretary of Defense Thomas Gates, Jr., supported the idea that the all-volunteer force was necessary to maintain security. Its recommendations were threefold: military pay should be raised, the quality of life for servicemen and their families should be improved, and a "standby" draft system should be established.[3] President Nixon signed the legislation to end conscription and to put the nation on the road to ending the Selective Service System on 28 September 1971. The draft formally ended on 27 January 1973.

MG Max Thurman became the commanding general of the US Army Recruiting Command (USAREC) in 1979. Under his leadership, the Army went in a totally new direction with regards to recruiting. Under the highly successful "Be All You Can Be" campaign, more qualified recruits were brought into the Army. Recruits were better educated, motivated, and sought to excel.

In 1981, under President Reagan's leadership, Congress voted for a significant 11.7 per cent military pay increase, as well as an increase in the defense budget to support it. This pay raise was followed in 1982 with another dramatic 14.3 per cent pay increase.[4] Paying a competitive salary and seeking soldiers who sought to excel, the Army became a well-thought-of organization by the American public.

The Development of a Smashmouth Army

The Army's reaction to the Yom Kippur War and ongoing Soviet expansion was one of orientation on one overriding principle—unparalleled LETHALITY on the future battlefield. Everything the Army of the 1980s did was meant to prepare soldiers and leaders to defeat a Soviet or Soviet-style force. This focus on lethality led to the development of new uniforms, protective equipment, vehicles, weapons, units, doctrine, and, perhaps most importantly, a new training philosophy. These changes resulted in the creation of the thinking and bone-crushing Army of 1990.

The Army Training and Evaluation Program

In developing the Tasks, Conditions, and Standards of the Army Training and Evaluation Program (ARTEP), the US Army ensured that units from squad to battalion level knew what tasks they were responsible for, under what conditions they had to execute them, and what standard they had to achieve. Beginning in 1975, the ARTEP system allowed commanders to evaluate unit training as a complement to individual training.

The Election of Ronald Reagan

Under President Reagan's military build-up, the US Army expanded to a force of eighteen divisions and 795,000 volunteer soldiers. The Army became competent, lethal, and robust. President Reagan had reportedly said, in talking about the Cold War with the Soviet Union and how it would end, "We win, and they lose."

Reagan was an optimist and a realist. His funding of the military would allow the Army not only to think about changes, but also to fund them and make them a reality. Reagan's optimism and realism seeped down into the US Army and boosted its self-esteem and its morale. The Reagan pay increases in 1981 and 1982 would also lead to an increase in morale as soldiers now felt they were being paid commensurate with the work they were doing.

Serious and Thinking Senior Leaders

After the end of the Vietnam War, the Army was blessed with senior leaders who were driven to correct what they saw as major weaknesses. The list included Abrams, Myers, Wickham, Starry, Depuy, Thurman, Lindsay, Cavazos, Otis, Richardson, and Schwarzkopf. These were officers who had fought in Vietnam as lieutenants, captains, and young field grade officers, had remained in the Army after Vietnam, and were dedicated to turning the Army around.

Recruiting

Army recruiting efforts in the 1980s changed direction to meet the new challenge of attracting the right people. Commercials and recruiting materials still talked about the benefits of military service—pay, travel, etc.; however, there was a significant change in the way that soldiers were portrayed in recruiting advertisements.

New television ads and posters showed soldiers parachuting out of airplanes, flying helicopters, and driving tanks. Ads featured Army Rangers in action, artillerymen firing howitzers, and infantrymen climbing cliffs and rappelling down again. The message was clear—the Army was full of action and was oriented on combat and the soldiers who engaged in combat—infantrymen, tankers, artillerymen, helicopter pilots.

New Equipment, Weapons, and Battle Dress Uniform

In 1982, the new Kevlar helmet and the Battle Dress Uniform (BDU) began to be issued. The Kevlar helmet would imitate, in many respects, the World War II German helmet, as its design and construction offered greater protection. The BDU would have outsized pockets for carrying equipment, a Western Europe camouflage pattern that replaced the solid green color of the earlier utility/field uniform, sturdy construction, and a shirt that would not be tucked in. A patrol cap would be issued to be worn with the BDUs. While the appearance of the Kevlar helmet and BDUs did not by themselves alter Army culture, it certainly announced that the Army saw itself as a combat force, not a spit-shine army.

In addition to the new BDU and helmet, new weapons and equipment began to make their way into the Army's inventory. The High Mobility Multi-Purpose Wheeled Vehicle (HMMWV) replaced the venerable Jeep. The HMMWV was larger and more robust than the Jeep and it could carry a greater payload. In addition, it was manufactured in several variants—command, cargo, ambulance, and anti-armor. New and improved weapons were also introduced. The M16A2 rifle replaced the M16A1 as the Army's standard shoulder weapon, and the M249 Squad Automatic Weapon provided more firepower to the infantry squad.

The "Big 5"

In the 1980s, the US Army purchased what was called the "Big 5" weapon systems: the M1 Abrams tank, the M2 Bradley fighting vehicle, the UH60 Black Hawk helicopter, the AH64 Apache helicopter, and the Patriot air defense missile. These systems were, at the time of development, the most advanced and lethal systems of their type in the world. They were so well thought-out and technologically advanced that they are still used in the US Army today. The "Big 5" would give the US Army an overmatch capability with any potential adversary in the world.

The Infantry Division (Light)

Another move towards the Army's more aggressive mindset was the establishment of several light infantry divisions in the mid-1980s. The Infantry Division (Light) was characterized by a lack of ponderous, heavy equipment, fewer vehicles, less heavy firepower, and a smaller support infrastructure. The result of cutting infrastructure was that the division could be deployed quicker and easier into trouble spots where large support facilities weren't available.

In all, five light divisions would be formed, four active divisions and one in the Army National Guard. The Infantry Division (Light) fit perfectly with the Army's focus on combat, offensive spirit, and lethality. The soldiers in these units developed their own ethos and prided themselves on their ability to operate in close terrain, such as forests, jungle, and mountains, without a large support apparatus. They ran their own "Light Fighter" schools, which were prerequisites for service in these divisions. A significant number of their junior enlisted soldiers were Ranger qualified, and almost all their officers were, too. They operated at night, lived out of their rucksacks, and constantly honed their cross-country movement, navigation, and close combat skills, as well as their ability to operate decentralized, in small units. The Army even made a television recruiting commercial about them.

Activation of the Ranger Battalions

In the immediate aftermath of the Vietnam War, the Chief of Staff of the Army, General Creighton Abrams, directed the formation of a Ranger Battalion. This battalion was to be the premier light infantry force in the Army and was to set the standard in training, readiness, and professionalism. The 1st Ranger Battalion was activated on 31 January 1974 at Hunter Army Airfield in Savannah, Georgia and, because of its success, was followed on 1 October 1974 by the 2d Ranger Battalion, which was based at Fort Lewis, Washington. By the mid-1980's the Army's focus on combat and lethality resulted in the formation of the 3d Ranger Battalion in 1984, with the 75th Ranger Regiment headquarters being formed in 1986. Coupled with the Light Infantry Divisions and the Big 5, the new Ranger Regiment showed the country, and the world, that the Army's philosophy had changed significantly.

Training and Education – AIRLAND Battle

In the early 1980s, a new offensive doctrine was created called AIRLAND Battle, which had as its tenets: Agility, Initiative, Depth and Synchronization. This "Blitzkrieg on Steroids" would theoretically enable the US Army to fight outnumbered and win against a Soviet or Middle Eastern adversary. In most NATO and Middle East scenarios, US forces would be outnumbered by their enemy. To defeat a numerically superior force, AIRLAND Battle doctrine called for the use of air and land forces to cut the enemy's lines of communication, destroy its logistics infrastructure, and attack its flanks.

The Study of the Operational Art

The study of the Operational Art, which is the level of war that ties the strategic to the tactical, became a passion for the US Army in the 1980s. The doctrinal recognition of the operational level of war in 1982 and operational art in 1986 was part of an overall post-Vietnam renaissance in the United States military's thinking. This thinking focused heavily on the Soviet threat and took Soviet doctrine into account. Emerging from its Vietnam experience, the United States Army had to shake off the lethargy of ten years of a war generally won at the tactical level but lost at the strategic level. It also had to recover from a generation wherein little doctrinal thinking beyond the tactical level had occurred at all.[5]

During the 1980s, The School for Advanced Military Studies (SAMS) was established at Fort Leavenworth to educate field grade officers on the Operational Art. During this time, FM 100-5 (1982) and FM 100-5 (1986) were written to promulgate the doctrine of AIRLAND Battle throughout the entire Army. The graduates of the SAMS program would fill important positions in division and corps staffs in DESERT STORM and would affectionately be called "Jedi Knights" by their superiors.

Combat Training Centers and Battle Command Training Program

The US Army's efforts to modernize and achieve unparalleled lethality would include the creation of "world class" force-on-force Combat Training Centers (CTC). These were the National Training Center (NTC) at Fort Irwin, California (desert), the Joint Readiness Training Center (JRTC) at Fort Chaffee, Arkansas (jungle), and the Combat Maneuver Training Center (CMTC) at Hohenfels, Germany (Europe). Here, US forces would train against a professional Opposing Force (OPFOR) which used Soviet doctrine, and which was outfitted with state-of-the-art "laser tag" equipment – the Multiple Integrated Laser Engagement System (MILES). This laser system gave validity to the use of proper tactics, marksmanship, and gunnery. These training centers established a "crucible" evaluation for units to test their readiness against an unforgiving opposing force in very difficult environments. The training centers were meant to recreate the rigors and stress of combat. Observer/Controllers (OC) were layered at all levels of command in the visiting unit to give feedback. The concept of "brutal" After Action Reviews (AAR) was implemented – nothing was sacred in discussing the faults and the strengths of the unit that was "in the box." This training was costly and man-power intensive, but it produced units that were highly trained.

The Battle Command Training Program (BCTP) provided advanced combat training to division and corps commanders and staffs through battle simulation. The concept incorporated an Observer/Controller (O/C) staff, a standardized threat, and a comprehensive After Action Review (AAR) package supported by the corps/ division battle simulation system. Mobile Training Teams (MTT) directed the evaluation process at designated installations and provided the necessary battle simulation system. The BCTP trained corps and division staffs in a manner similar to the CTCs, with tough and realistic scenarios.

Professional, Serious, and Thinking Junior Leaders and Soldiers

Of all the changes that occurred from 1973 to 1990, the improvement in junior leaders' and soldiers' professional development was the most dramatic. With the end of the draft in 1973, the all-volunteer Army was created. Soldiers wanted to be in the Army. The Army ensured that it recruited soldiers who had both the right aptitude and right attitude to serve well in the Army. Officers and enlisted soldiers were trained, educated, and treated as a "precious asset" that was the core of the Army's capability. The Army became, more and more, a professional force that could accomplish its mission and compete with the civilian job market.

Noncommissioned Officer Education System

In addition to recruiting high school graduates, toughening up basic training, and tightening discipline, the Army made sure that soldiers had a career path and education to go along with their job specialties. The Army's lethal equipment, workable doctrine, and rigorous training produced a solid core of soldiers that was made even more formidable by a professional Noncommissioned Officer (NCO) Corps. This corps of sergeants, the backbone of any Army, was itself made even better through an education system of sequential and progressive schooling requirements.

Towards this end, the Army developed a new Noncommissioned Officer Education System (NCOES) that was designed to educate, train, and prepare NCOs as they advanced through the ranks and took on greater responsibilities. This idea of not only recruiting the right soldiers, but also training, educating, and retaining them, resulted in good soldiers remaining in the Army and improving its overall level of experience and competence – a major tenet of Army philosophy in the 1980's.

Observations

During the 1980s the United States Army concentrated on one thing—LETHALITY. Individuals, squads, platoons, companies, battalions, brigades, divisions, and corps all had this focus. So, when the US Army was sent to Saudi Arabia in 1990 it was a professional, well-trained, well-educated, well-led, and well-equipped killing machine. The United States had never begun a war with an Army so formidable. The lopsided nature of DESERT STORM, in my view, was not because the Iraqi military was so terrible. As far as Middle Eastern armies went, it was big, modern, and a force to be feared. The battle was lopsided because the 1990 American Army was that much better.

Notes

1. Robert Citino. Blitzkrieg to Desert Storm.
2. LTC (Ret) Michael Lee Lanning. Battles for Peace. p.47.
3. Bernard D. Rotsker. "The Evolution of the All Volunteer Force." The Evolution of the All-Volunteer Force | RAND
4. "United States Military Basic Pay History" U.S. Military Pay Raise History (1794 to Present Day) (navycs.com)
5. Historical Perspectives of the Operational Art (army.mil)

CHAPTER 2

THE 101ST AIRBORNE DIVISION (AIR ASSAULT)

"Screaming Eagles"
Fort Campbell, Kentucky
1990

"We will crush our enemies by falling from the sky"
MG Bill Lee –
First Commander of the
101st Airborne Division

In 1990, the 101st Airborne Division (Air Assault) was the most unique division (approximately 18,000 soldiers) of the eighteen divisions in the US Army.[1] The division was unique because of its warfighting concept of flying soldiers into battle by helicopter and the prodigious quantity of helicopters it possessed.

The 101st was also the unit of choice for many young, enlisted soldiers and lieutenants. New soldiers were attracted by the division's focus on offensive helicopter-borne air assaults and its reputation of fighting heroically at Normandy and Bastogne during World War II, and the A Shau Valley in the Vietnam War. The 101st had its own Air Assault School, its own Air Assault Badge, its famous "Screaming Eagle" patch, and its own unique motto and song, *Rendezvous with Destiny*. In 1990, the training tempo of the 101st was high, its units trained all over the United States and the world, and it was well-prepared to go into battle. As the saying went, "It was a great day to be a soldier."

Concept of Air Assault

The 101st Airborne Division was constituted as an airborne division (being delivered to the battlefield by parachute and glider) in 1942. In 1965, the division deployed to Vietnam and would soon be traversing Vietnam by helicopters. In 1968, it was designated "Airmobile," indicating it was using the helicopter as its means of transportation. After the Vietnam War, the division would be re-designated as the "101st Airborne Division (Air Assault)," once again designating the helicopter as its means of entering a battle.[2]

The concept of Air Assault means that the 101st Airborne Division can, quickly and precisely, insert by helicopter large numbers of men and equipment to different parts of the battlefield. Once delivered to their objective, the soldiers will have the equipment and the lethality to complete their mission. One Gulf War briefer described this as, "flexibility plus lethality plus agility equals utility across the full operating spectrum," meaning the division was "free from the tyranny of terrain."[3]

Organization of the 101st Airborne Division (Air Assault)

In 1990, the 101st contained nine infantry battalions organized into three infantry brigades. Each infantry battalion had an authorized strength of about forty officers and 640 enlisted personnel.[4] An infantry battalion was organized into a headquarters company, three rifle companies, and an anti-armor company to provide extra firepower against enemy tanks. The anti-armor company had twenty TOW (Tube-launched, Optically-tracked, Wire-guided) launchers mounted on HMMWVs. The TOW missile had a maximum effective range of 3,000 meters and could penetrate and destroy any enemy tank. A scout platoon and an 81mm mortar platoon were also part of the headquarters company.

The division's artillery had three 105mm howitzer (11.5 km range) battalions (eighteen tubes in each battalion) and one 155mm howitzer (22 km range) battery (six tubes). The division's support command had a maintenance battalion, a support battalion, an engineer battalion, a signal battalion, a medical battalion, and an aviation maintenance battalion. The division also had a chemical company, a military intelligence battalion, a military police company, an air defense battalion (Stinger missiles and Vulcan cannon), and a light equipment company.[5]

The division's combat aviation brigade set the 101st apart from normal infantry divisions. In the aviation brigade were three assault helicopter battalions for lift transportation, each with thirty UH60 Black Hawks; two attack helicopter battalions with one battalion equipped with eighteen AH64 Apaches armed with a 30mm chain gun and Hellfire missiles (8 km range) and the other with twenty-one AH1 Cobras armed with TOW missiles (3 km range), 20mm cannon, and two 7.62mm miniguns. The brigade also had one medium assault battalion with forty-five CH47 Chinook heavy lift helicopters; a combat aviation battalion with thirty UH1 Huey lift helicopters; and an air reconnaissance squadron with sixteen AH1 Cobras. Additionally, the division had a company-sized long-range surveillance detachment and a sixty-man pathfinder detachment in the aviation brigade's headquarters company. For planning purposes, helicopters could fly out 100–125 miles before having to return to their base to refuel.[6]

Because the movement of the 101st was dependent on aviation assets, much training time was set aside to practice the pickup and the landing of personnel and equipment.

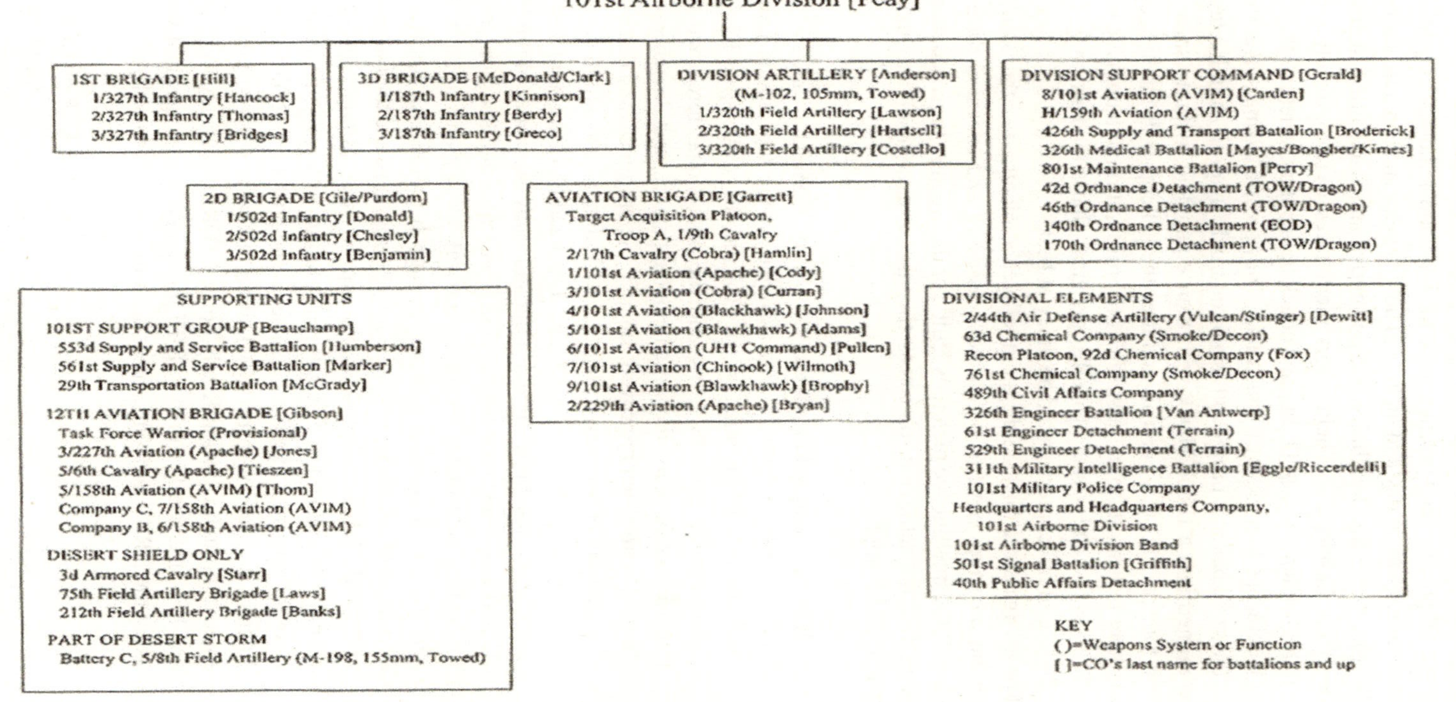

Divisional Organization for Operation DESERT SHIELD/DESERT STORM.[7]

Units would practice, and practice some more on how to hook up equipment, how to guide in helicopters in day and night, and how to enter and exit a helicopter.

Despite the agility, flexibility, and power that attack and utility helicopters gave to the 101st Airborne, the helicopters themselves were extremely vulnerable in mid- to high-intensity war. Utility and attack helicopters, whether the Black Hawk, Huey, Cobra, or Chinook, are flying trucks. They go fast and maneuver well but have about the same ballistic protection as a 5-ton truck. In an air assault, eleven soldiers are crammed into a Black Hawk with their equipment, with no safety restraints, while a four-person crew controls and flies the helicopter. If the helicopter is shot down, there is a catastrophic loss. With the proliferation of automatic weapons, air defense missiles, and rocket propelled grenades that a modern army such as Iraq had, the use of helicopters would be dicey at best.

For a large-scale air assault, the intelligence picture, weather conditions, and deception measures have to be correctly assessed and executed for a successful mission. If the intelligence picture is faulty, or the weather turns bad, or a deception measure does not achieve its objective, then the air assault soldiers may be in for a very hard day or night.

> Following completion of the US Army Command and General Staff College in 1989, I was assigned as the Operations Officer, 1st Battalion, 327th Infantry, 1st Brigade, 101st Airborne Division (Air Assault). The US Army and the operational force had truly transformed since my days as a lieutenant and captain. In general, the soldiers were much improved: smarter, better trained, and dedicated. The equipment was newer, better, and maintained to a high degree.
>
> Upon stepping into the position, I realized I had to get up to speed quickly. It is one thing to read about and study the tactics of the 101st Airborne Division (Air Assault) but it was quite another thing to plan for and execute them. My first year was spent planning air assault and live fire training at platoon through battalion task force level, execution of battalion task force defense missions, and the integration of lift and attack helicopters and fire support assets throughout. All this training culminated in a successful battalion task force air assault in a combined arms, live-fire exercise on the post's new Multi-Purpose Range Complex in April 1990. During this period, the battalion also rotated through Division Ready Force 1 (DRF 1 – Ready to Deploy) and Division Ready Force 9 (DRF 9 – the push package) that would assist the DRF 1 and subsequent units to deploy if so ordered.
>
> *MAJ John Chappell*
> *Battalion XO*

Observations

The 101st Airborne Division (Air Assault) in 1990 was a unique, powerful, flexible division that gave the US Army the capability to quickly and decisively outflank or strike deep into enemy territory. The division also had more vulnerabilities than any unit in Desert Storm. The use of the division in mid- to high-intensity combat was very much in question. The division's use and its survival would depend on the skill of its planners and the proper assessment of the enemy's capability.

Notes

1. LTG Edward M. Flanagan Jr. *Lightning*, p.35.
2. Ibid.p.34.
3. Ibid.p.35.
4. MG Binnie Peay. "Air Assault into the Gulf"
5. Flanagan. *Lightning*, p.35.
6. Flanagan. *Lightning*, p.36.
7. Peay. "Air Assault into the Gulf"

CHAPTER 3

1ST BATTALION, 327TH INFANTRY

Fort Campbell, Kentucky
Summer 1990

In the years immediately preceding my taking command of the battalion, a strong team had been formed. In effect, it was a "team of teams." The entire battalion was gradually coalescing around solid personalities at multiple levels—the soldiers themselves, the junior lieutenants and NCOs, the senior lieutenants and NCOs, the company commanders, the staff officers, and, at the top, the Battalion XO and S3.

> I graduated from Virginia Military Institute in 1987 and after the Infantry Officer Basic Course and Ranger School, arrived at Fort Campbell in July 1988, and was assigned to 1st Brigade. They assigned me to 1st Battalion, 327th Infantry. 1st Battalion assigned me to Alpha Company (ABU). So, I reported to A Company and met the guy who became, and still is, my best friend. George Glaze was a West Pointer and had 3d Platoon. I had 2d Platoon and my Platoon Sergeant was SFC Gene Wade, who was from Washington. What a great NCO he was and how lucky I was to have gotten him as my platoon sergeant. He was tactically proficient, in great shape, and incredibly articulate. He had his hands full with me, but he did his best to keep me out of trouble, to make sure the platoon was operating soundly, to make sure that he and I were mentoring our squad leaders and individual soldiers, and that we were doing our part. SFC Wright had 1st Platoon and 1LT Kent Milner, one of the toughest people I have ever known, was the Company Executive Officer (XO). The company commander was CPT Terry Duran.
>
> The company nickname "ABU" goes back many years, and there are several versions concerning where the name came from. The most common story is that it came from I Company, 3d Battalion, 187th Airborne Regimental Combat Team, when that unit was stationed in Japan in the early 1950s. The other companies in the battalion,

K, L, and M, had nicknames—"King Kong," "Lion," and "Mighty Mouse"—but I Company did not. So, the soldiers came up with the mythical "IBU," which was the body of a paratrooper, wearing fatigue pants and jump boots, but with the head of a lion, a moose's antlers, an alligator's tail, and carrying a .45 caliber pistol in one hand and a bloody knife in the other. Later, I Company, 3d Battalion, 187th Airborne Infantry was re-flagged as A Company, 1st Battalion, 327th Airborne Infantry, so "IBU" was changed to "ABU," which remains the unit's nickname to this day.

In short, the battalion was a great unit to be a part of—its core being a group of similarly motivated, profane, bulletproof, irascible lieutenants who had all the answers and who took advantage of any opportunity to mock and/or ridicule each other. One morning, we were playing softball for "Officer PT" and one guy showed up wearing one of those dark blue US Navy baseball hats with the silhouette of a ship and "USS Whatever" on it. So, Tom Guleff immediately asked him if that was the ship that his boyfriend was on. Commanding us must have been a challenge.

1LT Gerry Tertychny
Battalion S3 Air

My first assignment in the Army, the 1st Battalion, 327th Infantry, was a gem. The training and the leadership opportunities, culminating in combat operations, set the foundation for the rest of my 30-year Army career. The solutions I found in future challenges in my jobs and my postings came from the practical, common-sense approach forged in the sandbox of Desert Shield/Desert Storm.

1LT George Glaze
Support Platoon Leader

In March of 1989, I arrived at Fort Campbell about a month after being promoted to Captain. My wife, Yon, and I were coming from Fort Benning (now Fort Moore), where I'd attended the Infantry Officer Advanced Course. When we arrived, Yon was pregnant with our first child.

When I was assigned to the 1-327th Infantry in March of 1989, the Commander was LTC Donald Pavlik. He informed me there were no company commands immediately available and told me I'd be his Battalion Adjutant until a company opened. LTC Pavlik was a decorated Vietnam War Veteran, about 6ft 7in, thin as a rail, and chain-smoked Marlboro reds. He liked me and treated me well, but he could be extremely hard on everyone and anyone who worked for him.

I remained as the 1-327 Infantry S1/Adjutant from March until the end of December 1989. During that time, LTC Pavlik gave me the opportunity to either take command of the next rifle company opening or wait and take D Company, the battalion's anti-armor company. While I had always wanted a rifle company, the opportunity presented by D Company appealed to me.

D Company was part of an Army experiment in personnel management conducted between 1981–1995 in how to build more cohesive units—a COHORT Company (Cohesion, Operational Readiness, and Training). The defining difference between a COHORT company and other infantry companies during those years was that COHORT companies were filled on a unit-basis while all other companies were filled by the Army's Individual Replacement System.

So, what does that mean? In a COHORT Company, all the soldiers were recruited with the knowledge they would train together during their OSUT (One Station Unit Training) and AIT (Advanced Infantry Training) at Fort Benning / Moore, and then deploy to their first assignment as a unit, not as individuals. Their enlistments were for three years.

CPT Al Gill
D Company Commander

While many folks were new to the 101st and to 1-327 Infantry, some, like CPT Ken Russell, had been at Fort Campbell for a while and were familiar with the division's methods of operating.

Upon arrival at Fort Campbell, Kentucky, I assumed command of Headquarters and Headquarters Company, 3rd Battalion, 327th Infantry Regiment for a year, after which I assumed command of ABU (the A/1-327 Infantry nickname). Upon assuming command of ABU in the spring of 1990, I quickly realized that on a good day I could muster 90–100 men standing in formation and ready to train. On paper, a rifle company was supposed to have 132 personnel, but that was just a pipe dream for rifle companies in the Screaming Eagles. At that time, due to Army-wide manning priorities, most of the Screaming Eagle rifle companies were severely understrength.

CPT Ken Russell
A Company Commander

In February 1990, I got a call to go up and see MAJ John Chappell, the Battalion Operations Officer (S3). This was alarming because the S3 didn't typically interact with platoon leaders and I immediately thought that I was in some sort of trouble, though I couldn't figure out what it might be. We called MAJ Chappell "The Duke" (not to his face, of course) because he reminded us of John Wayne, and we loved the guy. He was competent and tough and would hand you your ass if you deserved it, but he didn't pick on or bully lieutenants. So, I headed up to my audience with The Duke, having no idea what it was about. I knocked on the door, stuck my head in, and said, "Hey, sir—you wanted to see me?"

"Yeah, T—come on up here and have a seat," he said. I, of course, did as commanded.

He got right to the point and said, "I need a new S3 Air and you're it—you're going to come up here and work for me. What do you think?" The S3 Air worked directly for the S3 and was responsible for moving the battalion around the battlefield by helicopter as well as deploying it overseas, should the need arise. In addition, he was responsible for unit movement certification and training throughout the battalion's subordinate companies. In any unit, but particularly in an infantry battalion in the 101st, it was an important job. I also knew that, because the S3 shop was short on personnel, I would also have to do training areas, ranges, ammunition, and the monthly Unit Status Report, which by itself was a royal pain in the ass.

I told him that I didn't want to be the S3 Air, that there was another job I wanted and thought I was best qualified for. He smirked and said, "Yeah, I know. But I really need you up here and that's the way it is. OK?" I realized right then that when he asked me what I thought, his question was a question only in the rhetorical sense.

I just said, "Roger that, sir. I'll give it my best shot. When do you want me up here?"

He told me to get myself cleared out of A Company, finish out my evaluations, go to the Strategic Deployability School (SDS), get my Expert Infantryman Badge (EIB)—the test for which was in late March—and report up to the S3 shop at the end of March, about a month away. I said, "Yes sir, I'll be up here as soon as I can."

1LT Gerry Tertychny
Battalion S3 Air

By early August 1990, I had been in command of 1-327 Infantry for seven weeks. I had previously served in the 101st, from 1980 to 1983, as the 1st Brigade Assistant

S3, Company Commander of D/2-327 Infantry, and Battalion S3 of 2-327 Infantry. The experience of these different positions made me very familiar with the division's air assault tactics and techniques. Before taking command of 1-327 Infantry, I had come from the 25th Infantry Division (Light) in Hawaii, where I had served from 1986 to 1990 in numerous "hard" infantry jobs. These included being a Brigade S3, a Battalion XO, the Division Secretary of the General Staff, and Division Deputy G3. The Army had also sent me to the US Army's Command and General Staff College and the British Army Staff College. As far as the Army was concerned, short of actual combat, I was about as well-trained and educated as it could make an infantry battalion commander.

> On 12 June 1990, LTC Frank Hancock assumed command from LTC Donald Pavlik. As with any change of command, it marks a time of anticipation, excitement, and some apprehension for the soldiers of the unit. LTC Hancock was no stranger to 1st Brigade. He had previously served in 1st Brigade and 2nd Battalion, 327th Infantry from 1980–1983. He immediately made a solid impression on his subordinates. He was confident and ready to take on the challenge of command. LTC Hancock was a family man, and he exuded a positive influence in all dealings with his subordinates and each soldier.
>
> LTC Hancock immediately immersed himself in getting to know the unit, his personnel, and the activities programmed over the summer. My assessment was that he had a solid officer and NCO corps within the battalion that would serve him well over the next two years of command. We had sound company commanders, smart lieutenants, and experienced NCOs. While there was always need for improvement in any unit, these men strove to be the best in the brigade and in the division. Little did we know that they would all be put to the test a little over a month into LTC Hancock's command.
>
> *MAJ John Chappell*
> *Battalion XO*

The company commanders, lieutenants, and battalion staff that I inherited were, in one word, outstanding. These were hard infantrymen, well-trained and thinking men. They would, and did, act on their own volition and make very good decisions without me micromanaging them. In retrospect, I was a very fortunate commander.

> By the summer of 1990, the battalion was in great shape. The soldiers were as good as ever, though we never seemed to have enough of them. The NCOs were sharp. Most of the platoon leaders were good and those who were lacking at least had good platoon sergeants

> keeping them on azimuth. The company commanders were all top-notch—CPT Mike Wright had Headquarters and Headquarters Company (HHC), CPT Ken Russell had taken A Company after having commanded HHC/3-327 Infantry, CPT Bill Simril had B Company, CPT Darcy Brewer had C Company, and CPT Al Gill had D Company, which was the anti-armor company. Their XOs were great, too: 1LT Bryan Blue was in HHC, 1LT Chris Chiarello was in A Company, 1LT Jay Peterson was in B Company, 1LT Jay White was in C Company, and 1LT Mark Pilkington was in D Company. These were strong teams at the company and platoon level.
>
> The other senior lieutenants were also very strong: 1LT Brian Bedell had the Scouts, 1LT Erik Valentzas had the Mortars, 1LT George Glaze had moved from B Company to take the Support Platoon, and 1LT Jim Kelley assumed command of the Medical Platoon in Saudi Arabia. At battalion, the senior staff officers were 1LT Tom Guleff, who was the S1; CPT Jose Delgado, the S2; and CPT Mike Landers, the S4. CPT Sung Lee, a real stud, was the Battalion Commo Officer. The Duke was the S3 and MAJ Bill Whitesell was the XO. In an incredible stroke of good fortune, I was able to bring my platoon sergeant, SFC Ray Juhnke, with me from A Company to the S3 shop to be the S3 Air NCO. Together, we tried to update and coordinate our movement plans, SOPs, and training so that we could help the commander and the S3 maneuver the battalion. That summer, we got to do just that.
>
> *1LT Gerry Tertychny*
> *Battalion S3 Air*

To augment my command and staff I received several officers and NCOs who were tasked to support the battalion. A Fire Support Artillery section, an Air Force Liaison section, an Engineer section, and an Air Defense Artillery section augmented our battalion. The Fire Support Officer (FSO) was CPT Jerome Hawkins from 2-320 Field Artillery, which, looking back, had the greatest of all mottoes—"Balls of the Eagle." Jerome was a skilled artilleryman, a no-nonsense officer, and a professional soldier. He knew his artillery business well. 2LT Tom Evans, who was new to the battalion, was the Battalion NBC Officer and would play a significant role in our upcoming deployment and operations.

> I arrived at Fort Campbell in early July 1990. Accompanying me were my wife of two years, Mayra, and our infant daughter, Kara. We quickly found housing in the form of rental property located just south of Hopkinsville, Kentucky.

The day I was to report for duty and meet the commander of 1-327 Infantry would prove more eventful than I could ever have imagined. I was up early spit and polished to make a good initial impression. I was anxious to get to work and start my first duty assignment as an officer. I was driving along Highway 41A toward Fort Campbell. It was still dark and the only other vehicle on the road was a motorcycle traveling immediately in front of me. Suddenly, for no apparent reason, the rider lost control of the motorcycle and laid it down. The rider slid off into the median while the bike slid down the highway. I stopped and located the rider, who I determined was unconscious. The rider was a young man and was wearing Battle Dress Uniform (BDUs) so I could safely assume he was a soldier. While I attempted to render aid to the best of my abilities the injuries proved extensive. The sun was now starting to rise, and with the added light, it was clear the rider had not survived. A Kentucky State Trooper arrived on scene, and I briefed him on what I witnessed. I took the soldier's dog tags and continued my journey to report to my battalion.

I arrived at Battalion HQ where I initially met Captain Jose Delgado. I did not know it at the time, but Delgado would later play a major role in my Army career and my life. As I stood covered in blood before Captain Delgado, the shock and confusion on his face was evident. I explained to him what had happened on the highway, and he seemed to feel a little more relieved that there was an explanation that did not include ax murders. I was escorted to Major John Chappell, the Battalion XO. Chappell was a solid matter of fact man and without hesitation he told me to return home, clean up and report later in the day. While returning home I tried to collect my thoughts about all that had transpired on this unnormal day. Little did I know the initial experience would only be a foreboding of what was to come.

2LT Tom Evans
Battalion NBC Officer

The Air Force Liaison Officer (ALO) was Captain Bill Reister. Bill was an F4 Phantom pilot. Every bit a fighter pilot, Bill was technically competent, confident, and experienced (he had called in airstrikes in Operation JUST CAUSE in Panama in 1989). He, too, would play a huge role in the battalion's success in the upcoming months.

My role, for those without military background, was Air Liaison Officer (ALO)/Forward Air Controller (FAC). My primary weapons were radios mounted in a HMMVW, which I used to ensure that air support assets understood first and foremost where our friendly elements were (so they would not accidentally hit them), and second to help them identify targets we needed removed. My team also included Sergeant Sabino and Sergeant Guererra, two fine men whose first names I've regrettably forgotten in the past thirty years. Apart from four years flying F-4E Phantoms, I had also participated in Operation Just Cause in Panama the year before where I had the dubious privilege of being hit by mortar shrapnel (no injuries, just on the vest and helmet)—making me one of only two people in the battalion with actual combat experience.

Why a fighter pilot? Fighter aircraft are fast, but they cannot stay airborne for long periods of time. Things look very different from 10,000 feet altitude than they do to soldiers on the ground. The job required someone who understood what it looked like from "up there," could communicate quickly to pilots where both friendlies and enemy were located and eliminate or suppress them to get the job done.

I will stipulate that the soldiers of 1-327 Infantry were primarily of the warfighter breed: professional, dedicated, and well-trained. When you happen across a unit like this in real life it is almost invariably because of strong leadership. Thus, I will share my first impressions of these men. I arrived at Fort Campbell about a month before we deployed to Iraq. I had never met them, and my first introduction was at a battalion meeting. Before the meeting began, a lean African American Command Sergeant Major Riley approached me and simply stood in front of me for a moment, looking deep into my eyes. I didn't sense any animosity, but I confess the hair stood up a bit on the back of my neck. After a moment's inspection he said, "You've seen a little, haven't you Air Force?" I intuited that he meant "combat experience," and so understood the inspection—and after a moment of looking back at him I realized he had been places I never wanted to go. I grinned back at him and said something to the effect that I doubted it compared to anything he had seen, which I was certain was true. I was soon to learn that Command Sergeant Major Riley, also known as "Sgt. Rock," had enlisted under-age to go serve in Vietnam—and liked it so much he re-upped for several tours there. Immensely respected by everyone in the battalion, he had turned down the role of Command Sergeant Major of the Army so that he could remain as the personal aid to the battalion's commander, LTC Frank Hancock (aka "The Warlord" to his troops).

He later told me that he expected the Warlord would one day go on to join the Joint Chiefs of Staff. That never happened, which was a loss for our country—but was sadly predictable due to the whole careerist vs warfighter theme I mentioned previously.

The briefing commenced, explaining that our initial mission would be to help defend the Saudi border (a "speedbump in the sand" as some described it), and then culminated with a lengthy intel briefing from the Battalion S2 (Intel Officer) about the Iraq Army—the world's third largest standing army with a total of about one million men in uniform. At the end of the briefing The Warlord gave a few closing remarks. He then very matter-of-factly said words to the effect of, "Oh, and one more order of business—we have a new ALO, Captain Reister. Captain Reister, come up here and tell us how the Air Force is going to help us beat the million-man Army." Caught completely off guard, I gathered my wits and stepped forward to speak.

I began by explaining that a Soviet-doctrine army does not use civilian transportation as we do—and thus fully 50 per cent of such armies are non-combatants—so it was really "only" a 500,000-man army. We would be stationed behind Saudi forces manning the border, about 200 miles from enemy troops. If the Iraqis decided to advance, they would do so only at about 30mph, and would have to stop to refuel before engaging us—meaning we would have many hours before any actual confrontation. I pointed out that every weapon in the Air Force inventory was tested at White Sands Missile Base—a desert just like we were going to, where their efficiency was at its best. Moving enemies raise dust, making them easy to target. I predicted that during this time they would call me over to the command center and would ask if I had any air assets (which I would not expect until the enemy was "danger close") and promised that I would offer them something better. I then pulled out my coffee pot from my backpack and held it up—and said something like, "We will have time. We will make a pot of coffee and you will tell me whether we want them dead, or to surrender." I finished my imaginings of how the battle would go, leading up to, "by the time they get to us (and if they don't simply abandon the attack) it shouldn't be more than 3 to 1 odds. Can you all defend against a Soviet doctrine military at those odds if you are already dug in?" Finally, I got a reaction from the team, "YES."

Apart from CSM Rock, who seemed to be struggling not to laugh, I really don't know what they all thought. While I meant every

> word, I'd said it because I was put on the spot and figured I may as well say something to raise their spirits. The meeting concluded, and I watched the Warlord interact with his men. I'd had commanders our pilots had respected, some they despised, some they thought simply incompetent. Frank seemed to be someone they truly respected and admired. That is a very special gift very few leaders attain. Some are feared, some despised—but to be loved by your troops AND be a great wartime commander is very rare. Filling out the rest of the cast with whom I had regular contact were the XO, Major Chappell, and Battalion S3, Major Dempsey. Major Chappell reminded me a bit of George C. Scott playing Patton. Not quite as hard-bitten, but that same determination. Major Dempsey was brilliant, spoke fluent Aramaic, and if he was a little bit eccentric, I suppose I was too. All in all, it was easy to have faith in our battalion leadership.
>
> *Capt Bill Reister*
> *US Air Force Air Liaison Officer/Forward Air Controller*

A short observation about some of the battalion officers. The Battalion Executive Officer (XO), John Chappell, was nicknamed "The Duke" because of his uncanny resemblance to John Wayne. He was extremely competent and very intellectually formidable. John had a big heart but could melt steel with his gaze. He was the ultimate "Bad Cop." When I needed a "hammer," John was it. If I became incapacitated, John could run the battalion without missing a beat.

> We were very fortunate that the command structure had the right personalities in the right positions. The Battalion Executive Officer was Major John Chappell. He was the heavy hand with a no-nonsense attitude in the headquarters. I liked him personally, and we were like-minded in how things should run. He basically was the chief of staff, the guy who made sure that the train was running on time. He instilled a sense of discipline with the staff and the company commanders. His approach to solving problems was more direct and straightforward. I was intensively loyal to Major Chappell, having worked with him previously in the operations area, and trusted his judgment and admired his dedication to the mission. I would run almost everything through Chappell before speaking with Hancock. It was important to me that the Executive Officer had an honest assessment. He never killed the messenger; he was steady and was never rattled. I respected his calmness and his directness, and it was easy to work under tough conditions, with such a command environment. Chappell also had the respect of many of the senior

lieutenants. Most had worked with him in some capacity and knew his expectations. These officers trusted him.

LTC Hancock seemed to be the perfect counterweight to Major Chappell. Hancock was free from the day-to-day grind of running the battalion and could focus on operational plans and the tactics of operating in the desert. He could also zero in on the needs of soldiers beyond just guns, ammo, and food. There was a good balance between the two. Hancock was personable and had great empathy for the young, enlisted soldiers in his command. He was more hands-on than our previous commanders when it came to understanding the plight of the grunt in the field.

With respect to the non-commissioned officers, the battalion had a ton of professionals, and it started with the Command Sergeant Major. LTC Hancock not only respected CSM Riley, but he liked him. He trusted him. Every officer knew their success was based on their NCOs' success. It was obvious to many of the senior lieutenants that much of their knowledge came from NCOs. There was a great deal of respect given to their capabilities.

CPT Tom Guleff
Battalion S1

All of my previous jobs at the Bastogne Bulldogs prepared me to be the Support Platoon Leader in the summer of 1990. I had been a rifle platoon leader, a company executive officer, and a mortar platoon leader in the years before becoming a senior lieutenant in the battalion, second only to the HHC executive officer in pecking order. And with this responsibility came great expectations of performance. The two takeaways from this were—I was the Battalion Executive Officer's action man, and that the leader is only as good as the men with him. You need to choose between focusing on being a great leader (inward focus) or having a great unit (outward focus). And you better be focused on having a great unit. Your men can tell which type of leader you are in this regard, and they will act accordingly.

1LT George Glaze
Support Platoon Leader

That summer, MAJ Whitesell left the battalion and The Duke moved up to be the XO. He was replaced as the S3 by MAJ Tom Dempsey, who was smarter than the rest of us put together and who spoke Arabic. Tom was intelligent and looked at situations from unusual points of view. Tom was not an "out-of-the-box" thinker; Tom *lived* outside the box. If I and other officers were looking at a problem through an X and Y axis, Tom was on the Z axis. Tom was a wonderful asset to run problems through, as he would see pitfalls that no one else saw. Tom, besides being an infantry officer, was also a Foreign Area Officer who had a two-year utilization tour in Saudi Arabia under his belt. He spoke Arabic and French, and when talking to the Arabs, he made them laugh with his understanding of the language. His linguistic talents and different viewpoints were very beneficial for the battalion.

My Battalion Adjutant (S1) was 1LT Tom Guleff. Tom was a very senior lieutenant who was close to making captain. He was also not planning on making the Army a career and had about one year left on his commitment out of West Point. He did not suffer fools lightly. If he had a filter on what he said, he rarely used it. To me, this was an outstanding trait for a staff officer. I would often say to the staff, "Don't let me do something stupid." Tom would be the first guy to say, "Hey Sir … that's stupid."

> It is important to understand the context of the times when discussing Desert Storm. This was pre-9/11. Iran and Iraq had been fighting a war with extensive use and threat of chemical weapons. The Iraqi Republican Guard was a formidable foe with combat experience. In addition, they were fighting in their own backyard with the advantage of logistics and knowledge of the terrain and the environment. It had the makings of nasty conflict in an unforgiving environment. The prior training years for the unit included training in Panama and Florida. At least for 1-327 Infantry, a desert war was not on our radar. There was no rest for the wicked.
>
> *CPT Tom Guleff*
> *Battalion S1*

My company commanders were CPT Ken Russell – A Company; CPT Bill Simril – B Company; CPT Darcy Brewer – C Company; CPT Al Gill – D Company (Anti-tank Company); and CPT Mike Wright – Headquarters Company. These were all seasoned captains and, in my view, good soldiers and commanders. None of them whined or ever showed any sign of not being able to get the job done. They were all tactically competent and none of them were leaders who abused their soldiers … which was not going to happen under me. I was very confident in all of them.

My S4 (Logistics) was CPT Mike Landers, another very hard guy who would accomplish amazing logistical feats during the deployment. My Signal Officer was Captain Sung Lee. Sung was of Korean extraction and had an interesting way of expressing himself. Technically proficient, he was also proficient in martial arts and looked like he could kill you with his eyebrow. Last was our fighting chaplain, Captain OJ Diulio. OJ was some type of Chaplain—rugged and fit and thoughtful. He was a great source of wisdom and courage.

One evening in late June, I was working in my office in the S3 shop. It was around 1800 and everyone else had gone home. I was crunching ammunition forecast numbers, I think. LTC Frank Hancock, the new battalion commander, came into my office, waved me to keep my seat, sat down, put his feet up on my desk, and just stared at me. I just looked back at him and asked, "What's up, sir—how can I help you?"

"Why won't anyone talk to me?" he asked.

I asked him back, "What do you mean, sir?" I knew full well what he meant.

He leaned forward and said, "You know damned good and well what I mean. Nobody talks to me. Everyone seems to want to avoid me. Why?"

I put my pencil down and said, "You really want to know what I think?"

He said, "That's why I asked you. Let's have it."

I said, "OK, sir, here it is. Your predecessor was a knee-jerk reactionary who jumped everyone's shit for any reason or for no reason at all. We never knew where we stood with the guy. One minute everything was fine and the next it was a four-alarm fire. After having our asses chewed so many times, we just tended to stay out of his bursting radius. At least, that's what I did. I think maybe the guys think you're just another version of him and that's why we're all just staying away from you." We stared at each other for a few seconds.

I just shrugged my shoulders and said, "I'm sorry if I crossed the line with that, sir."

He got up and said, "Nope, that's OK—but do me a favor."

I stood up and said, "Yes, sir—anything."

He said, "Tell everyone I ain't that guy," and he headed out.

Fair enough.

1LT Gerry Tertychny
Battalion S3 Air

We spent the remainder of the spring and summer executing local training exercises, mainly at the platoon and company level, and preparing to assume the responsibilities of the Division Ready Force (DRF) 9 battalion. The individual infantry battalions rotated the DRF responsibilities—DRF 1 through 9. The DRF 1 battalion would be the battalion to deploy immediately in the event of an emergency notice. It would be followed by the DRF 2 battalion, and so on. The DRF 9 battalion would be the last battalion to deploy and, as such, was the designated 'push' battalion, used to get the DRF 1 unit's personnel, vehicles, and equipment loaded properly, inspected, and marshaled at the airfield in the correct configuration to get it all on US Air Force aircraft for deployment. The battalion had done all this before and it really wasn't a major concern. Still, it was an important mission, one we couldn't afford to fail.

Because of Chappell and Dempsey, and the efforts of all the company commanders and XOs, 1LT Gerry Tertychny and SFC Ray Juhnke were able to brief the companies on their responsibilities, conduct leader rehearsals, and execute a recall alert to test the phone roster. Though we were technically "last," we had the same two-hour recall standard as the DRF 1 battalion because we had to push them out. The idea was to be ready at midnight on the designated day because you might get an alert one second after midnight. The DRF 1 and DRF 9 battalions could count on being alerted and having to go through the procedure. Sometimes the DRF 1 battalion would deploy to another area in the United States for an exercise and sometimes the exercise would end when everyone and everything had reached the airfield and was ready to deploy.

During the seven weeks I had been in command, I had the opportunity to take the battalion out on two different field exercises. In both exercises, it appeared to me that my lieutenants, NCOs, and enlisted soldiers were solid. As I remember, the battalion had about a 90 per cent Air Assault School qualification rate. Air Assault School was a ten-day course run by the 101st Airborne which emphasized hard physical training but, more importantly, taught the students the tactics and techniques for conducting a helicopter air assault—getting on and off the helicopter, rappelling from the helicopter, preparing vehicles and supply loads to be "slung" under helicopters, and guiding in helicopters to Landing Zones (LZ) were among the essential techniques taught at the school. All these activities/techniques were executed in both daytime and nighttime conditions. As a new commander, I believed that I had been handed a very competent unit.

> During the rest of the spring and summer months we had many more field training exercises from company to battalion level, a battalion change of command as we welcomed LTC Frank Hancock to the battalion, and all the normal company training on ranges, live fire exercises, etc. LTC Hancock was a breath of fresh air. Prior to his arrival, the command climate in 1-327 Infantry needed much improvement. All that changed with the arrival of LTC Hancock. The focus in the battalion shifted to readiness and training. Commanders and leaders at all levels were encouraged to exercise initiative and take charge. It was now OK to accept risk and allow soldiers and

> leaders to learn from honest mistakes without them fearing being crushed by higher HQ leadership. The new leadership embraced the doctrine of "train as you fight" and that was also a welcome change.
>
> *CPT Ken Russell*
> *A Company Commander*

> When LTC Hancock assumed command of 1-327, he was a very welcome arrival to the battalion. He was full of energy and enthusiasm, and he had a quality I've observed in many of the best leaders I had in the Army; he took his job very seriously—but not himself. He joked, had a great sense of humor, was self-effacing, and did not micromanage the companies. He was an athlete and an avid competitor—and I mean avid! The battalion really took on a very different persona after his arrival, for the better. Looking back now, I know we were fortunate to have LTC Hancock as our battalion commander. His CSM, Rock Riley, was a leader of character as well, a seasoned combat Veteran of several tours in Vietnam that everyone respected.
>
> *CPT Al Gill*
> *D Company Commander*

In a foreshadowing of future events, the only person who was certain that Iraq would invade Kuwait in early August 1990 was my Intelligence Officer (S2), CPT Jose Delgado. CPT Delgado was an interesting individual. He was studious, intelligent, and had the persona of a very professional soldier. I knew he had operational experience in South America, so I paid very much attention to his opinions about the crisis in Kuwait.

Before the 2 August invasion, the theory that "an Arab country would not invade another Arab country" was prevalent. There was no precedent of it happening before and the "talking heads" on TV news assured the American public that "Arabs don't attack other Arabs." On 1 August, CPT Delgado came into my office and said, "Sir, they are going to attack—all the indicators are there." I assured the young captain that this was not the case because, as everyone knew, "Arabs don't attack other Arabs."

Observations

You cannot micromanage a unit and have it be successful. There are too many variables and contingencies to take care of. I was blessed in that I took command of a unit where the staff, commanders, lieutenants, NCOs, and soldiers were well-trained and prepared to go into combat. If your command

structure is not prepared to go to war… then get it that way. War comes at you very quickly, as I found out, and you will deploy … ready or not.

In looking back at 1-327 Infantry in the summer of 1990, I believe it was transforming into having a highly functioning command climate. As an officer, I had been blessed to have several superb mentors and commanders. These include: 1LT Sam Pride from West Point and the 3d Infantry Division, CPT Al Todd from the 3d Infantry Division, LTC Joe Bolt and Colonel George Baxter from the 101st Airborne Division, and LTC Bill Craven, Colonel Tom Vaughn, and MG Charlie Otstott from the 25th Infantry Division. All these officers were hard, competent, smart, and took care of their soldiers and treated them with humanity. I certainly believed in how these officers treated their soldiers and in how the effectiveness of a unit is improved by that type of leadership. Officers and enlisted soldiers respected me but did not FEAR me. Fear breeds inaction and risk aversion, which can be fatal. I found CSM Riley and MAJ Chappell had the same attitude. This would lead to soldiers and officers doing things on their own volition, taking ownership of their actions without the fear of having their faces ripped off if they did something wrong. This would prove vital in future months.

CHAPTER 4

DEPLOYMENT

Fort Campbell, Kentucky
August–September 1990

"This will not stand" – President H.W. Bush
On Iraq's 1990 invasion of Kuwait

To fund its war against Iran in the 1980s, Iraq had borrowed vast sums from its Arab neighbors and was, by the end of the decade, severely in debt. By 1990, much of the Iraqi debt was being called in and Kuwait, specifically, was pushing Iraq to repay its loans and was publicly pressuring Saddam Hussein to do so. Hussein, having a battle-hardened army, decided to invade Kuwait and seize its oil wells.

Iraq's military, which made use of Soviet doctrine, was equipped with modern Soviet aircraft, surface-to-air missiles, armored vehicles, and, ominously, a very robust chemical weapons stockpile which it had used against the Iranians. It was a formidable force in the Middle East. In July 1990, Iraqi armored units began moving towards the Kuwaiti border.

On 2 August 1990, Iraqi tanks crossed the border and headed toward Kuwait City, 80 miles away. Iraqi special forces units infiltrated during the night to seize specific targets, one of which was the Kuwaiti royal family. In three and a half hours, Iraqi tanks were in Kuwait City and the country had been effectively overrun. The Emir of Kuwait and his family escaped to Saudi Arabia, and, by nightfall of 2 August, all the Emirate of Kuwait and its two million people were under the control of Iraqi forces.

Hussein, with the combined assets of Kuwaiti and Iraqi oil, would control a significant percentage of the world's oil supply. In addition, in the days immediately after the invasion, it appeared that Iraq would not stop in Kuwait but would also invade Saudi Arabia to seize its oil wells. After consultations with the Saudi leadership by Defense Secretary Cheney and the USCENTCOM Commander, General Schwarzkopf, President Bush received the go ahead to send US forces to the Kingdom to prevent an invasion and takeover of Saudi oil assets.

On 7 August 1990, the 101st Airborne Division (Air Assault) was notified that it would be deploying to Saudi Arabia as part of the XVIII Airborne Corps for the defense of Saudi Arabia. This would be the first time the 101st had seen combat since the Vietnam War. When the alert notice for the 101st to deploy came, 1-327 Infantry was the Division Ready Force 9 (DRF 9) battalion, which had the responsibility for "pushing" the division out to Saudi Arabia. The battalion was responsible for the flow of divisional units out of Campbell Army Airfield, providing drivers for convoys, and organizing the shipment of pallets and containers for loading on airplanes, trains, and ships. This is a thankless, albeit vital, task, as the remainder of the division is preparing to deploy while your troops are running the deployment stations.

> On 2 August 1990, Iraq invaded the country of Kuwait. Initially, the invasion half a world away did not register with me as significant, at least for those outside the region. Soon I would be aware of just how meaningful the events of 2 August were. Lieutenant Colonel Frank Hancock commanded the battalion I was assigned too. LTC Hancock, I would learn, was a West Point grad and was from a family of military men. While on an officer run, Hancock halted the formation on a softball field and made perfectly clear to me and the rest of the officers what I failed to grasp initially about the significance of recent events in Southwest Asia. LTC Hancock explained to us how world events such as we were witnessing in Kuwait could spiral and grow, engulfing others in the chaos. LTC Hancock instructed us to listen to a rundown of the situation presented by Captain Delgado, the Battalion S2 (Intelligence Officer). Delgado would tell us that the invasion of Kuwait was primarily about oil pricing and not only had Iraq invaded Kuwait in a blitzkrieg of sorts, but the Iraqi military had also repositioned and now presented a threat to Saudi Arabia. Approximately one month later the 101st Airborne Division deployed to Saudi Arabia. The prophesized spiral had indeed engulfed us.
>
> *2LT Tom Evans*
> *Battalion NBC Officer*

I was fortunate that the battalion practiced this DRF 9 mission recently in an Emergency Deployment Readiness Exercise (EDRE) that was designed to test the division's ability to deploy. The battalion was well acquainted with what needed to be done to deploy the division. Additionally, my two main "honchos" of this mission, 1LT Gerry Tertychny, the Battalion S3 Air, and SFC Ray Juhnke, the Battalion S3 Air NCO, were experts in DRF 9 responsibilities and techniques. During the deployment, on more than one occasion, 1LT Tertychny would call to let me know that he had "locked horns" with another unit's commander over that unit's loading out performance.

Speculation was rampant and we didn't know how this thing was going to shake out. Chappell, Dempsey, and I tried to keep the rumors under control, and we did the best that we could by letting the men know what we knew. Soon, we got the word that the Division Ready Brigade 1 (DRB 1), which consisted of the DRF 1, 2, and 3 battalions, their field artillery battalion, and some aviation assets and support troops, would be deploying to Saudi Arabia. This meant that we, as the DRF 9 battalion, had to execute the deployment Standing Operating Procedure (SOP) and push out the entire DRB. We were actually going to do this. For real!

> In my time in the US Army, I never saw an Army doctor outside of a hospital. Most of the unit's needs were taken care of by a Physician's Assistant and the medics within the battalion. So, it came as a surprise that we were assigned a real US Army doctor prior to the deployment. The doctor happened to be a good guy and the unit was lucky to have him.
>
> *CPT Tom Guleff*
> *Battalion S1*

> We were always training in 1-327 Infantry (81mm Mortar Platoon). One day we were conducting small/large deflections with our mortars and working on Fire Direction. When we came back from lunch, we found out on CNN that Iraq had invaded Kuwait. We all knew this was a big deal but always thought Saddam would pull out and this would all be over before it started. That never happened. As I said before, we trained all the time—tomorrow would be the same as the day before. We talked about this all week as we trained but we knew this would not be over till we had a show of force in the region and defended our friends, Saudi Arabia. The Iraqi army was the fourth largest army in the world, and all this could spin out of control.
>
> *PFC Rich Hagedorn*
> *Mortar Platoon*

Upon receiving the alert notification, the battalion moved to our assigned locations to get the deploying troops to the airfield. In the past, when we held rehearsals and training deployments, the deploying unit was usually a battalion, and the exercise concluded after a few hours or maybe a day. This was different—we were going to execute the Standing Operating Procedure until the entire DRB 1 force had departed Fort Campbell. This meant that we were going to have to work around the clock to make this happen.

As the deployment schedule began to get discarded, due to unavailability of aircraft, the DRB 1 guys started abandoning their vehicles to get chow or to go sleep. They jumped the line with other vehicle serials, thereby throwing the sequence off. Many vehicles were poorly loaded, with different kinds of hazardous cargo inappropriately mixed. One HMMWV was so overloaded with artillery ammunition that its rear axle was bent.

> One of the biggest offenders was the aviation brigade whose leaders didn't seem to want to take direction from me, a mere first lieutenant, or SFC Juhnke. They were convinced that they were headed for a fight and that the regulations didn't apply anymore. Things came to a head one afternoon when the aviation brigade commander, COL Garrett, came to our command post, near the railroad tracks by Kentucky and Tennessee Avenues, called me aside, and chewed my ass for not getting his vehicles and equipment inspected and on their way to the airfield in a timely manner. When I tried to explain why things were held up—because of his unit's deficiencies—he became irate and told me not to make excuses but to just get things moving. Not knowing what else to say, I saluted and simply said, "Air Assault, sir." He got in his vehicle and left.
>
> I was pretty pissed off. It was late in the afternoon, it was hot, and I wasn't making things happen like I thought I should have been. SFC Juhnke came over and gave me a Coke. That guy always had the answer to the problem. He said, "You should probably let LTC Hancock know what happened, so he doesn't get blind-sided." Good call. I got in contact with LTC Hancock and told him about my skirmish with COL Garrett. He just said, "OK. Are we doing the best we can?"
>
> I told him, "Yes, sir. The guys are doing their best and they know their jobs. Honestly, it's not us."
>
> He told me, "Got it. Keep at it. I'll be over there shortly."
>
> As I sat there with Ray, drinking my Coke, a vehicle with a star on the front bumper pulled up and out of it stepped BG Hugh Shelton, the Assistant Division Commander. Ray and I looked at each other and he said, "Good luck."
>
> I approached BG Shelton, reported to him, and gave him an update on where we were with regards to deploying the DRB 1. He listened patiently and let me get through my speech. When I was done, he asked me, "OK, lieutenant, what's the biggest challenge or problem you're facing here?" For a few seconds, I just stared at him. Ray Juhnke, who was behind BG Shelton, got my attention and began mouthing the words, "Tell him." He grabbed his crotch and again mimed the words, "TELL HIM." His message was clear—grab your balls and tell him what the problem was. In the space of about five seconds, I figured that I had nothing to lose at this point, that we weren't going to get anywhere the way things were going, and, well, he asked.

So, I said to BG Shelton, "Sir, it's the aviation brigade. They're skipping the line and throwing off the sequence, their vehicles are dirty and not prepped for air movement, they've got mixed loads of hazardous cargo, their vehicles are overloaded, their vehicle load cards aren't properly filled out, and they're not doing anything to fix their shortfalls." During my diatribe, he just looked at me and nodded. When I was finished, I stood there awaiting execution—I mean, who the hell was I to make such assertions? BG Shelton just said, "Got it. Do the best you can. And try to remember that we're breaking new ground here—we haven't done this before." I replied, "Yes, sir. We have a plan together to correct the deficiencies, we just need them to come to us so we can train them and get things moving again." He said again, "Keep at it," and left. I thought (incorrectly, as it turned out) that was the end of it.

A little while later, I got a call on the radio from 2LT Shawn Reger, who was a platoon leader in Charlie Company, from the Vehicle Marshalling Area. We had our military radios that everyone on Fort Campbell was tuned into, and we also had some hand-held civilian radios that we used to communicate with each other when we didn't want the whole world listening in. He called me on the civilian radio and said, "Hey T. What's going on over there? COL Garrett was over here chewing our asses when Shelton rolled up. He pulled him aside, locked his heels, and smoked him in place. Then he took off and Garrett left, and I think he's headed in your direction." Terrific. I saw COL Garrett's vehicle pulling up. Ray looked at me and said, "Well, here we go again."

COL Garrett motioned for me to follow him and said, "Lieutenant, come over here for a minute." I assumed I was going to get "Ass Chewing, Part 2." Instead, he said, "Look, we may have gotten off on the wrong foot earlier. I know we need to make some changes … but you guys are the experts in this, and we need your help. We need you to help us get squared away so we can get moving." I was stunned. Juhnke turned and walked away because he was laughing so hard. I just said, "No problem, sir. We've got training set up here to help your guys get straight. We just need them to come so we can get everything back on track." He said, "You got it. I'll make sure it happens. Thanks." True to his word, his folks showed up. We did some training and helped them out, and they returned to their units, corrected their deficiencies, and things ran a lot smoother.

1LT Gerry Tertychny
Battalion S3 Air

The DRF 9 operation was complex, complicated, ran 24/7, and took up almost all the battalion's time and soldiers before we deployed. While all the DRF 9 drama was happening, we learned that the entire division was going to deploy, not just the DRB 1. This posed some challenges because, while we were running the DRF 9 show and trying to get the DRB 1 units moving, we had to get ourselves ready to go.

> Soon, the Screaming Eagles received a prepare to deploy order, not just for our DRF 1 or our DRB 1, but for the entire division. It seems the XVIII Airborne Corps HQ was deploying as well. We were activated as the DRF 9 battalion and began our job of deploying other division units out of Fort Campbell. It was structured chaos, but due to exhaustive training we knew what to do.
>
> *CPT Ken Russell*
> *A Company Commander*

It was during this time that two significant events took place. First, we got a new Battalion Command Sergeant Major (CSM). CSM Johnny Riley was hard as nails, even-tempered, level-headed, and an absolute stud. Interestingly, CSM Riley had been King Fahd's Jump School instructor years earlier when the king was still the Saudi Crown Prince. CSM Riley processed into the battalion about three weeks before we deployed. He was a Vietnam veteran who had a distinguished himself with the 173d Airborne Brigade at the Battle of Dak To. I would find out, twenty-five years later, that he was written up in three different books for his actions as a mortar platoon sergeant in that battle. He was wise, a leader, physically imposing, tactically brilliant, and, as I would find out, a stone-cold warrior. He had two nicknames, "Combat" and "Rock," and was the heart and soul of the battalion. You can meet people and forget people but no one who met CSM Riley would ever forget him. I correctly gave CSM Riley complete latitude to "run" the first sergeants and the NCOs in the battalion. His knowledge, charisma, and competency made him worth, in my view, at least two infantry platoons.

> When my tour of duty in Korea was almost complete, the Department of the Army assigned me to a training brigade at Fort Leavenworth, Kansas. I called the Department of the Army and informed them that I was an infantry soldier and I wanted to end my military career in an infantry battalion. The person whom I spoke with at the Department of the Army informed me that the only battalion available was the 1st Battalion, 327th Infantry of the 101st Airborne Division (Air Assault) and that the division was preparing to deploy. I said I would take it.
>
> After leaving Korea, I arrived at the 1-327 Infantry Headquarters, 1st Brigade of the 101st Airborne Division (Air Assault). LTC Frank Hancock had just assumed command of the battalion. The 101st was

already preparing for deployment to Iraq. At that time, Iraq had the fourth largest Army in the world. I remember reading about the Iraq-Iran War in early 1989–90 before leaving Korea. Iraq attacked Iran, and both sides suffered heavy casualties. Finally, they agreed to a ceasefire, and the war ended in 1988 in a bloody stalemate, and neither side could claim victory.

LTC Hancock was a young, physically fit, very intelligent commander. I later learned that he was also a superior athlete. LTC Hancock was ready to lead his command into combat, and I was his Battalion Command Sergeant Major. I had served three tours of combat duty during the Vietnam War and was ready to serve in the Iraq War under the leadership of LTC Hancock. We were going to war and the commander had to have complete trust in his CSM, and I had very little time to prove my worth. My job as CSM was to advise and assist the battalion commander.

CSM Johnny Riley
Battalion Command Sergeant Major

Also of note, it was about this time that the 1-327 Infantry CSM moved on and was replaced by CSM Johnny "Rock" Riley. Of all the leadership changes within the 1st Brigade, this was perhaps the most beneficial for the 1-327 Infantry. The command team of LTC Hancock and CSM Riley instilled confidence and raised the morale of the soldiers of the battalion right from Jump Street. That made a huge difference to what was to come over the next few months.

CPT Ken Russell
A Company Commander

The second significant event was that we were relieved of the DRF 9 mission. One day, after the COL Garrett/BG Shelton affair, I was speaking with 1LT Tertychny about how things were going. By this time, we had worked out all the kinks and the division was moving units out much more smoothly. Gerry had been thinking about our place in the deployment sequence and asked me, "Hey sir—who is going to push us out?" I said, "What do you mean?" He replied, "Well, if we're the DRF 9 and the last to go, then nobody will be left on base to push us out when the time comes." I just looked at him for a few seconds and said, "Damn—you're right. We need to fix that."

It hadn't been thought of before because we had never deployed the whole division before, at least not since the Vietnam War. So, I brought it up to the "powers that be" and we got relieved of the mission—it got assigned to the 20th Engineer Battalion, a unit on post that was not part of the 101st. They sent some guys over, they watched the operation, and we handed over our SOP.

The number and variety of tasks that we had to accomplish was staggering. Vehicles had to be prepped and marshaled for convoy movement to Jacksonville, Florida, where they would travel by ship to Saudi Arabia.

> I joined the 101st after graduating from Fort Benning, Georgia in 1989. My first stop was with 1st Platoon, C Company. I was selected to go to HHC to be a driver around July of 1990. When we deployed for Iraq, I was the driver for CSM Riley. I was very grateful to be with a Vietnam Veteran that did three tours and was a complete badass. He was the coolest, calmest, and collected leader I had ever had the privilege of serving with. I remember us watching the news up at headquarters of the Iraqi invasion and thinking this could be our time.
>
> Not long after this, I found myself on a journey with the HMMWV to Jacksonville, Florida. I observed thousands of people along the side of the road and on the overpasses with flags and signs of encouragement. It was an amazing sight to see and was a bit emotional at times. That trip made me the proudest that I have been to be an American.
>
> *PFC Bruce Dittfield*
> *Battalion Commander's Driver*

> I had just been moved to (HHC 1-327th) Scout Platoon. In fact, three days into sniper school I was pulled back to the Mortar Platoon. I was told we had orders coming down to deploy. Platoon leaders said there was no time and that they needed seasoned soldiers back in the Mortar Platoon ASAP. I get back to the Mortar Platoon and things are ramping up quickly. Weapons maintenance, vehicle maintenance, combat drills, and lots of physical training. We were having formation after formation. Packing Conex boxes although we still had not received the final word to ship out. There were a lot of activities. Getting shots and boosters.
>
> *PFC Stan Banach*
> *Mortar Platoon*

> As the Battalion Chemical Officer, I was expected to be the resident expert on all things nuclear, biological, and chemical. The battalion was authorized one Chemical Officer and one Non-Commissioned Officer. I was fortunate to be assisted initially by an outstanding young Sergeant in Jose Vega. Vega was instrumental in showing me the ropes and introducing me to the assigned/detailed NBC Sergeant at each of the line companies. Together, Vega and I were charged with making sure soldiers were properly trained in basic preventive

skills like how to put on and wear their personal protective gear, which included their mask and overgarments in the event the unit is at risk of exposure to nuclear, biological, or chemical agents.

After the run when the battalion commander put us on notice that things could spiral quickly, I started learning all I could about the Iraqi army. It did not take long for me to come to the sobering realization that the Iraqi military had fought a long and bloody war against Iran in which the Iraqis employed chemical weapons. By all accounts, the Iraqi military was large, and battle-hardened. On the other hand, the United States had not been in a major conflict for a couple of decades. I remember there were only a handful of people in the 327th Infantry that had any combat experience. To me, it seemed like a fight between the inexperienced and the experienced and the rule-follower against the ruthless.

All of this would bring the chemical issue to the forefront of every soldier's mind and the Battalion Chemical shop would need to be prepared to provide recommendations and answers on a regular basis. Upon realizing I would need to hone my knowledge and skills quickly, I aligned myself with Captain Delgado, the Intelligence Officer. I did this for two reasons. First, he would be capable of tutoring me on Iraq's military capability. Specifically, I needed to know what weapons could deliver chemical or biological agents. Second, in approximately four years, I too would be an intelligence officer. Being close to Delgado would offer early insight into what that meant.

2LT Tom Evans
Battalion NBC Officer

LTC Hancock quickly put me at ease with his unique sense of humor and asked what I expected to accomplish as the Battalion S2. He also asked about my family, hobbies, sports, and schooling. He then began to recount how simple his expectations were. Specifically, he told me that he believed that intelligence drove operations, and, in this outfit, he expected me to direct the battalion's intelligence gathering and consumption. LTC Hancock told me that the XO and the S3 were expected to help him direct the battalion's operations and that I, as the S2, would serve as the principal staff leader for the intelligence effort. He expected me to be the expert in everything involving the intelligence activities of this battalion and his expectation was that I would help the leaders of the battalion visualize the enemy and understand what they could realistically accomplish.

As the S2, this meant that I assisted the battalion senior leadership to inform, shape, and direct the decision-making process and I was also one of the commander's chief architects in his preparation of the battlefield. I was responsible for the staff's efforts to understand the enemy and the terrain on which the battalion would fight and was also responsible for obtaining answers to LTC Hancock's priority information requirements (PIR). I was expected to focus on the reconnaissance and surveillance (R&S) effort to collect information that was essential to answering the questions asked in the PIR and that was also critical in helping ensure the targeting process met its objectives. Presciently, LTC Hancock told me that the S3 (or even he) would inevitably see the enemy situation differently than I would and that it was important that I aggressively argue my perspectives until the decision to act was made. This proved to be a critical point during our combat operations during Desert Storm.

CPT Jose Delgado
Battalion S2

For four weeks, our battalion ran the deployment stations for the division, while simultaneously preparing to deploy ourselves, until we were relieved of the DRF 9 responsibility. 1-327 Infantry would be the last infantry battalion to leave Fort Campbell. Of course, many of my soldiers were concerned that the whole thing would be over by the time we got there.

When we found out our division were deploying to Saudi Arabia, we were incredibly motivated and excited about this, but myself and many of my friends in the mortar platoon didn't think it would get as far as it did.

I remember when we received the operation order for the convoy to Florida. We were excited to make the two-day drive to drop off our vehicles at the port in Jacksonville. When we started the journey from Kentucky to Tennessee, we would see a few people on the side of the road, in front of houses, or standing on the hills of Tennessee and Kentucky holding American flags and signs. Some tried to hand us beers, which we could not accept because we were on duty, and others waved and smiled. As we went further into Tennessee towards Georgia that's when the crowds became prominent. The cheers, pats on the back, kisses on the cheek, and excitement from civilians made us feel so proud to be Americans.

It was an overwhelming sense of patriotism. I remember driving under a bridge in northern Georgia and standing on that bridge was what looked like the entire town waving American flags and chanting, "USA." It is a memory I will never, ever forget. One of the times that we stopped to refuel the vehicle, a police officer came up to us and talked about his father who served in World War II. The officer said he was proud of us and said that "all hell can't stop you airborne." Our group smiled and we all shook his hand, which only added to the mounting sense of patriotism.

Looking back on this time, that BDU uniform with the 101st Airborne Division patch on your shoulder made you feel so proud to be an American soldier. My father served during the Vietnam War for two years after being drafted. From 1967 to '69 he was stationed at Fort Benning, Georgia. He told me that he couldn't wear his uniform outside of the base because it was frowned upon by the civilian populous. What a change of times and American pride from then to 1990. The American public loved us and cheered us on to defeat Saddam Hussein.

The two-day drive that should have felt long and tiring was easy with all of the support we received from everyone waving flags and telling us that they were behind us. Our leadership did an outstanding job coordinating the operation and executing the mission. We dropped off our vehicles in Jacksonville and the next time we would see them would be in the hot sandy desert of Saudi Arabia.

PFC Rich Hagedorn
Mortar Platoon

Observations

This DRF 9 Mission was executed by young junior officers, NCOs, and enlisted soldiers. There had been numerous training sessions and dry runs in the months before this actual alert. You cannot fake competency for long.

Family Support Group and Morale

In 1990, the US Army was very much a married Army. To make sure that spouses and children were taken care of, the Army set up what was called the Family Support Group (FSG) network. The FSG was an informal chain of command where information was disseminated from an Army stay-behind officer to the FSG. Each level of command down to battalion level would have a stay-behind officer—division, brigade, and battalion. The head spouses would then get the information out to other spouses by a phone tree or, on occasion, an actual meeting.

Not sure how many units in the US Army had a live mascot. Our battalion had a bulldog that resided in the headquarters. The closest thing to a mascot I saw in the army was a penned-up alligator at Eglin Air Force Base during Jungle Phase of Ranger School and the Army Mules at West Point. I assume the alligator was alive, but maybe not.

> Our dog was one of a long line of other bulldogs, all named "Bastogne." Named after the Belgian town of Bastogne. Several regiments within the 101st were nicknamed "The Battered Bastards of Bastogne," due to their part in holding the important crossroads town during the Battle of the Bulge in World War II. During its defense, the 101st Airborne Division sustained casualties of which 341 were killed, 1,691 wounded, and 516 missing. Despite the entire division deploying, and possessing an illustrious name, Bastogne still had to stay behind.
>
> *CPT Tom Guleff*
> *Battalion S1*

I was very fortunate that my wife, Maureen, who oversaw our Battalion FSG, was organized, charismatic, and resilient. The battalion had about 500 spouses and children left behind. During our deployment, she had to deal with the death of a child, a rape, and a spouse sending a threatening letter to the President. Her ability to organize, take care of problems, get the word out to the company commanders' wives, and get appropriate support from Army assets was remarkable. She took care of problems that would have been otherwise transmitted to the deployed troops in the form of personal, pay, housing, and school issues. Nothing good would have come from that transfer of problems at Fort Campbell to the soldiers in the field who had little or no ability to solve them.

When the Department of the Army Inspector General Team came to Fort Campbell to look at the post's Family Support Groups, Maureen was asked to be interviewed, to showcase how the battalion had set up its FSG. This taking care of business by my wife and other wives in the battalion was a tangible force enhancer for the battalion.

Observations

In uncertain situations, the willingness of spouses to help ameliorate any problems at home, especially for junior enlisted spouses, cannot be overrated. My advice to future soldiers is to marry well, if you can.

Linda Patterson

In mid-August 1990, I received a telephone call from Linda Patterson from San Mateo, California. Linda, unbeknownst to me, had been supporting the 1-327 Infantry since 1968. During the Vietnam War, her brother, Joe Artavia, had been serving with A Company (ABU), 1-327. On 24 March 1968, Joe was killed in action during the Tet Counteroffensive.

After Joe's death, Linda began her 50+ year odyssey of supporting first ABU, then later the entire 1-327 Infantry, and then starting her own non-profit organization to support all American soldiers. Her support would include a non-sponsored and on-her-own visit to Vietnam during Christmas in 1968; bringing gifts in the form of City Seal medallions from San Mateo to the troops in ABU personalized with their names engraved and noted 'Adopted Son;' a 1972 Welcome Home parade in front of 50,000 people in San Mateo for ABU; and a 1980 Welcome Home celebration for Vietnam Veterans in San Mateo.

> In early 1968, while serving with A Company, 1st Battalion, 327th Infantry, 101st Airborne Division in Vietnam, my younger brother asked me to have the city of San Mateo, California formally "adopt" his rifle company.
>
> On March 4th of that year, San Mateo's city council formally "adopted" A Company and, henceforth, A Company would become and be known as San Mateo's Adopted Sons. Tragically, my brother, SGT Joe Artavia, was killed in action later that same month. Several months later, during Christmas and without government approval, I traveled to Vietnam to personally deliver Christmas gifts to the men of A Company. To this day, the relationship between the soldiers of A Company and San Mateo continues.
>
> In 1990, America was once again at war and San Mateo renewed its commitment to the soldiers of A Company, 1-327 Infantry. I immediately contacted LTC Frank Hancock, the commander of 1-327 Infantry, and shared with him the history of San Mateo's support. LTC Hancock recognized the value of this relationship, and he directed his staff to establish the mechanism to incorporate San Mateo's support. Such was LTC Hancock's enthusiasm, and, at his request, the entire battalion would be included in San Mateo's adoption. As was the case with LTC Hancock, good officers recognize the value of such a unique relationship. San Mateo rallied its citizens, businesses, and schools and, as a result, thousands of letters and packages were sent to and received by the soldiers under his command. The relationship and connection with LTC Hancock's soldiers and San Mateo were overwhelming. What it did down the line was to help create other city adoptions for hundreds of other military units through the formation of the America Supporting Americans (ASA) Adopt-a-Unit Non-Profit Organization. I recall teachers telling of their students' interest, sensing a new patriotic climate in their classrooms, and receiving letters from their Screaming Eagles.
>
> *Linda Patterson*
> *America Supporting Americans*

When I first answered the phone to Linda, I knew none of this. I just knew that some woman named Linda Patterson was asking if she could help support the battalion as it deployed. At the time, there was no guidance or expectation on how long this deployment would last. Looking to get as much support for the battalion as possible, I asked her if I sent a roster of the soldiers in the battalion to her, could San Mateo provide each one of the soldiers with a pen pal. Her response was a classic example of support and love. Not only did every soldier get a pen pal, but every soldier in the battalion had several letters from several pen pals from San Mateo residents when we arrived. This effort by Linda was a very, very significant morale boost for the soldiers in the battalion. When I arrived in Saudi Arabia, I was queried by the Division G1 (Personnel) on why the unit was getting so much mail compared to the rest of the division and I replied, "a lady in San Mateo, California is making this happen."

Observations

The Gulf War would be the first time that the United States deployed over 100,000 men into combat since the Vietnam War. The support of the American people would be significant. The support that 1-327 Infantry would receive from Linda Patterson and San Mateo would be extraordinary.

Uncertainty

The looming deployment to Saudi Arabia would cast a net of uncertainty on deploying troops and their families that was almost unbearable. The scope of an immediate deployment of hundreds of thousands of soldiers was something that had not happened since the Korean War. The following are a few of the unanswered questions that would make the stressors on the deploying soldiers so formidable as soldiers got on their plane to Saudi Arabia.

1. What is the length of deployment? UNKNOWN
2. When will we attack? UNKNOWN
3. Is the Iraqi Army that good? UNKNOWN
4. Will our modern equipment work in the desert? UNKNOWN
5. Will the Iraqis use their chemical weapons? UNKNOWN
6. Will the volunteer Army work with the estimated 10,000 or more casualties? UNKNOWN
7. Will a Coalition army and its countries withstand an oil embargo by Iraq? UNKNOWN

8. How long could an American Army stay in a Muslim country without a collision of cultures? UNKNOWN
9. Could American soldiers withstand the extreme climate conditions in Saudi Arabia (125-degree temperatures) without breaking under the strain? UNKNOWN
10. Would the American population turn its back on its soldiers as it had during the Vietnam War? UNKNOWN

Getting on the Plane

The final week before deploying was interesting indeed. CPT Chris Reed had left the battalion to go to Fort Benning, Georgia, in late July. Chris was going to the Infantry School's six-month Advanced Course when the deployment order came down. Days before we deployed, Chris called me at the office and said he was back at Fort Campbell. When I asked him why he had come back to Fort Campbell he said, "Colonel, I need to go to war with my mates." When asked what his plan was, he had none—other than his former battalion commander (me) getting him on the plane. I cannot remember what process I used but I managed to get him equipped, manifested, and into Saudi Arabia, where he stayed until the battalion came home. The Army had no sense of humor about this, nor about his going "AWOL," and proceeded not to pay him for nine months.

A second incident occurred the day before leaving, when a young specialist was brought into my office saying he had just broken his ankle falling down the steps at his girlfriend's house and could not deploy. His platoon sergeant, who was there with him, said his girlfriend hit his ankle with a hammer and broke it so that he could get out of the deployment. I sided with the platoon sergeant's story. I believed then, and still do, that "being stupid" was not a valid excuse to get a soldier out of deployment. The young specialist deployed to Saudi Arabia and was then sent to Germany where surgery was performed on his ankle.

> My company and soldiers were in high demand to drive vehicles, load pallets, and about a thousand other jobs required to move an Air Assault division thousands of miles. Our own vehicles, twenty hard top TOW HMMWVs and eight soft top HMMWV carriers, had to convoy from Campbell to Jacksonville Florida, a mission conducted by my company XO, 1LT Mark Pilkington. Mark was an excellent officer, smart and knowledgeable, and a great XO.
>
> *CPT Al Gill*
> *D Company Commander*

While there were some who actively attempted to avoid the deployment, there were others who resorted to subterfuge to ensure that they didn't get left behind.

> I must fess up to one thing I hid from LTC Hancock and "Rock." Five days prior to our departure to Saudi, I was instructing and demonstrating hand-to-hand combat with CPT Brewer to our company. During one of the throws, I injured my right ankle bad enough that I had to visit the aid station. X-rays showed I had fractured the damn thing. The doc said I wouldn't be able to deploy, and he had to inform all injuries to battalion because of the deployment. Like a good 1SG, I talked him out of it and said I would take care of it. CPT Brewer and I made a "command decision" to not inform LTC Hancock and CSM Riley. We were concerned that those two Combat Heroes might not allow me to deploy, and there was no way in hell that was going to happen. I had no plans on letting them have all the fun and claiming that they had won the war all by themselves. Besides, someone had to keep those two straight.
>
> *1SG Butch Schwoyer*
> *First Sergeant, C Company*

Finally, in the last week, the battalion officers and their wives had a "Hail and Farewell" dinner at a local restaurant. As can be expected, it was a melancholy affair. As I got up at the end of the dinner to say what needed to be said as the battalion commander, I looked at the teary eyes and distraught faces of the wives and the young officers and matter-of-factly said, "We are ALL coming back." Whether that was the right or wrong thing to say to this day I don't know but I did know I was going to do everything I could to make it come true.

> Then we got the word to deploy. We loaded up all of our gear. Boarded a civilian plane and left for the Middle East. I remember being both concerned and excited. I was fortunate to be with the best soldiers and Leaders around. Most soldiers never get to experience the brotherhood that we all had at the time.
>
> *PFC Stan Banach*
> *Mortar Platoon*

CHAPTER 5

OPERATION DESERT SHIELD

Camp Eagle II

September–October 1990

The battalion began its deployment on 14 September 1990 and closed twenty-four hours later, deploying 715 soldiers to Saudi Arabia, along with seventy-one vehicles. The battalion was initially stationed at King Fahd International Airport and then moved to Camp Eagle II along with the rest of the division. Camp Eagle II was located about 80 miles north of Dhahran on the east coast of Saudi Arabia.

> I remember boarding the Tiger Airlines plane that took us overseas. The Battalion Executive Officer, Major John Chappell, turned to me and said, "Now you know you are not coming back to see the birth of your son in three months, George—you know that, right?" Of course, I said, "Roger that Sir!" when all I was trying to do was to find my seat. It was this shift in focus from the silly to the mission critical problems that really put this young soldier in a daze. I am grateful for the training we had prior to deployment because you fall back on it when other things catch you drifting away from the mission. Compare it to "muscle memory" in weapon training. We trained to quickly pop our weapons to our cheekbones and scan for targets when we are alerted. It becomes second nature. It becomes something that you no longer have to devote mental energy to perform, because it happens easier than a sneeze. Realistic training like that ingrains behavior that becomes second nature and ultimately saves lives. The Bastogne Bulldogs trained this way.
>
> *1LT George Glaze*
> *Support Platoon Leader*

> After we had been there a few days, CSM Riley took a detail of soldiers and put up locally made cotton tents for us in our section of a big field of sand outside of the airport grounds. I believe that

these tents were originally made for the pilgrims when they made the annual trip to Mecca. So, we had tents with rough carpet floors, Army cots, and, eventually, locally made, wooden latrines and showers. This place was called Camp Eagle II, as the original Camp Eagle had housed the 101st in Vietnam.

1LT Gerry Tertychny
Battalion S3 Air

We were some of the first to get there. In fact, there was not much of anything. We stayed in a newly constructed airport garage. We were closer to the bottom where it was cool, and then day by day they moved us up to get acclimated to the heat. I can remember we were also some of the first to start building the camp which later became tent city. When we got to the area it was extremely hot. I looked around and the emptiness, the heat, along with the terrain made me feel like we were totally on a separate planet. We began erecting tents while more soldiers were arriving.

PFC Stan Banach
Mortar Platoon

MAJ John Chappell's diary provides us with a chronicle of the week of our departure and arrival in Saudi Arabia:

16 Sept 1990
After hours upon hours of continuous preparation since 10 August, we finally departed Fort Campbell at about 0830 local enroute to Saudi Arabia. As a unit, we witnessed for the first time the massive requirements it takes to deploy such a force. Operation Desert Shield is probably the largest deployment for the 101st Airborne Division (Air Assault) since Vietnam. By my calculations, we will land in Saudi Arabia on the morning of 17 Sept. Ironic that this is the same day that the 327th Infantry Regiment went into Holland during World War II. It was difficult leaving families behind. Many thought that we would never go. Others thought that we'll only be gone for a short time. Lots of sad faces as we told family and friends goodbye. The Air Assault will be greatly tested in the coming months. It's an opportunity to prove it works. We shall see before this is over.

21 Sept 1990
We made it in and settled down. The days are becoming somewhat bearable. That's partly because we are becoming more acclimated

and partly because the heat is decreasing as we approach winter. Temperatures are topping out around 110–115 degrees now—much less than when the other units arrived in August. Our vehicles are coming in now—a few trucks which is at least enough to do something with. We are starting to build a routine now with training. Our daily routine consists of first call at 0430; personnel hygiene from 0500-0600; a day full of activities until 1800. After 1800 it is dark and hard to get anything done. Tempers have already gotten short. There's frustration about the unknown. We have to be hard about cleanliness. No one has dysentery yet and hopefully they won't. The dust covers everything, every day.

23 Sept 1990
My first week in the desert now. It's interesting as personalities have developed. I have garnered the nickname "The Duke" and the Company Commanders have slightly revolted over me being so hard about discipline, training, and safety. Guess I have been pressing them too much. LTC Hancock talked it over with me and asked me to back off a little. CSM "Rock" Riley is very strong. He is a solid force for supporting LTC Hancock and he gets things done.

MAJ John Chappell
Battalion XO

Shortly after returning to Fort Campbell, it was time to head to Saudi Arabia's King Fahd airport. The very first thing that hit me was the oppressive heat. We eventually set up tent city before taking our rotation north where I would soon figure out that I was no longer driving for CSM Riley, but I was now driving for LTC Hancock. Driving the HMMWV on Tapline Road was an adventure that I would never want to do again. There were more than a few times I thought I was going to die on that road and would never make it to see the war.

PFC Bruce Dittfield
Battalion Commander's Driver

In mid-September of 1990, 1-327 finally deployed to Saudi Arabia. After saying goodbye to my wife, Yon, and daughter, Andrea, who was an infant and not yet walking, we boarded aircraft for the desert on the airfield at Campbell. We flew in contracted commercial aircraft with civilian crews and flight attendants. It was strange getting on a commercial aircraft with our weapons, but those were not normal times.

When we arrived in Saudi Arabia, at King Fahd International airport, the thing I remember most vividly is the heat as we disembarked the aircraft. I mean it was like a wall of heat hitting me in the face, like being in an oven as we crossed the tarmac. I'd never experienced that kind of stifling, dry heat. We moved into the airport's parking garage and didn't do much of anything except acclimate to the heat for several days. It was cooler in the shade of the parking garage, but still damn hot.

CPT Al Gill
D Company Commander

At the onset of Desert Shield/Storm, on 14 September 1990, I deployed to Saudi Arabia assigned as RTO/NBC NCO/Driver to the Headquarters and Headquarters Company (HHC) Commander. I fondly recall the HHC Commander, CPT Michael Leon Wright, from Chicago, Illinois. CPT Wright was a "soldier's soldier."

CPL Frank Bills
NBC NCO, Headquarters and Headquarters Company

By the time the battalion had closed into Camp Eagle II, the division had been given the mission to be the covering force unit in the XVIII Airborne Corps' defensive scheme. The division rotated its infantry brigades into the covering force area while keeping one infantry brigade at Camp Eagle II for base protection. 1st Brigade was the last brigade to deploy, so it was the last brigade to rotate to the covering force area.

At Camp Eagle II from 15 September to 30 October, the battalion concentrated on acclimatization to the environment and preparing for combat. The battalion trained heavily on breaching minefields, vehicle identification, combat lifesaving techniques, chemical decontamination, and physical fitness. There was a real sense of impending battle which helped make the training very productive.

Finally, ABU moved out of the parking garage and into our portion of Camp Eagle II. Our 1SG and the soldiers of ABU worked hard to do their part in building this base camp, and there was no time to rest. We had to continually acclimatize to the desert, while being prepared to do our part in the defense of Saudi Arabia. Orders came down that we would rest and stay in our tents during the worst part of the heat of the day, but that during the cooler hours we should conduct physical training.

CPT Ken Russell
A Company Commander

To acclimatize the battalion, our work regimen mirrored the Arabs. Our daily routine would start at 0530 and would end around 1800. The heat was still unbearable in September and October, routinely being 125–135°F during the middle of the day. There was no respite from it. Soldiers would "microwave" their MRE meals by throwing them on the white tents and letting the sun do the rest. The first time I saw a cloud to block the sun was 22 October, thirty-nine days after we arrived in-country. No work was conducted between 1100 and 1600 hours, as soldiers stayed in their tents, drank water, and rested.

> Acclimatization took many forms. ABU soldiers weren't used to carrying around live ammunition 24/7, so TLs and SLs constantly checked on ammunition carried on the body and stored in the tents. We settled into base camp living while acclimatizing to the heat of the desert. Sleeping with sweat pouring out of every pore in your body became normal. ABU soldiers wrote letters, played cards, conducted individual training within squads and teams, learned to wash their uniforms by hand, and of course speculated on what was going to happen.
>
> *CPT Ken Russell*
> *A Company Commander*

Shortly, the Battalion S4 guys went out and bought a bunch of plastic basins and a lot of laundry soap that we used to wash clothes. There was no infrastructure there, as there was in later deployments to the Middle East, so we had to do our own laundry. We were only issued two sets of desert camouflage uniforms, which we called "Chocolate Chips" because they looked like that kind of cookie. We'd wear one set for a few days and then put on a clean set and wash the dirty one, which, in the outrageous heat and sun, would dry in just a few minutes. As the days wore on, the men learned to live in the harsh desert conditions.

> When we reached our staging area, which seemed to be in the middle of nowhere, it was obvious that we needed more supplies to perform our upcoming mission. The logistical support was incredible; however, the system couldn't deliver everything. Such items as batteries, rope, etc. were in short supply. Chris Reed and I were tasked to drive to a small town to acquire the listed items. This was really out of the ordinary, since most American soldiers were sequestered from the general population of Saudi Arabia. But, before we just "go out and get stuff," we first had to have some money. So, with a driver and 2½ ton truck, we headed to an administrative building several miles away to sign for $20,000 in cash for our shopping spree. What

I quickly noticed, was that most of the shopkeepers were not Saudis, but foreign nationals who were working for them. On our way back with the supplies, we stopped at a fast-food place that served chicken. I am confident that was not part of the tour. To be sure, we used our own money for the lunch break—the MREs could wait. We had to keep our weapons in the truck, which seemed weird, but it was the protocol at the time. We didn't want to upset the sensibilities of the host country (Kingdom).

It was late afternoon in the desert. Far in the distance, we could see something moving toward us, but not at a very fast pace. At first it appeared that it would bypass our position and continue on its way. We were not quite sure what to make of it. We were close to the Iraqi border, but still in Saudi Arabia. As it got closer, we could see a vehicle or two trailing the cluster. Several minutes later, it was clear they were headed straight toward us. With all this vast space around us, a goat herder had brought all 400–600 of his animals through our position with his water trucks following. There was nothing that we could really do about it without causing an international crisis with the Saudi government or with the Brotherhood of Goat Herders Union Local 1067.

Having water is essential. Our water supply was supplemented by packaged water from within the region. It was odd at the time to see water in the clear packages with Arabic writing on them, it seemed like a novel idea. The writing translated as, "Gift from the King".

CPT Tom Guleff
Battalion S1

Individual soldiers were experiencing problems as well. We had been issued only two sets of desert uniforms and two pairs of jungle boots for the deployment (the desert boots not yet being in the system for issue). Additionally, we had only the dozen or so pairs of socks and half-dozen t-shirts that were on our clothing packing list. To maintain hygiene, this limited amount of clothing had to be washed frequently. The laundry and bath units of earlier wars had largely been relegated to the reserve components that had yet to deploy to Saudi Arabia. A contract laundry service would eventually appear, but that was only available when we were back at Camp Eagle.

The solution was two-fold. The immediate response was to purchase items locally. MAJ Chappell designated me the battalion purchasing officer and Tom Guleff, our S1 was the Class-A-agent

> (carried the money). In short, I ordered the supplies, and he was the bank carrying the cash. Accompanied by MAJ Tom Dempsey, the battalion S3 and a former Foreign Area Officer and fluent Arab speaker, we ventured out into the city of Dammam in search of supplies. We quickly found a stationery store that met our needs for office supplies. We also made the acquaintance of a Pakistani shopkeeper from whom we purchased many large, plastic wash basins which we distributed to the soldiers for washing clothes.
>
> *CPT Chris Reed*
> *Battalion Assistant S4*

We continued to eat MREs for a couple of weeks until the mess hall (tent) got set up and then we would get heated Tray-Rations, or "T-Rats," once a day, typically for breakfast or dinner. The roast beef and rice was good, but they were all better than MREs. Initially, the mess guys opened all the T-Rat trays to save time as the line moved through. This, of course, led to a massive swarm of flies crawling all over the food—flies that we knew had just come from our open-air latrines. The result was predictable—we all got the shits. After a couple of days, they stopped this practice.

> I was in a tent with 1LT George Glaze, 2LT Tom Evans, CPT Sung Lee, who was the Battalion Commo Officer, and CPT Jim Knickrehm, who worked in the battalion S3 shop. We'd do PT in the morning or late afternoon and try to get a shower in the evening. When the sun went down, around 1800, it got dark fast and, since we didn't have any lights, we sat around talking and then went to sleep. Mail started pretty soon, and we spent a lot of time writing letters, many to folks back home who sent letters addressed to "Any Soldier." I recall that it took about twelve days for me to get a letter mailed from the States or for my folks to get one I sent to them.
>
> Gradually, we got acclimated to the weather and the companies increased their physical activity—we'd do PT during the day, and they would go out into the desert to do local training and to get used to having full-strength platoons and companies. In the past, rifle platoons were always short of men and had an average strength of about twenty-five to thirty guys. Now, with all the reinforcements we had gotten before deploying, they were at full-strength, about forty men. One day, a bunch of us played a marathon game of volleyball in the middle of the day. Most of us were lieutenants but LTC Hancock, always the competitor, and The Duke were out there, too. We got sunburned pretty good and a lot of us had the white outlines of our sunglasses on our faces and temples where the sun didn't hit us.

George, who always had his hair cut in a “high-and-tight,” looked particularly ridiculous.

We got used to constantly drinking warm water and our bodies adjusted to the environment, so we didn’t need to drink as much. The rule was that you always had to have with you, at a minimum, your gas mask and your weapon. So once, George went down to the showers, about 50 meters from our tent, wearing nothing but his boots, his gas mask carrier (which he moved around to his front), and carrying his rifle and his shower stuff. Unfortunately, the sight of his bare ass heading towards the shower point has been indelibly etched on my memory, along with the unprintable comments that were directed at him. In his defense, he had, technically, met the minimum requirement, as he had both his mask and his weapon.

1LT Gerry Tertychny
Battalion S3 Air

I was in 3d Platoon, A Company, 1-327 Infantry and at the time I was in a weapons squad. I was a SAW gunner/anti-armor gunner and carried the M-249 Squad Automatic Weapon and, if it was needed, the M-47 Dragon anti-tank missile.

When we arrived at Camp Eagle II, our days were spent taking long walks out in the open desert getting used to the heat and patrolling in the sand, PT to build up endurance, weapons cleaning, and flash card training on armored vehicles and aircraft. I remember my late Uncle Rudy, who was a member of the Special Forces, visiting me. It brought me great comfort to see him and the advice he gave me to help with coping while being deployed was great. He told me to “trust in my command staff, trust my officer’s decisions, trust in my fellow soldiers, remember my training, and that, if I should fall, I would not be forgotten.”

Once we went on a two-mile road march with full combat gear and we all joked, “just two miles … come on, make it more of a challenge.” We could not have been more wrong about how easy we thought it would be—those were the toughest two miles ever! The heat and combat load kicked our asses.

PFC Jesse Hernandez
3d Platoon, A Company

Your mission, should you choose to accept it (right out of a James Bond movie), is to get some real food and not just the standard MREs day in and day out.

Initially at the tent city, I bunked with HHC leadership, to include CPT Wright (Commander), 1LT Brian Blue (Executive Officer), 1SG Cleveland Terry, and SPC Tilas Law (Driver for the Executive Officer). My battle buddy was Specialist Tilas Law.

After several days in this tent, 1SG Terry directed that, as the junior personnel in the tent, SPC Law and I had to clean the tent. Law and I were not thrilled about cleaning behind some grown a** men, so Law replied to 1SG Terry that "respectfully" that was not our job. With a big grin, 1SG Terry replied, "Well boys, that is protocol. I say again, that is "Proooootoooooocooooollllllll." He made the word "protocol" last for what felt like an hour. So, suffice it to say that SPC Law and I made it our mission to find another tent to lay our heads as soon as we could. That is just a funny recollection that I will never forget. Sometimes trivial things are memorable.

Often we got near the Air Force dining facility and saw in amazement real food being cooked, griddled, and fried. We thought it was a Shoney's Buffett. We salivated like puppies but were turned away because we were in the Army. Well, guess what? We knew the mission. We went to the Air Force BX store and bought Air Force physical training (PT) gear. So, each day after we washed the trucks, we parked them, switched into the Air Force PT gear, and dined on a heavenly American breakfast. Working Smarter not Harder, but sooooo worth it! It was such a step up from MREs. Many years later, we found out that others in HHC had also learned that trick and would sneak over there for some good home cooking, as well. Again, the petty things are often embedded in our memories.

On 19 October 1990, the chaplain invited all True Believer Christians to come for Baptism, which I did confidently. It was an uplifting period in my life after receiving Jesus Christ my Lord at the age of 9 years old and has kept my foundation solid even in the most challenging of times.

CPL Frank Bills
NBC NCO, Headquarters and Headquarters Company

Perhaps the most important part of our stay in Camp Eagle II was the nurturing of the troops' morale. At this time (late September and early October) there were three areas that I believed were critical to bolstering morale. First was making sure the soldiers knew that the country was behind them and that what they were doing was right. Fresh in everyone's mind was the legacy of the Vietnam War and how many soldiers felt abandoned by their countrymen. The rationale for our deployment was drummed into the troops; why they were in Saudi Arabia and that what they were going to accomplish was not only right, but much appreciated by the American people. The thousands of letters the battalion received from San Mateo, California, helped reinforce this theme. Similarly, a small Catholic school in Morganfield, Kentucky, Saint Ann's Elementary School, adopted our battalion and sent thousands of letters to us.

Back at Fort Campbell, the battalion's Family Support Group was established and functioning well. My wife, the company commanders' wives, and the NCOs' wives were doing their best to make sure that personal and family problems were solved. The married personnel knew that their loved ones were being well taken care of by the stay-behind personnel and Family Support Group. This helped take some of the pressure off the back of the married soldiers, as they had little to no recourse in affecting what happened at Fort Campbell.

The second area for bolstering morale was convincing our soldiers that we would defeat the Iraqi Army. The media made much of how the Iraqis were masters of desert warfare and were "battle hardened." Intelligence briefings reinforced the idea that they were the world's fourth largest army and that they were well equipped; nerve gas, Mig29s, SCUDs, triangle trench defenses, and T72 tanks were part of their inventory. In the Middle East, the Iraqi Army was a very formidable force.

To offset this aura of Iraqi invincibility a concentrated effort was undertaken to look for Iraq's weaknesses in equipment and tactics. Studying the Iraqi order of battle, tactics, and equipment gave our soldiers confidence that when push came to shove, we would be victorious. The saying, "We're not Iran," which our brigade commander first echoed before going to Saudi Arabia, became the phrase which summed up our confidence.

> One force multiplier that I frequently used prior to and during Desert Shield/Storm was my access to classified information. While most of the battalion did not usually need access, the intelligence available provided key leaders and staff the clarity they needed to make decisions. Prior to deploying, my access provided the battalion's leadership with a "heads-up" that things were serious and that it would likely require us to deploy. Once deployed to Saudi Arabia, I frequently walked miles to brigade and division headquarters (while in garrison at Camp Eagle II, King Fahd International Airport in the desert's blazing heat) for their classified updates, then I would report back to LTC Hancock what I had heard and seen. During those trips I also liaised with outside organizations and had access to other systems and capabilities that required Top Secret clearances.
>
> *CPT Jose Delgado*
> *Battalion S2*

During our stay at Camp Eagle II, we trained—for my company, lots of vehicle identification. We had decks of cards with various armored vehicles, tracked and wheels, in profile. D Company soldiers got so proficient with the cards it was no longer a challenge, so we thought of ways to make it harder. We buried part of the cards in sand, so only a part of the vehicle was visible, and then made the soldiers use binoculars from 25 to 50 feet away—and they mastered that, too. We worked on this so hard because between Iraq and the alliance of countries opposing them there was just about every type of armored vehicle built in the last thirty years or so; we considered fratricide a serious threat. We also did some ruck marches and air assault training, but the air assault training with helicopters was cut back to almost nothing because the sand was eating away the edges of the rotor blades at an incredibly fast rate.

During that time my platoons assisted in airfield security, running mounted patrols in their HMMWVs around the perimeter fence that surrounded the King Fahd flight lines, and using their TOW weapon sights, day and night sights, to scan the perimeter from on top of a building in the airport complex.

Early on, we learned about several issues and came up with innovative ways of operating in the desert:

First, we did not have time to have our green vehicles painted with desert camouflage paint, and they stuck out like sore thumbs even from a long distance away. We quickly found some light-colored dirt / clay and after mixing big batches of mud, we smeared the vehicles with that slurry—which worked well as it was not raining, at all, when we arrived. At least we weren't green in a desert that was 100 per cent brown.

Second, in the areas we were training around King Fahd, there were several areas of very soft sand. The drivers were not used to driving in that stuff, and, early on, we had several TOW HMMWVs stuck. We could self-recover the ones that got stuck with sling ropes, chains, and other vehicles from the company, but we worried about what might happen when vehicles were dispersed, and other vehicles weren't readily available. One of my NCOs found that an 8–10-foot section of chain link fencing worked wonders—unroll it, stick it under the spinning tires, and out they came. So, we acquired rolls of chain link for all the TOW vehicles and had few problems after that.

Third, I got a message to bring all my TOW sights (the TOW system had separate sights for day and night —forty sights total) to a division maintenance facility. The sights were large and, at

> the time, technologically advanced. When we got the sights to the maintenance guys, I asked them what they were going to do; they said the sights needed to be pressure tested and completely inspected—something that had to be done every six months with TOW systems. I told them we'd had all that done before we left Campbell. One of the maintenance NCOs told me the pressure testing had to be done with nitrogen, and they hadn't had any back at Campbell, but now they did. When they did the pressure testing, almost half the sights blew seals and had to be repaired, resealed, and retested. It took a while, but every sight eventually passed the tests, and every issue was addressed / repaired.
>
> Last, the desert is incredibly hard on equipment, especially vehicles. Sand and fine dust gets everywhere, clogging air filters and getting oil dirty fast. We used panty hose to stretch over our air intakes as a kind of additional filter to keep dust and sand out of the engines, and this seemed to help, but we still needed oil and air filter changes frequently.
>
> *CPT Al Gill*
> *D Company Commander*

The last piece of maintaining morale was to kill rumors. "We're going home by Christmas," "the 82d is pulling out," "the 10th Mountain is replacing us," were some of the rumors that were circulating. Some had a little validity, but most did not. Many were bits of data that the soldiers received in their mail from home. Rumors are at best bothersome but can severely sap morale, especially of troops who are on an open-ended and dangerous mission.

The way I handled this was to hold a weekly battalion formation with the sole purpose of killing rumors. Using a bullhorn, I would invite one soldier from each of the five companies to come to the front of the formation and relate what the rumor was in their company. I would then address each of the five rumors. I would not equivocate but tell the truth as best I knew it on each of the rumors. This seemed to work and helped, I believe, build trust between the soldiers and their leadership.

Observations

Morale is a tricky and important matter for leaders. How do you maintain morale when there are such harsh conditions and no end in sight for the mission? I found telling the truth, being hard but not stupid, and fixing as best you can the soldiers' complaints was a step in the right direction.

As the battalion continued to train at Camp Eagle II, the rest of the division and XVIII Airborne Corps were active. The division had started to move brigades north to the covering force area. The first move was to establish FOB BASTOGNE at the city of An Nuayriyah, which was on Tapline Road and about 115 kilometers south of the Kuwaiti border. By the end of September, the 2d Brigade had established a second site, FOB OASIS, at the abandoned desert town of Qaryat as Sufla, which was 75 kilometers west of FOB BASTOGNE. The division would ultimately have a covering force area that stretched 115 kilometers from An Nuariyah, west along Tapline Road, to the town of Al Wariah.

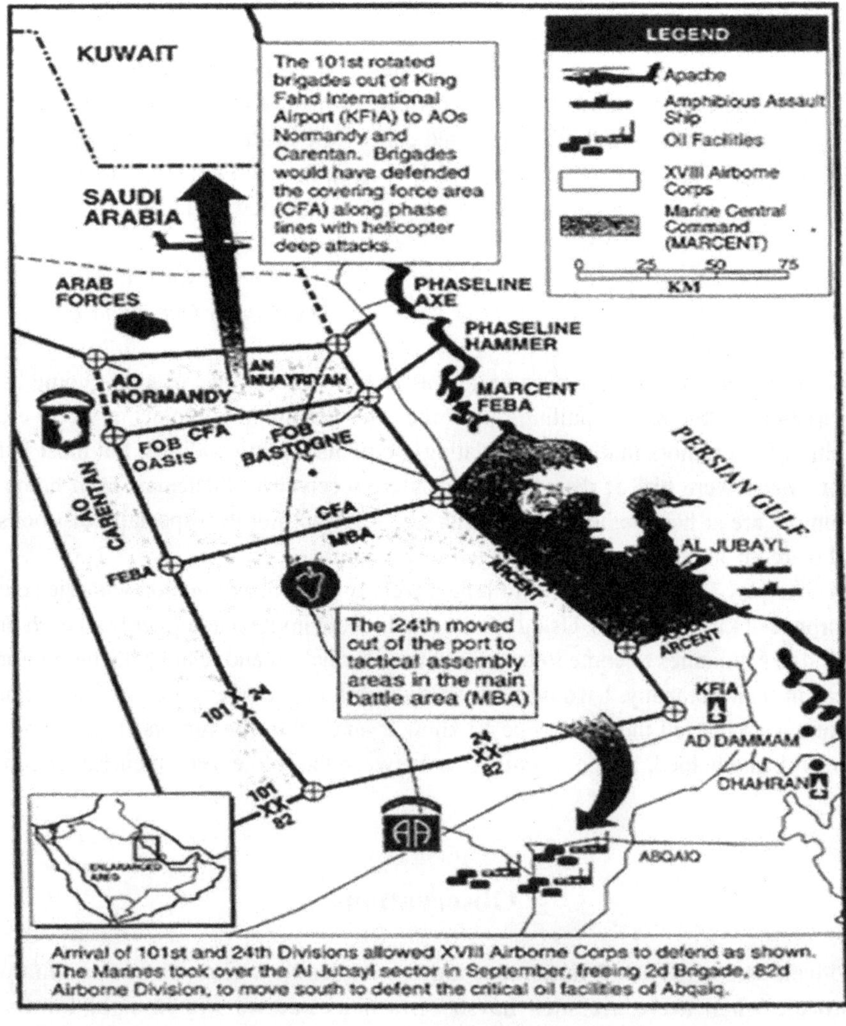

Arrival of 101st and 24th Divisions allowed XVIII Airborne Corps to defend as shown. The Marines took over the Al Jubayl sector in September, freeing 2d Brigade, 82d Airborne Division, to move south to defent the critical oil facilities of Abqaiq.

101st Airborne (Air Assault) Covering Force Disposition Sept 1990 – Jan 1991.

CHAPTER 6

COVERING FORCE

AO NORMANDY

October 1990 – January 1991

At the end of October 1990, the battalion prepared to take its place in the division's covering force mission. The area given to my battalion was the most western and northern portion of the XVIII Airborne Corps sector. Our mission was to be the forward element of the division's covering force, to guard the division's western flank and, if attacked, to fall back through the 2d Brigade's sector to another defensive position, some 40 kilometers to our rear. The Iraqi force arrayed against our brigade's sector was one armored division. The threat arrayed against the entire division sector was two armored divisions and one mechanized division.

> In early October, I had another stroke of good fortune. Back in May, before any of us even knew who Saddam Hussein was or the location of Kuwait, the XO of A Company, 1LT Chris Chiarello, had put in a request to branch transfer from the Infantry to the Quartermaster Corps. His request was approved, and he got notification that he was to move out of our battalion and over to a support battalion, which left the A Company XO position vacant. This revelation was passed on to us at a battalion staff meeting. When I heard the news, I looked directly at the Duke and then to MAJ Dempsey. They looked at each other, grinned, and just nodded to me as if to say, "Yeah, yeah … keep your pants on—you can go."
>
> *1LT Gerry Tertychny*
> *A Company XO*

For the next three months, we rotated up to the border for three- or four-week periods, keeping an eye on the border area and training in the desert. The weather started to get increasingly cool, and eventually got downright cold. We were issued "desert parkas," long coats printed in a black and dark green pixilated pattern that came with a hood and a liner made from the same material as a field jacket liner or poncho liner. Great piece of gear—we never went anywhere without them. Throughout this period, we continued to receive replacements to fill vacant positions.

> After graduation from West Point in May of 1990 and commissioning as a 2LT in the Infantry, I completed the Infantry Officer Basic Course at Fort Benning, Georgia. During my time at the Officer Basic Course, Iraq invaded Kuwait and the 101st was deployed to support Operation Desert Shield. I had completed Airborne and Ranger training during my summer assignments at West Point, so I was sent directly to Fort Campbell after completing IOBC.
>
> I met my platoon that first evening and spent the night with the platoon in our assigned tents. Within a few days of my arrival, I participated in the first major rehearsal of the battle plan that eventually became the initial mission to establish FOB Cobra. I spent those first few days getting to know the platoon and understanding the current situation. NCO leadership in the platoon was tremendous and very supportive of a young lieutenant arriving mid-stream into the war effort.
>
> *2LT Dave Esposito*
> *1st Platoon Leader, Alpha Company*

Once, we went to a deserted desert village and practiced company-level attacks there. We spent the hours reading and writing letters and playing cards. Gradually, we received "supplements" to augment our MREs—fruit, Cokes, bread, and candy. Looking back and comparing it with the amount of support that soldiers in a combat zone get I am amazed with how little we got along. We lived out of our rucksacks, slept on the ground or a cot, had zero electricity, ate MREs, did our own laundry, and learned how to make the best of it. One thing that was irritating was that we didn't know when it would end—our deployment was open-ended. Today, and even in Vietnam, soldiers know exactly, or within a week or so, when they will re-deploy and go home. Back then, we had no idea—speculation, and rumors, ran rampant.

> In the months following our arrival in Saudi Arabia, a massive coalition of forces went to work setting the stage for what would be historical in nature. The buildup and deterrent phase dubbed Desert Shield. In my opinion, Saddam Hussein and his military let their window of opportunity close if they had ever planned to use chemical weapons against coalition forces. The use of weapons of

mass destruction (WMD) would, I believe, have significantly altered the Coalition's ability to build a force as quickly.

2LT Tom Evans
Battalion NBC Officer

I can sound intelligent in describing all this now, with the benefit of time and experience. However, at the time, as a junior officer with three years of service, we seemed consumed with too much to do and not enough time to do it. It was chaotic at times as the unit sorted through the real-world scenarios we found ourselves in and some of the old ways we did stuff. But we had several things going for us in that we had the best training a unit could have at that time in our country and, I believe, in the world. Additionally, the upper echelon of the Army leadership had made some future weapon systems choices in the Bradley Fighting Vehicle, the self-propelled howitzer, the HMMWV, and the Blackhawk Helicopter—all of which were part of this fight.

Last, we had good, solid leadership throughout our unit—from platoons to companies, from the battalion staff to the brigade staff. We had leadership that made practical, on-the-spot calls that, I believe, took bravery and risk to personal careers. And then that same leadership gave room for initiative and growth at the platoon level. This was super important. And I say so because, in the other twenty-six years of my career, I witnessed other types of leadership that was not so focused on the important stuff.

1LT George Glaze
Support Platoon Leader

On 8 November it was announced that VII Corps from Germany was deploying to join the Coalition Force in Saudi Arabia. VII Corps was a big, powerful, mechanized and armored corps. VII Corps' deployment was meant to increase pressure on Iraq. No war plan had VII Corps deploying from Germany and fighting in the Middle East. Its deployment was a major move.

Once VII Corps arrived, the US Army would have over 50 per cent of its fighting force in Saudi Arabia. If the pressure on Iraq failed, in my opinion, there would be war. There was no way the Bush Administration or its military leaders were going to allow American forces to rot in the Saudi Arabian desert.

While VII Corps deployed to Saudi, we continued to execute the covering force mission, along with the two other infantry brigades in the 101st. We spent Thanksgiving and Christmas up on the border and the mess hall guys outdid themselves both times—we had absolutely fantastic meals on those days.

Again, MAJ John Chappell's journal provides some insight:

5 Oct 1990
The Command Group left on a reconnaissance mission up north (3 Oct) and are due back tonight. We anticipate that we will head up north to our defensive area of operations. It will work out that we will be 60 days forward and about 30 days back in our new home "Tent City". A lot of speculation continues about whether or not we shall do something offensive in November. Nothing solid yet.

8 Oct 1990
The Commander's Reconnaissance returned from up north. Our new area of operations will be AO Normandy. It's farther out in the desert to the west than any of us have been before. We will be the western most flank in a second defensive array behind our Arab Allies (Egyptian, Kuwaiti, Syrian, and Saudi). The Company Commanders have settled down and realize how important discipline really is. They are getting more mature by the day. CSM "Rock" Riley is the absolute best CSM that I've seen in my limited years of service. He's got the respect of all and is just what the Battalion needed on this deployment.

14 Oct 1990
Things have continued apace here. There is talk of increased threats from terrorists now. Luckily, no one has hit any of the American forces yet save one MP soldier. However, it's possible that he may have shot himself. I'm sure there is an investigation underway. Worries of the Iraqi chemical threat is always in the back of our soldiers' minds. Hopefully we won't have to deal with that. We will move up north at the end of the month.

20 Oct 1990
Have been up north on a reconnaissance mission. The Battalion will move north on or about 31 Oct and stay until 20 Nov. We're then supposed to return to Tent City for twenty-five days and then go back again. We're going to rehearse the covering force mission. As far as the home front, wives and families are not getting any mail and they believe no one is writing to them. Of course, that is not true, but they think that. I think that most are starting to realize that their husbands are not going to be home for Christmas or any other near-term holidays. Sadly, we've had a few deaths back home—mostly children—and we've had to send people back on emergency leave. We continue to plod along.

27 Oct 1990
In the past week, our biggest efforts have been spent getting rid of an intestinal virus. Everyone here gets amoebic dysentery sooner or later. Hopefully, it will all pass by the time we must move north. Rumors continue to abound here, and the Battalion leadership tries to keep them under control. We are to become masters of the defense as we prepare. Later, I guess we'll prepare for the offense. We still think the American people are generally behind us. Hopefully, that will not change.

11 Nov 1990
As time moves along, we approach two months in the desert now. The weather has cooled significantly. The days are 80–90 degrees and nights at 50–60 degrees. The soldiers are thankful for the change in the weather. The dysentery has passed for now. We moved up north to our position for the current operations plan. Everything is focused on the defense with the 101st set up as a covering force. 1st BN, 327th Infantry is the northern most US unit. We're executing this mission to the best of our ability. It helps keep the soldiers occupied and their minds off home.

27 Nov 1990
Thanksgiving is over and we've returned to Camp Eagle II. The training period went well but most of us are happy to be back at Tent City. Whether we admit it or not, this place is slowly becoming our home. Comfort for every soldier consists of a warm meal, a cot, an occasional warm shower and mail. Mail is truly a morale booster. We've got a lot of people writing to us to include family, friends, supporters from San Mateo, CA and others we've never met.

11 Jan 1991
Been a while since my last entry so I'll bring things up to date. The weather began to turn poor with areas of intermittent rain. We redeployed back to sector after a stint at Camp Eagle II. While in sector, Iraq fired a Scud missile or two in the direction of Israel. The missiles impacted in Iraqi territory, but this was an effort to send a message that Iraq would attack Israel if the Coalition Forces did anything. Christmas has come and gone. It was sad for everyone, but we made it through with another big holiday meal. It's been cold up here this time—really turned bad after Christmas.

MAJ John Chappell
Battalion XO

There were numerous challenges in accomplishing our covering force mission. The first was the sheer magnitude of our battalion sector, which was 20 kilometers wide and 25 kilometers deep. Just the surveillance of the area was difficult for the force structure of an air assault infantry battalion. With our few vehicles, we found our ability to defend this large area, and our ability to be mobile, limited.

> My platoon was always working to maintain the unit supplies including food, fuel, and ammunition for the Bastogne Bulldogs. It was my boss' job as the Battalion Logistical Officer, the S4, to order and arrange pickup. But my job was to make the pickups and deliveries of said supplies to our units. The support platoon had the only hauling capability in the battalion, with seven M35 2½ Ton trucks, known as "deuce and a half." We had five cargo trucks for hauling and one maintenance truck for the Maintenance Platoon. And finally, we had one truck with fuel pods for refueling the HMMWVs throughout the battalion—with the primary mission of supplying our tank killing capabilities in the twenty TOW HMMWVs of D Company.
>
> *1LT George Glaze*
> *Support Platoon Leader*

A second challenge was the lack of any armor in our defensive scheme. The closest armored formations were the 3d Armored Cavalry Regiment, 75 kilometers to the east, and the 24th Infantry Division, 80 kilometers to the south. We were given six inflatable Ml dummy tanks as a deception measure, but we found these were of limited use because we had no real armored force to exploit the deception. Our sector, as the most western unit in the covering force, had no unit to tie into on our western flank. The lack of any armored force to counter an attack on our exposed western flank was a serious problem.

A third challenge was the barrenness of the terrain we were occupying. The battalion sector was in a desert without water, shade, vegetation, or identifiable terrain features and with temperatures over 100 degrees. Efforts were made to keep the soldiers as comfortable as possible by bringing pup tents for shade and providing gravity showers. However, it was harsh going for everyone throughout our time in the covering force area. Soldiers observed nomadic Bedouin sheep herders with their Toyota pickup trucks and seemingly luxurious tents with rugs for flooring and wished for such amenities.

The final challenge was the possible passage of lines with the Saudi brigade to our immediate north. In a liaison meeting, the Saudi brigade commander said his unit was going to defend its position and would not fall back through our defenses. It was my brigade commander's opinion, and mine, that an Iraqi attack in November could have punched through the Saudi lines and done considerable damage to the Coalition build-up. How we were going to handle any Saudi retrograde movement was never realistically discussed with them and never resolved.

To meet these challenges, the battalion's scheme of maneuver for the covering force was focused around our twenty TOW anti-tank vehicles and the one 105mm artillery battery that was in direct support of the battalion. The battalion area was divided into two sectors, with a company commander placed in charge of each sector. Each of the company commanders received eight TOW vehicles for their sector, while four TOWs were held in battalion reserve. The remainder of the battalion's HMMWVs transported infantry soldiers around to provide close-in protection for the TOW vehicles. TOW vehicle firing positions were dug by the engineers throughout the two sectors and the company commanders were expected to fight their TOW force through their sector.

The remainder of the battalion was put in a battle position at the rear of the battalion sector. After delaying the attacking Iraqi force, the battalion was to conduct a passage of lines through the 2d Brigade to our south and then establish another defensive position. In performing this covering force mission, the battalion had to stay mobile. All personnel had to have a dedicated vehicle to move on the battlefield; otherwise, they would be cut off, bypassed, or left behind. The use of the TOW vehicles to delay enemy forces as we moved back through our sector was the only feasible course of action we found to accomplish the mission.

> LTC Hancock had already taken us up into the covering force area on a recon. The area of AO Normandy was incredibly barren, mostly flat, and had zero vegetation. To me, it looked like what I had always imagined the surface of the moon, or Mars, would be.
>
> During the recon into the AO, one of our vehicles broke down, and LTC Hancock was invited, along with others, to have a meal with the local Emir in a small town along Tapline Road while we waited for mechanics to assist with the vehicle.
>
> We had a good meal, lamb and vegetables, and I was seated at a table with the Emir's oldest son, a big guy in his middle twenties, I'd guess. He spoke perfect English. I asked him how he had learned English so well—he smiled and said, "well, I spent four years and received my degree from Ohio State University." Strange days.
>
> AO Normandy was bisected by the Tapline Road—the straightest road I'd ever seen, two lane, undivided, which I think was built to support an oil pipeline running adjacent to it, buried in most places. There were some hills from which you could easily see the road stretching out for more than 10 miles into the distance, and Saudis

travelling along the road often drove at excessive speeds of 100 mph, or even more, on the Tapline.

Once we occupied AO Normandy, D Company platoons were out in front of the rifle companies and the BN CP, facing northwest on either side of Tapline Road. They picked battle positions for their TOW vehicles oriented in the direction from which any Iraqi incursion, attack, or armored forces would come from, and division engineer assets soon showed up to dig one or two positions for each TOW vehicle. These were three-sided berm positions into which the vehicles could drive, open on the rear side.

While we were in the covering force mission, we received a visit from General Peay, the Division Commander. LTC Hancock was also there. General Peay was a very calm and reserved man. He spent most of his time talking to soldiers and LTC Hancock. At one point, he asked me if I knew that the 101st was, at that time, the most forward US unit, closest to Iraq. I told him I did. He asked me if I realized that 1st Brigade was the most forward unit in the division. I said I did. He asked me if I knew 1-327 was the most forward unit in the brigade. I said I did. And he said, "well then, I guess you realize your company is the most forward unit in 1-327 and will be the first ground unit engaged if the Iraqis come here." I said, "Yes Sir." And he then asked if we were ready. I told him we were, with confidence, because I believed that we were. Kind of sounds dramatic now, but at that time, the perceived threat of an Iraqi attack into our battalion was considered entirely possible.

One day I saw four or five 5-ton trucks approaching, loaded with pallets of wooden boxes, and when they arrived, I said, "what the hell is this?" One of the drivers said, "these are your TOW missiles."

We took the missiles off the pallets and stacked them on the desert floor, and let me tell you, it was a hell of a big stack. Twenty x TOW vehicles; racks for seven missiles in each vehicle; 140 missiles. Every missile had to be uncrated. The platoons had become used to having the rear of the vehicles and missile racks empty and had stored rucksacks and other equipment inside their vehicles. That had to change. Rucksacks and various other equipment had to be tied to the outsides of the vehicles to make room for the missiles. There was something about receiving those missiles that removed any doubts about whether we were going to war. In a peacetime Army, TOW gunners were authorized/required to fire one live missile per year—and those training missiles did not have explosive warheads. We'd just gotten 140 new TOW IIA missiles in one issue.

At some point during the covering force mission, the date I no longer remember, we conducted a battalion live fire exercise; I believe this happened before we were issued our full combat load of TOW IIA missiles. The live fire included rifle companies taking down a simulated Iraqi strongpoint, consisting of berms and trenches, and after seizing the enemy strongpoint, the scenario included an Iraqi counterattack with armor. Delta company TOWS would be called up and deal with the armor threat by firing live TOW missiles. We'd be firing from a low ridge overlooking the battalion strongpoint.

When we got the missiles, one per gunner, NCOs brought to my attention that the missiles were all very old, from a previous generation of TOW missiles. They had dates on the crates/missiles, akin to expiration dates; we were well past those dates—by years, in fact. I remember discussing this with members of the battalion staff, and perhaps LTC Hancock, and voicing reservations about firing these things over the heads of the soldiers in the rifle companies who would be occupying the Iraqi strongpoint in front of/at the base of the ridge from which the TOWs would be fired. I thought nothing would be lost by having the soldiers vacate the strongpoint before we fired, and we might avoid an accident. Eventually, that was the decision made.

When the date of execution arrived, we got to the range and BG Shelton, the ADC was there—as was Colonel Hill and LTC Hancock. When we were ready to fire the TOWs, the scenario called for me to get a radio call about an enemy armor counterattack, and then call up the TOWs, by section (two vehicles in a section) to fire their missiles.

The first two vehicles fired, and both hit their targets (there were old car hulks out on the range from about 2,000 to 3,500 meters). When the second section fired, however, one of the missiles came off the launcher, and immediately began tumbling, hitting the ground and going airborne again several times before exploding near the unoccupied strongpoint. I'll always remember looking to my left, and seeing one general officer and two field grades looking at me, at the same time, with looks that said, without words, "what the fuck?" All I could do was shrug, and say, "looked like a broken wire after the missile was fired." By the time all gunners had fired their missiles, four or five had malfunctioned. But no one was injured, and

I passed the word to other D Company commanders of 1st brigade that something wasn't right with those old missiles.

It was also during the covering force mission that my driver and I witnessed a horrible accident on Tapline Road. We were in our HMMWV, D-6, early one morning when we noticed a thin stream of black smoke rising on the horizon, towards Tapline Road. I asked Jon to drive in that direction, and when we arrived, we saw two tractor trailers, one a gasoline tanker and the other with a flatbed trailer—full of sheep. They'd been driving in opposite directions at probably at 70–80 miles per hour. I suspect one of the drivers went to sleep, drifted into the other lane, and hit head on.

When we arrived, you could feel the heat of the burning gasoline on your face at 100 yards. One of the drivers had been thrown clear, a good 30–40 yards from the trucks, and was lying dead in the sand, with apparently most of his bones broken. The other driver was immolated in his truck. The flames were rising about 30–40 yards in the air. Many sheep had been killed outright and were lying around in every state of dismemberment. Others seemed to be in shock and stood near the burning vehicles with their wool smoking.

The flames began to die down as the gasoline was consumed, and an ambulance arrived. They got a body bag out and approached the dead driver's body. The man had been tall, and when they laid his body on the bag, it was clear it wasn't going to fit. With a shrug, one medic simply folded his legs up on to his torso—the bones in both being shattered.

As Jon and I turned to leave, he spotted the emblem from one of the truck's grilles that had been thrown clear and was undamaged. It was a big Mercedes emblem. Jon promptly tied it to the front of D-6 and we drove around with it for weeks.

CPT Al Gill
D Company Commander

By mid-November, the belief that we were going to go on the offensive started to prevail in the battalion. As already mentioned, President Bush had ordered, on 8 November, the deployment of VII Corps in Germany to Saudi Arabia. Additionally, the Air Force was receiving reinforcements and had just flexed its muscles in Operation IMMINENT THUNDER on 17–18 November.

One of the highlights of my career as an infantry officer was the battalion night live fire exercise we did during this time. A to-scale model of an Iraqi triangular strongpoint was built in the desert of this training area. Our battalion had the opportunity to conduct a night live fire assault on this strongpoint, and then conduct a passage of lines with a 24th Infantry Division mechanized battalion as it moved into a live fire assault. Our battalion had to breach the 20ft sand wall with a Bangalore torpedo, then the infantry companies had to assault through the breach and secure each of the corners of the strongpoint. Once the strongpoints were secured, a dismounted TOW team attached to each infantry company would set up a TOW for firing. We did a couple of daytime dry-fire rehearsals prior, and then we executed the night Live Fire Exercise (LFX). ABU soldiers did a great job and once our corner of the strongpoint was secure with the TOW set up, we had a ring-side seat for the night passage of a mechanized battalion as they moved into their own LFX. It was a spectacular sight.

CPT Ken Russell
A Company Commander

The reality that the only way to go home was to go through the Iraqi Army was slowly but surely dawning on our soldiers. The battalion was starting its fourth month in the desert and the idea of spending a year or more there in that hellhole waiting for the economic sanctions to work was repugnant at best.

As the months would go by, we would get closer to the air war. We traveled many times as a Mortar Platoon and practiced our hip shot missions, direct fire missions, and air assault operations. We were prepared for anything and ready to fight at any time. I remember that time before the air war thinking that Saddam would give up and pull out of Kuwait. When we would get close to the Kuwait/Iraq Border we would hear over the radio the Voice of Peace from Baghdad, "American Soldiers in the Arab land, give up now or you will come back in coffins." All of us in the Mortar Platoon would just laugh. One time, Baghdad Betty said our wives and girlfriends were sleeping with Bart Simpson and Iraq has hidden surprises for us if we escalated our aggression. That's funny—if the 101st Airborne Division has another Rendezvous with Destiny, you will get your asses killed. This motivated us. One more thing that motivated us was Thanksgiving dinner and Christmas dinner up north in the field. The food was good but spending this time with my Army Family was really special. We still talk about this after all these years. I remember CSM Riley visiting us and telling us that we (81mm Mortar Platoon) were his favorite! How about that/Motivation 101. December 31st at 2359, many of us stayed up to say Happy New Year. One of those men was our platoon sergeant, SFC Levesque. He was a great leader. Many years later, me and five of his 81mm Mortar Platoon Gulf War Veterans would be folding his burial flag at Fort Campbell. MSG (Ret) Thomas Levesque, July 13, 1953—June 1, 2007.

PFC Rich Hagedorn
Mortar Platoon

Observations

I have always been grateful to the Iraqi Army for not attacking our Covering Force Area. The battalion was limited in mobility, had an open flank, was responsible for way too much terrain (500 square kilometers), and had no armored counterattack force. Once air assault soldiers leave their helicopters, they become light infantry and are ill-suited for a covering force mission in a desert environment against a mechanized force. Until VII Corps arrived, there were few options for CENTCOM planners, as the forces available were limited for the Covering Force mission. But it was a dicey proposition for the battalions from the 101st who were executing it.

Vietnam Stories

In late September 1990, news reporter Joe Galloway published an article in *US News and World Report* magazine concerning the Vietnam War's 1965 Battle of the Ia Drang. Galloway participated in the battle as a reporter. The article, titled "Vietnam Stories," described how the 1st Squadron, 7th Cavalry Regiment, under LTC Hal Moore, air assaulted by UH1 helicopters to conduct a search and destroy operation against North Vietnamese forces. The article would lead to the 1992 book, *We Were Soldiers Once ... and Young*. The book was written by Galloway and LTG (Ret) Hal Moore. Later, in 2002, the book was made into a movie starring Mel Gibson as Hal Moore.

In late October, by pure chance or serendipity or divine intervention, someone put the magazine on my cot. I had heard of the Battle of the Ia Drang, but I did not know any specifics. I'd never heard of Hal Moore, Galloway, LZ X-RAY, LZ ALBANY, or the casualties the battalion took. I certainly did not know that 1-7 Cavalry was the test unit for using helicopters to bring soldiers into battle and then for supporting the soldiers once on the ground. 1-7 Cavalry committed 411 soldiers to the Ia Drang operation and would have, at the end of the battle, 79 dead and 121 wounded – a 49 per cent casualty rate.[1]

After reading the article, I was deeply, deeply disturbed. It appeared to me that the intelligence for that operation was so flawed that it certainly should have been rethought or cancelled. Upon landing, 1-7 Cavalry would have to fight around 2,000 North Vietnamese Army regulars.

That night, I called the battalion staff and the company commanders to my tent, told them to bring an MRE, and talked about the article. As I remember, I told them I would do my best to avoid putting them into a situation where they would have to fight immediately after getting off the helicopters. As the company commanders and staff left, I pulled aside CPT Delgado, our Battalion S2, and said, "We are not fucking doing that." In four months that statement to CPT Delgado would come back to haunt me.

MAJ John Chappell once again summed up the situation:

> 11 Jan 1991
> In the last few days, we've gotten the final plan of what our unit is going to do. However, that is now in a state of flux. As Division and Brigade were getting ready to issue the operations plan (OPLAN), rumor is that a British Officer got the details of the OPLAN stolen from his car in London. Also, there was supposedly an Egyptian Officer detailing the OPLAN over the radio in the clear in Arabic. Unclear that either of these are true but changes are ongoing as I write. It still looks like we'll move to a tactical assembly area (TAA) southeast of Rafha. It's a little unnerving as stateside begin to beef up the units with extra people. This of course would back fill units in the event of casualties. In a letter, my mother told me to keep Psalm 91 around me and believe. The Psalm describes the cloak or armor of God that he can put around you during the worst of times. Our Chaplain, by coincidence, had cards in his possession with Psalm 91 printed on them which he subsequently passed out to the soldiers.
>
> *MAJ John Chappell*
> *Battalion XO*

Observations

Joe Galloway's article was a severe wakeup call for me. In October of 1990, the battalion had no idea what our ultimate mission, or missions, would be. However, after reading that article and thinking it through, I was determined

not to have a tragedy/disaster like the Ia Drang. The most vulnerable time in an air assault is the landing and the initial organization at the Landing Zone. A unit that is air assaulting must do everything in its power to avoid being surprised and overwhelmed on the Landing Zone. It was assumed that, because the terrain was open desert and the Allied Coalition would have satellite and overflight observation, it was unlikely an air assaulting unit could be surprised by an Iraqi force. This turned out to be an incorrect assumption.

> At the time, I was responsible for distributing random magazines that were sent to Headquarters Company. That morning, one magazine had on its cover "Vietnam Stories." The article covered the Battle of the Ia Drang in Vietnam by a journalist named Joe Galloway. I asked the Chaplain, Captain Delgado, and SGT Gonzalez who they thought should get the magazine and all agreed the battalion commander, LTC Hancock, should get it. As I was taking the magazine to LTC Hancock's tent, SGT Gonzalez yelled out, "Don't get caught in his tent without a good reason," and then grinned at me. As I got to the commander's tent, Major Chapell, the Battalion XO, asked me, "Why are you going into the Old Man's tent?" I replied, "Paperwork, sir." Collecting my wits, I walked in and LTC Hancock was not there, so I placed the magazine on his cot. Thirty-four years later, I found out the contents of the story in the magazine would have a profound effect on both LTC Hancock and on the February 24, 1991 takedown of FOB COBRA.
>
> *Corporal Frank Bills*
> *NBC NCO, 1-327 Infantry*

Note

1. After Action Report, IA DRANG Valley Operation 1st Battalion, 7th Cavalry 14–16 November 1965.

CHAPTER 7

AIR ASSAULT – THE PLAN

Camp Eagle II
December 1990

When VII Corps received the order to deploy from Germany to Saudi Arabia on 8 November, two Army corps were now available for CENTCOM to force Iraq out of Kuwait. I believed that the ejection of Iraq from Kuwait meant battles in Kuwait, and not Iraq. Our forces would simply enter Kuwait and push the Iraqis out. VII Corps and all its mechanized and armored units would give the Coalition enough firepower to do that. I also believed that the vulnerability of our helicopters, flying in a high intensity battle against the vast array of Iraqi air defense weapons, meant no air assaults. I was wrong in both deductions.

The planning for the ejection of Iraq from Kuwait would find XVIII Airborne Corps and the 101st moving to the western part of Saudi Arabia. From there, the 101st would launch multiple air assaults into Iraq. This movement and the mission of the 101st was top secret and, therefore, not disseminated to lower echelons.

The initial plan for the 101st, code named DESERT RENDEZVOUS ONE, had the division launching an air assault deep into Iraq, northwest of the Saudi town of Rafha. The 2d Brigade was to assault the town of As-Samawah and establish a forward operating base (FOB) there. The 3d Brigade was to follow the 2d into As-Samawah and then conduct an assault into An-Nasiriyah in conjunction with 1st Brigade. The assault was aimed at cutting Highway 8, a major thoroughfare that runs through central Iraq, roughly parallel with the Euphrates River. The 2d Brigade would then move southeast and attack Talil Air Base.[1] After looking closely at this plan, the division and corps planners decided that it was too ambitious.[2] The idea that the division would have to do some heavy fighting in cities was not appealing to anyone.

The plan was altered, and the following mission was given to the division:

> When directed, the 101st Airborne Division (Air Assault) moves by air and ground to TAA Campbell and prepares for offensive operations commencing G-Day, conducts Air Assault to establish

> FOB Cobra, and attacks to interdict, block, and defeat enemy forces operating in and through AO Eagle and, on order, conducts attacks to the east to assist in the defeat of the RGFC Forces.[3]

This second plan, named RENDEZVOUS DESTINY TWO, called for the entire division to move out of the covering force area and back to Camp Eagle II. The division would then move by C130, helicopter, and convoy to Tactical Assembly Area (TAA) CAMPBELL, which was 900 kilometers to the west near the Saudi city of Rafha. From TAA CAMPBELL, the division would stage for its air assault into Iraq.

MG Peay would explain it this way:

> We had been working a war plan out there since mid-December. In fact, we called it DESERT RENDEZVOUS I and then DESERT RENDEZVOUS II, as I recall. The first plan had us far, far to the west. That was logistically unsupportable, because of the distances, and secondly, it did not meet the timelines, logistically, from the viewpoint of the rest of the theater. We could not use up the theater's haul [transportation] assets to push us that far west, because if you

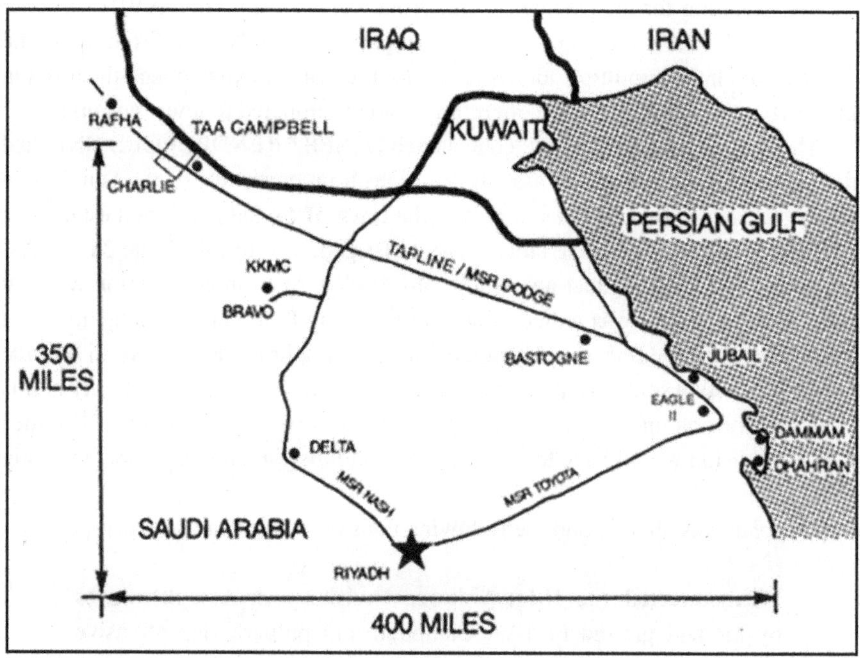

Relocating the 101st Division from the coast to TAA Campbell.[4]

> take away from those haul assets, they would not be able to move the rest of the corps, or the rest of the theater. So we developed a RENDEZVOUS II plan, which brought us a good thirty-five miles east of Rafha where we eventually launched our attack from assembly areas in that location [Tactical Assembly Area (TAA) CAMPBELL].[5]

In early December, my brigade commander, COL Tom Hill, received the division's plan for the attack into Iraq and developed the 1st Brigade's concept of operation. To disseminate the division's plan and 1st Brigade's concept of operations, COL Hill brought the battalion commanders—myself, LTC Gary Thomas (2-327 Infantry), LTC Gary Bridges (3-327 Infantry), LTC Jim Donald (1-502 Infantry), LTC Glenn Hartsell (2-320 Field Artillery), and LTC Russ Adams (5-101 Aviation) into the brigade headquarters tent for an overview briefing. As the briefing began, the map was uncovered and immediately I had three thoughts that jolted my brain:

A. "Where in the hell are we?" I have no idea where this area is, no recognizable cities or terrain. The division's area of operations was shifting approximately 500 miles to the west.
B. "Good Grief! We're going to air assault!" The big crossing arrow indicating an air assault was on the map. We are not going by trucks and following mechanized forces into Kuwait. We are flying into Iraq.
C. "Damn! We're going first" – 1-327, 2-327, 3-327, and 1-502 were flying in that order.

COL Hill, perhaps noticing that I was perplexed and red-faced, asked me, "Frank, what do you think?" I answered with the weakest, most unenthusiastic, and barely audible "hooah" ever uttered by an American soldier.

In the scheme of maneuver, the 1st Brigade would be the lead 101st unit and would be air assaulted into Iraq to set up FOB COBRA. FOB COBRA would be used as a refuel point for the rest of the division in its operations in Iraq. The 2d Brigade was to follow the 1st Brigade, on G-Day, into FOB COBRA and then posture itself to assault Talil Airbase. The 3d Brigade would follow the next day, G+1, and fly to the Euphrates River Valley, into Area of Operations (AO) EAGLE, and cut Highway 8. The helicopters which took the 3d Brigade to the Euphrates and Highway 8 would then fly back and refuel at FOB COBRA.

MG Peay's Intent for RENDEZVOUS DESTINY II was as follows:

> Reposition Forces (Safety/OPSEC).
> Conduct aggressive pre-G-Day armed reconnaissance.
> FOB Cobra must be established rapidly.

Interdict in AO Eagle as combined arms team.
Operations are enemy force oriented.

Success is:
Defeat ingressing/egressing enemy forces.
Disrupt Iraqi Combat Service Support (CSS) operations.
Deny Iraqi Lines of communications (LOC) in Euphrates Valley.[6]

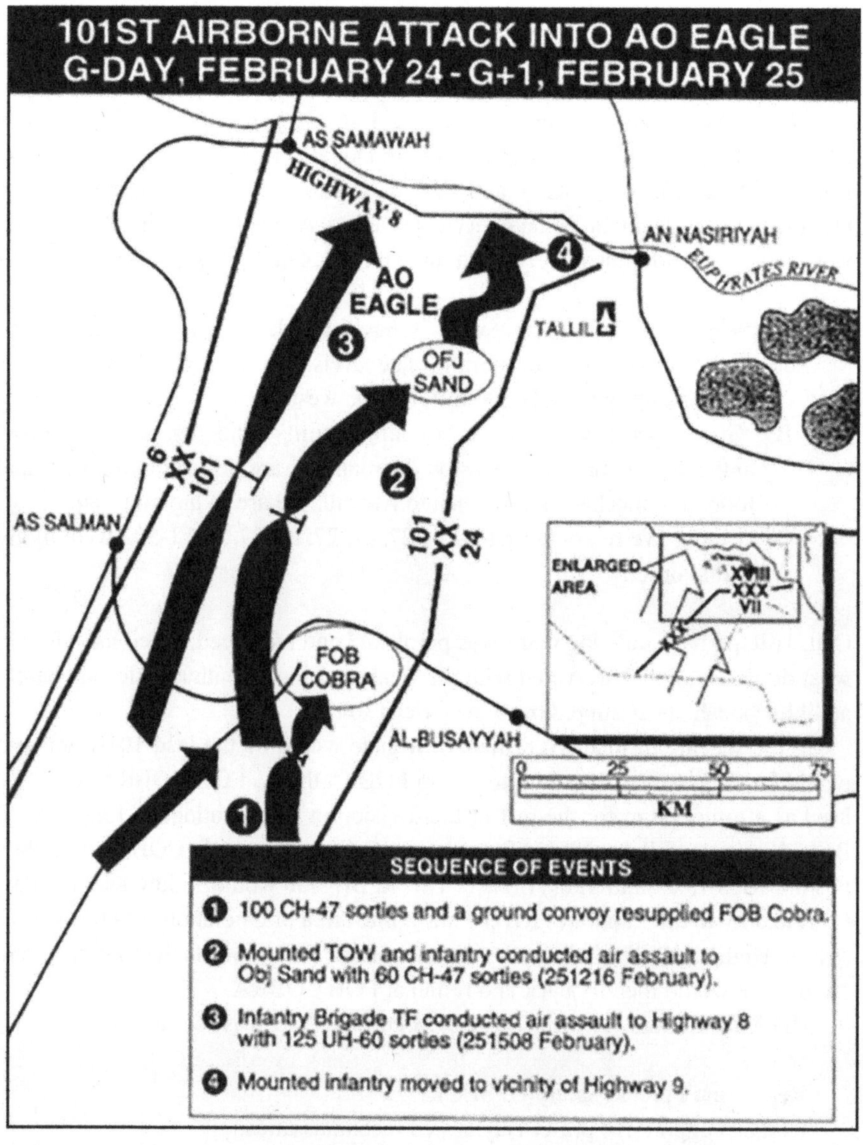

Desert Storm Master Air Assault Plan.[7]

By mid-December, the plan for the assault on FOB COBRA was fairly solid. To validate the concept of the setup of FOB COBRA, the division executed a major Command Post Exercise/Field Training Exercise (CPX/FTX) to see if the FOB could be established and operational in one day. The operation went fairly well, and it appeared that the concept was valid.

From the CPX/FTX, the battalion determined the maximum load capacity of the Black Hawk helicopter in the desert environment. The exercise showed that a Black Hawk could carry fourteen fully combat-loaded soldiers along with a Kevlar blanket on the floor of the helicopter for bottom protection. The seats on the Black Hawks would be removed and soldiers would sit on the floor.

The battalion also found how much water (five 5-gallon containers), overhead protection (plywood, metal pickets, sandbags), and individual equipment (food, grenades, chemical gear, ammunition, etc.) could be taken. Rucksacks would weigh well over 100 pounds. This data was used to determine how many soldiers could fly into FOB COBRA on G-Day. Of course, with all the equipment it was possible to "weigh out" before "cubing out" the helicopter; that is, we would have too much weight on the helicopters before we ran out of space. The Black Hawk and Chinook pilots would have to do "power checks" before taking off to make sure they could lift the weight on the helicopter.

On 18 December, the battalion headed back north to its covering force position after a three week stay in the base camp. At this time, the division had decided to pull the 2d and 3d Brigades back into Camp Eagle II, leaving only the 1st Brigade in the covering force area.

> Some of the fondest and funniest moments of being isolated in the desert occurred when receiving packages from home. I remember receiving one such package that felt like home. It was the biggest package I had ever seen come to our unit in the middle of a barren desert. Even, one of the soldiers who handed it to me said, "Sir, you must know a general or two, to receive this." It was easily a 3-to-4-ft box. This grossly surpassed the weight and size restrictions on all packages by a mile. Once I saw the return address, I just laughed. The return address listed Larry Lowdermilk. It was from the person who encouraged me the most to attend West Point. He never gave a shit about rules or regulations. I shared the contents of that box with everybody around me that day. His audacity was always infectious to me. And that box was every bit of him. Larry died of Covid in 2021, and during his celebration ceremony, I rose to tell everyone this story. I could have shared a million other stories about him that day, but I wanted others to know that he outranked any general, and that's how he probably thought.
>
> *CPT Tom Guleff*
> *Battalion S1*

I recall moving up to the border on Christmas Eve for another stint up there and unloading gear as the sun went down. One item was a case with a clip-on lid that had "1SG" stenciled on it in big, white letters. We didn't know what was in it and one of the artillery forward observers said, "Maybe it's the First Sergeant's box of whoop-ass?" At any other time, that might not have been so funny, but at that moment it was hilarious and helped to lighten the moment.

1LT Gerry Tertychny
A Company XO

Notes

1. Sean Naylor, "Flight of Eagles: 101st Airborne Division's Raids into Iraq," *Army Times* (22 July,1991).
2. Ibid.
3. 101st Briefing Charts
4. 101st Briefing Charts.
5. Peay. "Air Assault into the Gulf" p.27
6. Ibid.
7. Ibid.

CHAPTER 8

OPERATION DESERT STORM

The Air War Starts

17 January 1991

On 16 January, our brigade commander called the battalion commanders together and informed us that the air war would start in the early morning of 17 January. COL Hill was unsure as to how long the air campaign was going to last, but he was fairly sure it would last at least two weeks. COL Hill also gave us the order that the brigade would be pulling out of the covering force area on 18 January, one day after the air campaign started. Since my battalion was the furthest west, we would be the last unit to pull out.

After the meeting, I returned to my CP and told the S3, MAJ Dempsey, that I wanted to see all the officers at 1600 hours and for each of them to bring an MRE and a bottle of water for a "Desert Dining In." When I had all the officers together, I told them what COL Hill had told me about the air war starting that night. Although everyone had anticipated that we were going to war, the stark reality was now setting in. Giving my best "Knute Rockne" speech, I told them again what we were fighting for and that I was proud of them. CSM Riley also gave a fiery speech about leading their men from the front. The meeting broke up after about an hour and I told the officers that they could tell their men that night that we were going to war.

Around 0200 hours, we heard the first wave of fighters and bombers going overhead. At that time my XO, MAJ Chappell, opened a new can of coffee called his "Victory" can and CSM Riley came in the TOC singing a song called "Kick that Booty." At about 0430 hours, we heard over the BBC shortwave radio station that Baghdad was being bombed, so we knew the first wave had gotten through and that the war had started.

We would later find out that the initial air strikes were very successful and that one of our divisional units, the 1st Battalion, 101st Aviation, a battalion of Apache helicopters, had played a huge role in the success of the first night attack. The Apaches, led by their battalion commander LTC Dick Cody, whose call sign was "No Mercy 6," punched a hole in the Iraqi early-warning air defense radar system.

Following Air Force Pave-Low helicopters and firing the first shots of the war, they attacked and destroyed the Iraqi radar system with Hellfire missiles, allowing Air Force planes to go through undetected. Dick Cody was my West Point classmate. I had known him for twenty-two years and I considered him a "Legitimate Badass" because of his competency in leading soldiers and his expert ability in flying attack helicopters.

> As night fell, we eventually saw waves of B-52 bombers with F-15 Eagles arrayed to the flanks flying overhead. We saw flashes of light on the horizon. Gentle vibrations and low rumbles were all we felt or heard of the explosions since they were quite a distance away. We watched most of the night through night vision goggles (NVGs) and wondered what the cost to the pilots and air frames would be for this night's mission. It wasn't until much later we learned it was a huge success and that the Screaming Eagle attack battalion led by LTC Dick Cody actually struck the first blow.
>
> *CPT Ken Russell*
> *A Company Commander*

The morning of 17 January was to be punctuated by several exciting events. First was watching the second wave of aircraft fly over en route to Iraq. In one flight were three B52s escorted by sixteen F15 fighters. To most of us it was a sight we wouldn't quickly forget.

The second event was the threat of attack on our position by Iraqi aircraft. Over the brigade command net, we were alerted with a SKYWATCH codeword, which meant inbound enemy aircraft headed to our location. The incoming aircraft never made it to our position and the alert was cancelled. After the alert was over, I noticed with some amusement the shovels of dirt coming out of everyone's fighting position as we all (me included) tried to get down another foot or two. It was a vista worthy of a Lawrence of Arabia movie, with 700 shovels throwing dirt out of fighting positions in a desolate desert environment. The rest of the 17th was spent breaking down our positions and preparing for our pullback to Camp Eagle II.

On Tapline Road, which bisected our defensive sector, we could see the increased tempo of vehicle traffic, as VII Corps was now moving out to the west. Earlier, we had seen the 1st Infantry Division move to the west down Tapline Road, and now the 1st Armored Division and the 3d Armored Division were using the two-lane highway to move to their attack positions. Trucks, lowboys with tanks and fighting vehicles, ammunition, and artillery pieces rolled past our positions with no break in the convoy. If the description "Heavy Metal" ever needed a photo, it would be of the continuous 150-mile convoy of VII Corps vehicles moving to the west on Tapline Road.

Return to Camp Eagle II

On 18 January, we assembled in two areas for buses to pick us up for the movement back to Camp Eagle II. As the battalion was the most western unit in the covering force area, it was the last unit of the 101st to leave and head back to Camp Eagle II. Our movement plan called for six double-decker buses to move approximately 500 personnel with the rest of the battalion moving by HMMWV and 5-Ton truck. Because we were sometimes short of buses to transport our soldiers, we had come up with an innovative way to load the buses to maximize their space. Our NCOs had found that the most efficient way to load a bus was to put part of the eighty-six personnel on the top deck of the bus, then load rucksacks on the floor of the bottom deck, and then load the remaining soldiers through the bottom windows of the bus.

> In mid-January, I think the 18th or 19th, we came off the covering force mission and returned to Camp Eagle II, driving our HMMWVs back to King Fahd International. We pulled out the day after the air war began, I believe. I can remember the first night of the air war, we could hear, far in the distance, low rumbles of exploding munitions. I went to the top of a sandy ridge with, I think, a couple of the Lieutenants, with our NODS. Looking north toward Iraq, with the NODS on, the entire horizon was a green tinted mass of flashes, each of which was an exploding munition in the far distance, not visible to the naked eye.
>
> *CPT Al Gill*
> *D Company Commander*

When our buses finally arrived at around 1400 hours on the 18th, we found that we were 1½ buses short, as we received four double-deckers and one regular bus instead of the six double-deckers. Since we were the last 101st unit left in the covering force and the rest of the brigade was already back or on the way back to Camp Eagle II, this was a serious problem.

To rectify this, my S4, CPT Landers, showed great initiative and perhaps not so great judgment by going out on Tapline Road and stopping an empty bus by pulling his HMMWV in front of it and commandeering it to our assembly area. I would later find out that he also pulled his pistol out and threatened the driver. At this point in DESERT STORM, this seemed totally reasonable to me. When COL Hill eventually found out about how we commandeered our last bus, he did have some remarks about it.

Loading our troops on the buses, the battalion headed south down the 200 miles to Camp Eagle II. The battalion was the last 101st unit to pull out of the covering force and was alone on our side of the road. On the other side was half of VII Corps, bumper-to-bumper, going to the northwest. Our ride home was most interesting.

The battalion returned to Camp Eagle II around midnight on the evening of 18 January. The division by this time was well into preparing for the movement to TAA CAMPBELL. The 2d Brigade had already moved out of Camp Eagle II on 11 January. They were sent to Hafar Al Batin in order to reinforce VII Corps. Intelligence estimates had shown that a possible Iraqi attack was headed toward the Hafar Al Batin basin on 13 January. The 2d Brigade was attached to the 1st Cavalry Division and given the mission to guard the Al Qayusumah airfield, which was 25 kilometers southeast of Hafar Al Batin. The 2d Brigade was commanded by Colonel Ted Purdom. His battalion commanders were LTCs Dave Benjamin, Jim Donald, and Joe Chesney.

We came back to Camp Eagle II and got issued with a full load of ammunition. While we were there, a soldier from one of our sister battalions, 2-327 Infantry, accidentally discharged an AT4 antitank rocket. Many of the soldiers, myself included, thought a SCUD had hit the camp. The missile screamed into another tent and exploded, injuring several soldiers. Fortunately, no one was killed. In another incident, we barely avoided a disaster.

> One event of note happened during those months which factored into a delay of the ground war, but probably did not appear anywhere in the news. On the ramp at the airfield, an entire row was dedicated to parking just about every unique airplane in the Air Force inventory. Side looking radars, imaging aircraft, ELINT, you name it—probably several billion dollars' worth of R&D. For some unknown reason, someone thought it would be a good idea to use a space at the end of that row to park attack helicopters. Cobra helicopters have two missile rails on each side—one facing straight ahead, and one angled up about 15 degrees. On this particular day they were loading missiles on one of the helicopters, and somehow the missile ignited. Had it been on the rail pointed straight ahead, at least one of those tremendously expensive aircraft would surely have been destroyed. Fortunately, or so it seemed, it was on the rail canted up. At the far end of the airfield about two miles away there was a bunker, with an immense steel door heavy enough to shrug off a hit from that missile—had it been closed. It was not, and the missile scored a perfect hit through the door and detonated. Inside that bunker were stored a vast quantity of "dumb bomb" nose fuses. Those went off in a rather spectacular secondary explosion.
>
> *Capt Bill Reister*
> *US Air Force Air Liaison Officer/Forward Air Controller*

In the days just before deploying to TAA CAMPBELL, the area around Camp Eagle II and the King Fahd airfield would be subject to SCUD attacks. On the first night of attack the SCUDs were identified by radar and a high-pitched alarm came out over the warning siren. Everyone donned their protective mask, as no one knew if the SCUDs contained chemical weapons. The soldiers then waited in their tents. At Camp Eagle II, there were no bunkers built for self-protection, so a soft fatalism set in. If you were unlucky, then that was that.

The attack was in the early evening and the two incoming SCUDs were clearly identified by their red-looking trajectory. The SCUDs seemed to being going at a slow rate of speed. I walked out of my tent to watch what was going on, again being somewhat fatalistic about it. Off to my left, two Patriot missiles were launched from the King Fahd airfield about 3 miles away. The Patriots were traveling near MACH 7. The two missiles, streaking like "bats out of hell," hit or blew up in the vicinity of the two SCUDs and both were destroyed. As I walked back into my tent, I reflected to myself, "Ain't this some shit ... I go to one war and they're shooting ballistic missiles."

> When a SCUD was detected, an alarm would sound, and we would put our gas masks on and go to our tents so that we could get a count and make sure we had everyone. The problem was that the alarm was synched to a central system which set off the alarms regardless of where the missile was heading. We usually reacted to missiles hitting targets miles away from us. One night, the alarm went off after we had gone to bed. Since we were already in our tents, we rolled over, put on our gas masks, and went back to sleep. We woke up hours later, still in our masks, wondering if the "all clear" signal had been given.
>
> *1LT Gerry Tertychny*
> *A Company XO*

Personally, I had to make a tough decision at this time. One day, LTC Hancock and COL Hill sent a runner to my tent and asked me to come and talk to them. Once I arrived, they told me that an emergency Red Cross message arrived stating that my mother in Tennessee was hospitalized. I lost my dad back in 1988, so Mom was my sole surviving family. COL Hill and LTC Hancock sent me to a phone center to call home and then come back and talk it over with them. I got in touch with my cousin Gene and was able to talk to my mom for a short while. She was back home and no longer hospitalized. She assured me she was OK, but I was worried. Gene relayed to me that when she learned about the coalition air attack, that she had suffered a mild heart attack. Obviously, it was out of concern and worry for me.

> After the phone call, I went back to my two Commanders and talked to them regarding the situation. COL Hill offered to send me home on emergency leave, however it would mean giving up my command, and not just 1LT Tertychny taking over for a couple of weeks. With war looming, he wanted a qualified CPT in command.
>
> I went back to the ABU company HQ tent and confided in Gerry about the talk with COL Hill, and then spent some time mulling over things in my mind. Lots of things factored into my decision, but the two I kept coming back to was that my mom was home being looked after by my cousin Gene and I didn't want to disrupt the ABU cohesion and team this close to the ground war. Simply put, I had faith in my God, my mom, and my cousin but I didn't feel right about leaving ABU at that time, especially after all the other personnel disruptions we had weathered. Later that day, I went back to my two commanders and told them I would retain command of ABU and stay with my men.
>
> *CPT Ken Russell*
> *A Company Commander*

The day after the air war began, the division initiated a massive movement to the northwest in preparation for the ground war. Within seven days, the division moved, in ground convoys and C130 Hercules aircraft, about 900 kilometers from Camp Eagle II to TAA CAMPBELL. TAA CAMPBELL was approximately 75 kilometers southeast of the Saudi town of Rafha and 10 kilometers southwest of the Iraqi border. It was from here that the division was to launch its assault into Iraq on G-Day.

Deployment to TAA Campbell

My battalion was the last infantry battalion to depart from Camp Eagle II and closed into TAA CAMPBELL on 25 January. Like most of the division, we went by C130 and drove our vehicles. The C130 flight was close to being a rollercoaster ride, as the airplanes flew nap of the earth to avoid giving off a radar signature. I estimate the planes were flying 200 to 300 feet off the ground the entire route.

> We departed AO Normandy after a relief in place conducted by the US Marines. Back at Camp Eagle II, we reorganized and prepared to kick out by C-130 Aircraft and Ground Convoy to the Division Tactical Assembly Area (TAA) vicinity of Rafha. CSM "Rock" Riley and two soldiers were immediately dispatched via C-130, along with other Quartering parties, to mark off the Battalion TAA. LTC Hancock, most of the staff, and soldiers prepared to be transported via C-130 to Rafha while the

> remaining parts of the Battalion prepared for the Ground Convoy. On 17 Jan, the Air Campaign began and would ostensibly provide cover for the Division and XVIII Airborne Corps move to the north and west. From 20-21 Jan, the Ground Convoy moved west around Riyadh and then north (over 700 miles) to get set up in our new TAA.
>
> *MAJ John Chappell*
> *Battalion XO*

CSM Riley had gone to TAA CAMPBELL on 18 January as part of a brigade advance party and had our company positions well laid-out when we arrived. In TAA CAMPBELL, we were the most western unit in the 101st and had the French 6th Light Armored Division on our western flank. During the month that we were in TAA CAMPBELL we had to concentrate not only on the upcoming air assault mission but also on the defense of our sector.

Our brigade sector was adjacent to the Iraqi border, so we were in a location where we had to be constantly aware of possible Iraqi incursions. Complicating this was an Iraqi border position that was 1 kilometer north of the brigade border. MG Peay had decided not to capture or destroy this enemy position until right before the ground war began and not to fire any artillery into our sector. This constraint was meant to deceive the Iraqis as to how large a unit they were facing. The brigade kept one infantry company on patrol directly in front of the Iraqi area.

> After some additional adjustments on positioning the division, our unit eventually took the position at TAA Campbell in mid-January 1991, about 10km south of the Iraqi border. Our unit was on the extreme western flank of the division and my platoon, 1st Platoon, was positioned as the last infantry platoon that connected with the French 6th Division to the west of the division.
>
> *2LT Dave Esposito*
> *1st Platoon Leader, Alpha Company*

> We got back to our rear area at Camp Eagle and prepared for the next major move of the division—about 500 miles west, just south of the Kuwaiti border with Iraq, near the Saudi town of Rafah.
>
> When we got to TAA Campbell, it was another area of zero vegetation and empty desert, a little rockier and a little more elevation than it had been on the covering force mission. Once again, Tapline Road was in our AO, though we were 500 miles further west than we had been in the covering force. That damn road runs across all northern Saudi Arabia.
>
> *CPT Al Gill*
> *D Company Commander*

As it happened, our Commander CPT Wright, was leading a convoy to our Tactical Assembly Area. In the lead vehicle, I was driving. CPT Wright was in the passenger seat, and SPC Jackie Alexander was in the air guard position perched atop the Humvee. As we were driving down Tapline Road, we spotted a civilian vehicle driving head-on towards the convoy and not stopping, slowing, or yielding. SPC Alexander kept yelling, "Do I shoot? Do I shoot? Sir, Do I shoot?" CPT Wright's adrenaline and brain was going a mile a minute. He made the split-second decision not to shoot. The vehicle passed the lead vehicle without incident and the entire convoy continued without harm or incident. Our concern was that the vehicle was a possible hostile or VBIED (vehicle borne improvised explosive device). CPT Wright's instincts were spot-on and continued to be throughout the conflict. The full convoy arrived at Tactical Assembly Area Campbell safely.

My battle buddy, SPC Jackie Alexander, told me another funny (fateful) story in that same period. Jackie was driving for 1LT Bryan Blue, who was the Executive Officer at the time. 1LT Blue was in the passenger seat. Also in that vehicle was SPC Tilas Law, who was the RTO for 1LT Blue. 1LT Blue kept asking SPC Alexander if he was hot. Jackie kept saying, "No Sir, I'm good." 1LT Blue kept saying, "I don't know what's wrong with me. I am super-hot. I am burning up for some reason."

The convoy reached their designated location per the order. 1LT Blue and Jackie got out of the vehicle. Within minutes, while they were standing next to the vehicle, the vehicle battery that was located under 1LT Blue's seat blew up and spewed a lot of caustic battery acid. It turns out that the reason 1LT Blue was so hot was because that battery was overheating, and he was just lucky to have gotten out of the vehicle and not be sitting on it when it did blow up. Just in time!

CPL Frank Bills
NBC NCO, Headquarters and Headquarters Company

We then moved by C130, sitting on our rucks and crammed in like sardines, to a small airfield near Rafha, in northern Saudi Arabia. From there, we moved by truck to Tactical Assembly Area (TAA) CAMPBELL to prep for our role in the upcoming ground operation, should it come to that. We got dropped off just as the sun was going down. As the trucks pulled away, it started to rain. In the desert. Of course.

1LT Gerry Tertychny
A Company XO

CHAPTER 9

TACTICAL ASSEMBLY AREA CAMPBELL

Northern Saudi Arabia

January–February 1991

We arrived at TAA CAMPBELL on 21 January and spent the following weeks after arriving getting updates, improving our defensive positions, and watching Coalition planes heading north to strike targets in Iraq. We all war-gamed possible scenarios and many thought that our air power alone would be enough to get the Iraqis out of Kuwait. However, as January moved into February, the Iraqis were still in Kuwait, so we began to get briefed on our offensive mission.

> On 21 Jan, we linked up with CSM Riley. He had the entire area marked off upon my arrival and had done a tremendous job while waiting for the rest of the Battalion. We got the Battalion logistics set up and awaited the arrival of the soldiers. The Brigade troops started to flow in on 23 Jan with the arrival of COL Hill.
>
> *MAJ John Chappell*
> *Battalion XO*

Sarin and Mustard Gas

On 28 January, some of the battalion staff and I went to recon a sector of the battalion defensive position where enemy forces had been observed. CPT Delgado, the S2; MAJ Dempsey, the S3; and 2LT Tom Evans, the Battalion NBC Officer, came with me. While on the reconnaissance, 2LT Evans started receiving positive readings for nerve agents on his detection equipment. 2LT Evans alerted the rest of us to put on our gas masks. We didn't see any aircraft, or any artillery, mortar, or SCUD impacts anywhere nearby. Because of the lack of any impact from enemy artillery or missiles, we only donned our protective masks and did not break out the rest of our chemical gear.

CPL Frank Bills, the Battalion NBC NCO, radioed 2LT Evans and told him that the M8 Chemical Alarms in the battalion's company areas were going off. Here again, there were no enemy aircraft sighted and no mortar, artillery, or missile impacts. At 1st Brigade headquarters, CPT Stephen B. Leisenring, the Brigade NBC Officer, remembers 28 January 1991 as the day twelve chemical alarms sounded. In addition, he then got several positive readings for chemical agents. In reality, there had been positive readings in other 101st units, starting on 22 January and going up to 31 January.[1] Additionally, positive readings were reported by both the 82d Airborne Division and the French 6th Light Armored Division, both to our west.

> As part of my duties with HHC, I served as the Battalion Nuclear Biological Chemical (NBC) Non-commissioned officer (NCO). This was a job I took seriously, as I felt the weight of knowing that the lives of every soldier in HHC, to include the Command Group, rested with me doing my job effectively, consistently, and without fail. I ensured training of all battalion personnel and emphasized the importance of keeping the issued Mission Oriented Protective Posture (MOPP) gear in the highest working order to be ready for the worst (chemical exposure) if (God forbid) that would ever occur. I preached the necessity of maintaining atropine injectors on hand and knowing how to use them. I preached about ensuring the right chemical protective gear was issued, ready, and available. I preached about having the right type of canteen cap to allow a soldier to drink water and maintain the coverage of the MOPP gear.
>
> As happened on the morning of 28 January 1991, I was having my coffee. Suddenly I heard (we all heard) the M8 chemical agent alarm sound off! For those that have no idea what I am talking about, the M8 alarm notifies all in the vicinity of detection of chemical agents in vapor form, and its sound is unmistakable. My heart raced and I am sure this human reaction of anxiety and what's next was common among all who heard this M8 alarm.
>
> To verify the M8 alarm, I utilized the M256A1 chemical agent detection system and M8 paper litmus test. It "streaked yellow." That yellow streak was confirmation of a "G-type" chemical nerve agent. That system confirmed the presence of a chemical nerve agent as indicated by the initial M8 alarms. All this testing and double-checking that I share with you happened quickly, VERY quickly.
>
> I put gloves on and ran back to the Headquarters tent and screamed "GAS, GAS, GAS!" CPT Wright said, "We are gonna kick your ass, quit F*c*ing around." I gave the "Gas Gas Gas" signal again and

> I will remember that look in everyone's eyes and reaction, dropping everything and donning their gas masks. CPT Wright ordered me to immediately go test it again! This time, the litmus test did not streak yellow, but the M8 alarm was still going off. All personnel were ordered to MOPP Level 4. This is the highest level of protection, but it is a pain in the ass to do work in that gear. Eventually, two German Fox NBC vehicles arrived on scene and conducted soil samples. That German NBC team gave us the "all clear."
>
> *CPL Frank Bills*
> *NBC NCO, Headquarters and Headquarters Company*

After about an hour, 2LT Evans told me that the positive readings were for sarin gas and mustard gas. Some more time went by and 2LT Evans said he was not receiving any more positive readings and that we could take our masks off. I asked 2LT Evans to take his mask off first and see if he had any reaction. Unflinchingly, he took his mask off, rolled his eyes, and said, "I'm good." Fortunately, no casualties occurred from this incident.

> There had been some Iraqi patrols crossing the border on recon missions. Most of these patrols met with large artillery responses. LTC Hancock, the Battalion S3, Major Tom Dempsey, Captain Delgado, several other slice (personnel attached to our battalion from support units) officers, and I went just south of the Iraq border to assess where the patrols were moving. I remember we were outside of our vehicles and standing on a small hill that offered some distant observation. While the staff was talking, I started taking measurements of the air with a chemical agent monitor (CAM). Suddenly, I started getting a positive reading for nerve agents. I immediately put on my mask and gave the signal for the others to do the same. Within seconds we were all standing there with masks on. I knew the threat must be vapor in nature and therefore a mask was sufficient protection. CPL Frank Bills, the Battalion Chemical NCO, radioed and informed me that nerve agent alarms, known as M8 alarms, were also sounding back at base camp. After spending some time with masks on, I was finally able to determine the vapor threat was gone. The protocol for giving all clear called for one soldier to take their mask off to determine if they became affected by nerve agents. LTC Hancock chose me to be the canary, so to speak. I took my mask off and fortunately was not rendered a casualty. The base camp was able to go through the same process and all clear was given. We would later learn we had been

in the downwind hazard area for nerve agents that had been released as the result of friendly forces bombing a storage bunker located at an Iraqi facility.

2LT Tom Evans
Battalion NBC Officer

Also, while in TAA Campbell, ABU experienced a NBC event. One sunny day we heard a light ringing from our right flank that kept getting louder. We immediately understood that it was M-8 alarms detecting nerve agent, and it was approaching ABU. We masked up and continued going to MOPP 4 as our own M-8 alarms joined in the cacophony. The Brigade HQ sent a Fox NBC Vehicle to the area. The Fox vehicle crew shared with us that they were detecting trace elements of nerve, blood and blister agent. We physically saw the print-out from the detection equipment. Evidently, the agents had carried on the wind across the battalion front, from our right to left.

CPT Ken Russell
A Company Commander

Our time at the TAA was spent writing letters to all the "Any Soldier" mail we would get and living in a hole in the ground. A few times we would go on full alert because we had enemy tanks rolling towards our position, but now I think it was just training. When the air war started off it pretty much solidified in our minds that we will be called to do our jobs in a ground assault. We were still thinking Saddam Hussein would come to his senses and not take on the whole coalition. I remember our M-8 Chemical Detectors going off a few times, and going into MOPP Level 3 for a few hours. Once we had some explosions go off not too far from us and we were told the Air Force had to drop unused bombs if the planes were damaged during their mission because it was too dangerous for them to land with a damaged aircraft with bombs on them.

PFC Jesse Hernandez
3d Platoon, A Company

Observations

At the time, this exposure to chemicals seemed just another "shitty day" in the desert. No investigation was carried out that I know of, and no report was asked for. It was assumed that a chemical weapons stockpile in Iraq must

have been bombed north of us and the chemicals had drifted down into Saudi Arabia. As I remember, the 3d Brigade of the 101st had their alarms go off, the 6th French Division had theirs go off, and the 82d Airborne had theirs go off. The 6th French and the 82d were west of our position. Because the chemicals were in a trace amount and had no immediate effect on soldiers, the incident was chalked up as a reality check for the air assault. What if the Iraqis used their chemical weapons after the unit air assaults? The really hard part of thinking through the air assault was figuring out how to decontaminate a unit that had gotten hit with chemical weapons. The Army's way of decontaminating was to use dirt/sand and water and make a slurry to help clean and decontaminate equipment. Of course, there was no water where we were going to land. My conclusion was there was no option other than marching out of the contaminated area and decontaminating as best we could in the desert. The same conundrum occurred with casualties and KIAs in a chemical environment. There was no easy way of handling contaminated casualties.

Indirect Fire

On 13 February, our mortar platoon received about four to six rounds of what was believed to be enemy mortar fire. It was never determined if that was a correct assumption, as it could have been American fighter planes dropping unused ordnance. Around this time, the division's 3d Brigade, which was adjacent to our brigade, reported enemy armor moving near their sector. The unconfirmed armored movement led to the 3d Brigade (Rakkasans) being given the joking nickname "Irakkasans." Nevertheless, the mortar fire and possible enemy armor kept everyone on their toes.

> One day, LTC Hancock came to our position to speak with us and check up on us. I remember him saying that if we were to take fire, we were allowed to engage. SSG Cisco was my Team Leader, I was the gunner, and PFC Mackert was the driver. We also had a medic with us.
>
> After LTC Hancock left, we got hit with artillery. One round landed right behind us, about 75 meters away, just at the bottom of the ridge we were on. I think that literally saved us from shrapnel. The explosion was amazing, and I saw a big plume of black smoke right behind our position. Another round landed near one of our other positions and I believe the scouts got some in their area as well. The French were to our left flank, and I believe they were hit as well.

It's crazy because on that day, we were getting relieved and the next platoon was moving up from the rear to relieve us.

While all this was happening, I remember seeing a trail of dust and I saw enemy movement directly to our north and started tracking with my TOW. I went through our fire commands, kept tracking, and I had my missile armed and ready. The vehicle moved to the Iraqi outpost that was about a click away. I saw enemy commanders dismount and go into the Iraqi outpost. I reported what I saw to my squad leader and waited for the fire command.

As far as I knew at the time, there were no friendlies in front of us. We were the most northern unit. I was ready to engage, but I was not allowed to. The Iraqi troops got back in their vehicle and headed back to where they came from. I tracked them until I could not see them anymore.

Minutes after the artillery and spotting Iraqi movement, we had a few Apaches fly over us and head into Iraq. One Apache was flying so low I saw the pilot's and gunner's faces. So low, if I was tall, I could have reached up and touched one of its tires. He flew right above our position. These boys were flying low and fast and were about to whoop someone.

At first, I was thinking, "Damn, the ground war is starting, and Iraqi tanks are going to come over that ridge any moment." We were ready and well-trained by Captain Gill and our leaders. If the war was about to start, we would be ready for them, and I knew Delta Company was going to give them hell. I was going to take out as many as I could.

I guess on a good note, that was an isolated incident, and the ground war did not kick off. On a bad note, I almost got to engage an Iraqi vehicle with troops in it. Unfortunately, I wasn't allowed to engage the target.

PFC Larry Maroto
5th Platoon, D Company

While we occupied TAA Campbell, we were within visual distance of the Iraqi border from my Company CP (that CP consisting of my vehicle, my driver, Jon Nordin, and maybe the XO and one or two soldiers/NCOs). Using binos, I could see the border, and a Saudi Border Guard post, as well. For a couple of weeks, we ran mounted patrols up near the border—I think with soldiers either from the BN Scout Platoon or one of the rifle companies. These patrols were led by one of the D Company Platoon Leaders. I believe I went on the first mission, during which we contacted and spoke to the commander of the Saudi Border Post. They reported frequent contact and some firefights with enemy soldiers from an Iraqi Border Post that was a few kilometers away. The patrols were conducted for the most part without incident and were good training for the PLs of D Company.

There was one incident I remember well, and that was a near fratricide of one of my platoons. From the ridge I was on, with binos, I could watch the progress of the mounted patrols—even though the patrols were several kilometers north of my position, the vehicles and rising dust were visible. One day, as a patrol was out, there was a large explosion, and I saw the dust and smoke of it rising in near proximity to the patrol. Through my binos, when the smoke cleared, it looked to me that the explosion was within 20–50 meters of one of our HMMWVs. Quickly getting on the radio, I asked them what the hell was going on—my fear was a mine or some engagement by Iraqis or Saudi Border guys.

The Platoon Leader/Patrol Leader, who I think was Lieutenant Chris Richardson, immediately reported that they didn't know what had happened, but that no one was injured—other than ringing ears and maybe some wet fatigues…. The explosion had been quite close, and they thought it was some sort of rocket or bomb dropped by an aircraft. Moving to where the munition exploded, they found parts of it—with English writing and nomenclatures. Bringing it back, we passed it on to the BN S-2.

Once again, during this mission, my memory is that 1-327 was the westernmost 101st unit in TAA Campbell, and as such, we shared a border with the French 6th Light Armored Division which was to our west. These guys had some strange looking vehicles, and to help prevent possible fratricide, we invited them over and asked them to bring one type of each vehicle so my TOW gunners could get a close-up view of them.

While in TAA Campbell, Jon Nordin and I witnessed another bad accident. Again, we saw smoke maybe five miles away. We drove to the site and found a CH-47 helicopter completely ablaze. The aircraft, which I found out came out of Germany and was brand new with something like only nineteen hours on the airframe, had one engine explode in flight, and had to make an emergency, hard landing at high speed.

This helicopter had a HMMWV and a towed 105mm artillery piece, the crew of the gun, and a basic load of 105mm ammunition, all internally loaded. It hit the ground so hard, and with so much forward momentum, that the wheels dug 18–10-inch ruts in the hard packed desert for about 75 yards before it came to a stop. All members of the crew and the artillery guys made it out just before it burst into flames. Within minutes, the only thing left of the aircraft were the lumps of the motors, the frames and engine block of the HMMWV, and the tube and frame of the 105. Everything else had melted, exploded, or burned up. The interior portions of the rotors had burned, closest to the helicopter, dropping the remains of the rotors in the cardinal directions of the remains of the helicopter.

All the soldiers were evacuated to a nearby British unit who fed them and checked them out. Everyone was OK other than the battery 1SG. He'd been told by the Crew Chief to sit in the flight seats lining the sides of the aircraft, which are designed to collapse slowly on a hard landing, and not to sit in the HMMWV. He sat in the HMMWV. He got compression fractures of the spine.

CPT Al Gill
D Company Commander

As companies rotated through the border observation and security mission, eventually it was our turn. Battalion trucks pulled up to ABU one afternoon and we loaded up to go up to the border. ABU made a long line of vehicles as SPC Stephens and I led the convoy in our HMMWV. Suddenly, the desert exploded off to my right as an Iraqi shell landed near our convoy. We immediately accelerated the convoy towards our link-up site with the company withdrawing from the border mission. CSM Riley met us wearing MOPP gear and as we stopped the convoy, we donned our MOPP gear as well. A few minutes later we heard the "all clear" over the radio.

CPT Ken Russell
A Company Commander

Rules of Engagement

Before the air assault into Iraq, the division arranged for Rules of Engagement (ROE) cards to be printed to ensure all soldiers understood what they were able to do and what limitations there were. The ROE card made perfect sense to me. It was simple, direct, and easy to understand. To support the ROE dissemination, 1st Brigade arranged to have the Brigade Judge Advocate General (JAG) officer, a young captain, address the battalion commanders on the ROE to make sure we understood it. I brought MAJ Dempsey, the S3, with me and we listened to what the captain had to say.

The only sticking point for me in the briefing was that the captain alluded that there was a point where a unit could apply too much force. In the air assault mission that the battalion was given, I could not see that being valid. When the battalion landed, it would be deep in enemy territory, operating with no connection to any other unit. If I had firepower, whether artillery, mortars, close air support, or attack helicopters, I planned on using it on any enemy in my vicinity. It is easier to kill with a bomb than a bayonet. As we walked away, MAJ Dempsey asked, "Boss, what do you think?" I replied, "Fuck him. If there is an enemy squad and there's a flight of B-52s available, I'm using the B-52s on them."

Observations

An easily understood ROE is a necessity for soldiers. Under stress and strain, soldiers must be able to retain their humanity and refrain from acts that are flagrantly wrong. ROE helps the soldiers understand what they can or can't do so no war crimes are committed. At the same time, soldiers cannot be handcuffed by restrictive ROE that makes no sense and micromanages their movements and actions. That is a sure recipe for disaster.

Meeting the French

One day, a group of soldiers from the French 6th Light Armored Division, which was out to our west, came over to the battalion area and brought some of their equipment with them—tanks, armored vehicles, a helicopter, etc. The French 6th Division was formed in Saudi Arabia in September 1990 and was built around the headquarters of the 6th Division but included elements of over fifty other French units, including some elements of the French Foreign Legion.

We spent the day with the French, showing them our weapons, vehicles and equipment and learning about theirs. Most importantly, we wanted to know what each other's vehicles looked like so that if we saw them on the battlefield we would recognize them and not have any fratricide. As I was talking to the French captain who was in charge of their vehicles, I asked him what he thought about our air assault plan. Without blinking an eye he said, "It sounds like the movie *A Bridge Too Far*." This of course referred to the failed British/American airborne drop in Holland in 1944 where a British airborne division was cutoff and decimated. Brilliant!

> I could speak some French, so I was able to translate for the guys. It was a great day, and we learned that the French soldiers were pretty much the same as us. I remember two characters, Bruno and Eddie, who were tank crewmen on an AMX30 tank. They couldn't speak

any English, but they were damned funny guys. George and I thought it hilarious the way they rolled their eyes when their helicopter pilots started strutting around. One of them, Bruno or Eddie—I can't recall which one—pointed at them and said, "Tom Cruise." Thinking back on that day, I wonder what happened to them. I hope they made it through the fight and are well.

1LT Gerry Tertychny
A Company XO

New Soldiers

As close as we were to the ground war commencing, we were still receiving new officers and soldiers. As with any other time, we did our best to welcome them to the unit, learn a little about their backgrounds, and orient them to their responsibilities. The learning curve was steep—we were only weeks, and sometimes only days, away from a massive air assault operation. They wouldn't have much time to get settled.

I joined 1-327 Infantry as a First Lieutenant on 31 January 1991, when the battalion was positioned near the border between Saudi Arabia and Iraq. Due to the battalion being overstrength on assigned officers, I was assigned to a non-authorized position on the MTOE (Modified Table of Organization and Equipment) as the Assistant Battalion Adjutant. I took on responsibilities and duties as directed by the Battalion Adjutant (S-1), Captain Tom Guleff. As the timeline for the initiation of the ground war became clearer, the battalion made final plans for accomplishing its portion of the brigade mission to secure Forward Operating Base (FOB) Cobra. Part of the battalion would air assault in helicopters, and the rest would participate in the "Convoy from Hell" in wheeled vehicles. Due to limited air assets and the need to maximize combat power, only two spaces on the helicopters were allocated to the S-1 Section. CPT Guleff decided those two S-1 spaces would go to me and Sergeant Walker, an infantryman from one of the line companies assigned to the S-1 Section. CPT Guleff and the rest of the S-1 section would ride to FOB Cobra in the convoy. I was pleasantly surprised (and extremely grateful!) that CPT Guleff chose me to lead the S-1 Section on the air assault and gave me the opportunity to participate in the largest air assault in history

CPT John Santini
Battalion Assistant S1

I was commissioned out of The Citadel on 12 May 1990 and reported to Fort Benning for Infantry Officers Basic Course (IOBC) on 14 May 1990. I was already pinpointed for assignment to 327th Infantry Regiment in the 101st Airborne Division. In August of 1990, my IOBC classmates and I were in the field and heard about Iraq invading Kuwait.

I reported to Fort Campbell on January 9, 1991, and encountered a town and installation deserted due to the deployment. Things were so uncertain during that time that the Post Office would not let me get a PO Box "in case I didn't return" and local merchants would not take personal checks for the same reason.

On January 24, 1991, as an individual replacement, I boarded a Civil Reserve Air Fleet (CRAF) 747 out of Fort Benning with stops in New York and Rome before landing in Dharan, Saudi Arabia on the afternoon of January 25. Coming down the external stairs of the aircraft there was an Army O-5 greeting everyone as they got off the aircraft. The Lieutenant Colonel stopped me, looked at my shoulder patch, rank, and branch insignia and said, "You're really asking for it, aren't you?" This was a heck of a way to start off in Saudi Arabia for a young Second Lieutenant.

I got to sleep around midnight that night and at 0345 I was awoken to air raid sirens followed by three Patriot Missile launches, followed immediately by three explosions of destroyed SCUD missiles. Rushed into MOPP 4 and not getting an "all clear" until 0420, we were again put into MOPP 4 at 0515 but quickly given "all clear" again but remained in MOPP 2 until 0720. It was an appropriate reality check for us as we entered a combat theater for the very first time.

Soon thereafter we were put on a C-130 to move to a location; to this day I do not know where we ended up. This was another appropriate introduction to a combat environment for this young Lieutenant as there were no seats in the C-130 and the air crew packed it completely full of soldiers and equipment. We were instructed to sit on the floor of the aircraft across its width, and the air crew simply used ratchet straps across our laps to secure us for the flight like cargo.

Upon our arrival at our destination around January 29, the group started to get split up based on where they were being assigned. As the morning went on, I was the last person sitting on the outside of the command post perimeter. Like a scene out of a war movie, the two Humvees pulled right up to me, and one young officer looked out the window at me and asked "are you Karres?" It turns out this was the 327th Brigade S-1, and I loaded my gear in the Humvee and got in for the ride to the 327th. The next words out of the Brigade S-1's mouth were, "Congrats, you got the *last* platoon in the Brigade." This experience just got that much more real for me.

Around January 30, I was dropped off at the Headquarters of 1st Battalion, 327th Infantry Regiment and was immediately ushered into tent that was the living quarters of Lieutenant Colonel Frank Hancock, aka "Warlord", the Commander of 1-327 Infantry. The tent was not big, and it was not well lit. Frank Hancock was clearly deeply involved in operational planning with maps and notebooks on his small field desk in the tent. Dressed in his "Chocolate Chip" desert camouflage pants, a classic wool Army issue pullover sweater, and a black watch cap rolled up tightly befitting the warrior he was, Frank Hancock stood up with a big smile, stuck his hand out, and immediately said, "Welcome to 1st of the 327th, LT. We are invading Iraq in ten days, and your platoon is waiting on you." Just when I thought this experience couldn't get more real, it just did. THIS warrior standing in front of me was the personification of what I had envisioned since the day I realized I wanted to be a warrior someday, and immediately instilled confidence in me. Warlord was confident, no-nonsense, serious, and focused while being personable and I immediately had a feeling that I had just landed in the exact right unit.

After that introduction, I walked out into the sunlight and was met by Captain Darcy Brewer, the commander of Charlie Company. The first thing Brewer said to me was "you're coming at a bad time LT," and then Brewer and First Sergeant Art Schwoyer took me down to 2nd Platoon, "Outlaws," where I would take over as Platoon Leader on the eve of the invasion of Iraq.

Darcy Brewer and Art Schwoyer took me to 2nd Platoon and introduced me to Sergeant First Class Ken "Mac" McCooley the Platoon Sergeant. At this point, I realized that the Army had prepared me over the years for this exact moment, to take over a platoon in a hostile fire zone on the eve of embarking on the largest combat air assault in history. From the many lessons while enrolled in ROTC, to the numerous lengthy talks with ROTC Cadre who were Vietnam vets, imparting their combat experience, to IOBC and, in particular, Ranger School, the basics of Infantry small unit leadership were well inculcated in me. When I met Ken McCooley, the sun was setting, and it was getting ready to get very dark in the desert with no ambient light for hundreds of miles. Mac and the squad leaders wanted to get me set up with a primitive sleeping hooch so I could get out of the elements, but instead I immediately prioritized troop leading procedures as I had been taught, particularly recognizing that the stakes were high in a combat zone and I needed to establish the standards immediately. I trooped the front trace of the platoon with Mac, checking each fighting position and meeting the men. I checked sector sketches, sector stakes, and in particular the M60s in the weapons squad.

Sergeant First Class Ken McCooley was a bit of a legend in 1st Brigade. He knew Tom Hill well and prior to Iraq invading Kuwait, Ken had turned over his platoon sergeant duties in the Outlaws and was moving to a division staff position. Once Ken saw the news of the invasion of Kuwait and that the Brigade was going to deploy, he immediately went to Tom Hill to ask for his platoon back. His only request was that he would lead the platoon through the deployment and would not get a Platoon Leader. Under these conditions, Ken went back to the Outlaws and deployed in September. Ken was the consummate professional NCO and exactly the perfect Platoon Sergeant for a brand-new Platoon Leader to be paired with.

2LT Matt Karres
2d Platoon Leader, C Company

The Run-Up to G-Day

By the first part of February, the plan for the air assault into Iraq was solidified. 1st Brigade (1-327 Infantry, 2-327 Infantry, 3-327 Infantry, 1-502 Infantry, and 2-320 Field Artillery) was to air assault 90 miles into Iraq to seize FOB COBRA in the early morning hours of G-Day. 1st Brigade would be given two lifts of sixty-seven Black Hawks, thirty Chinooks, and ten UH1 Hueys to accomplish the mission. On the afternoon of G-Day, the 2d Brigade (-) would fly into a secure FOB COBRA.

I remember LTC Hancock asking us at a staff meeting, "OK, who thinks we're going to Kuwait?" Most of us raised our hands. He said, "Nope—we're headed to Iraq." Now, most of us raised our eyebrows. Ken Russell and I exchanged glances. This was exactly what the 101st had been organized for—a deep strike, using the mobility provided by our helicopters, to disrupt the enemy's rear echelon and lines of communication and supply. "Oh, and by the way," Hancock added, "we're the lead battalion." A few months earlier, we thought we would miss the whole thing because we were the DRF 9 and we wouldn't get here in time.

We were briefed on the plan and on our role in it. 1st Brigade, augmented by 1-502 Infantry from 2d Brigade, would conduct an air assault into an area about 100 miles inside Iraq, seize it, establish Forward Operating Base (FOB) COBRA for follow-on forces, and prepare to conduct future operations, as needed. The idea was to lift a force into Iraq to establish a base for the next brigade to stage out of to move north to cut Highway 8 from Baghdad and disrupt the enemy's ability to communicate with and resupply his forces in Kuwait, which would then get hit by Coalition armored and mechanized forces. The 101st was designed to be able to execute a brigade-level air assault every twenty-four hours by massing its aviation assets—helicopters. However, it had never been done before.

1LT Gerry Tertychny
A Company XO

Once I had received the mission, I briefed the ABU command group, mortar section leader, and platoon leaders. As I and the ABU leaders developed our plan, we had some constraints to consider. First, we would conduct the company air assault in two lifts of sixty men each. Because of the distance, it would be approximately two hours between lifts. This meant I would go in on the first lift with a partial company HQ, the company mortars, and one ABU platoon. Two hours later another ABU platoon would arrive by air assault. My third ABU platoon would be part of the battalion ground assault convoy (GAC), led by Major Chappell, that would convoy from Saudi Arabia into Iraq to get to FOB COBRA. Second, with seats out each Blackhawk could transport fifteen ABU soldiers. Each lift would consist of four Blackhawk helicopters.

CPT Ken Russell
A Company Commander

The elements of the 1st and 2d Brigades which would not participate in the air assault, along with Division Support Command (DISCOM), would infiltrate into Iraq by way of a Main Supply Route (MSR) called NEW MARKET and would link up with the assault units on G+1. The MSR would be cleared by a composite 1st Brigade unit called Task Force (TF) CITADEL, led by the Brigade Executive Officer, LTC Jim McGarity.

In late January 1990, the 101st Airborne Division (Air Assault) was positioned in western Saudi Arabia, way out west with the French Foreign Legion on our left and the 24th ID on our right. I had discovered a fissure in Saddam's defense line there, along the "Darb al Haj" (Route of the Pilgrimage) from Baghdad to Mecca, that fell across our sector. I found it named on old geodesic maps from the oil searching days and matched them to our USMIL maps. General Peay took a gamble on this tip and requested that Special Forces check it out. They reported it as a good route for our HMMWVs vehicles up to HEMTT (Heavy Expanded Mobility Tactical Truck) size. That gave 1st Brigade the nod to be the lead combat unit into Iraq.

I was initially given four infantry companies, one from each of our task organized battalions, to form into four combat teams, along with MP platoons, anti-aircraft batteries, medics, etc. We totaled over 2,300 soldiers in TF Citadel. Our mission was to carve out the division's Main Supply Route (MSR) and deliver enough fuel to Cobra to support follow on air assault operations into Iraq and the Euphrates Valley.

LTC Jim McGarity
1st Brigade XO

I was tagged by MAJ Chappel to be "S3 Ground" and plan the battalion's ground movement into Iraq where it would link up with the elements that had air assaulted in.

We received word that our vehicles would convoy across the open desert and link up with the elements that had flown into FOB COBRA. Now came our second surprise. Surely, we thought, no one was crazy enough to send us out in soft-skinned vehicles with no protection. We thought we would get a company of tanks to escort us and provide security. This was not to be the case. We would venture out escorted only by two platoons of TOW anti-tank missile HMMWVs per battalion and whatever small arms and AT4 anti-tank rockets we carried for protection. Now it felt like we were planning a suicide mission! Discussion over the wisdom of the convoy got quite heated over the next several days. MAJ Chappell took us to task and told the planners that we had to show a positive attitude about the mission, as our negativity would transmit to the troops. He was right, but I still harbored doubts as we worked out the details of the convoy. During one talk that MG Peay and COL Hill gave us about the mission, they told us that we would likely see no enemy other than lone, disorganized Iraqi elements that were trying to get

> out of the way of the VII Corps advance. Upon seeing our numbers, they predicted these Iraqis would avoid any contact. That sounded plausible but what worried me was running into the lone Iraqi tank commander who decided that he would take out as many of us as he could before he was destroyed.
>
> *CPT Chris Reed*
> *Battalion Assistant S3*

On G+l, the 3d Brigade would air assault its three infantry battalions into three landing zones, called Area of Operations (AO) EAGLE, which was just south of the Euphrates River near the town of Al Khidr. Securing FOB COBRA was the key to the division's plan, and absolutely critical. Without the refuel point, helicopters carrying the 3d Brigade to its objective—Highway 8, which connected Baghdad with the Iraqi forces in Kuwait—would run out of fuel long before they returned to home base at TAA CAMPBELL. FOB COBRA had to be secured and operational before the 3d Brigade could launch on G+l.

My battalion's mission was to seize the northwestern part of FOB COBRA, which was about 40 square kilometers in area. Additionally, we were expected to conduct a linkup with the French 6th Light Armored Division on our western flank on G+2. For the air assault, the battalion was given two lifts of twenty-four Black Hawks and two lifts of six Chinooks to bring in its troops, vehicles, and equipment. The remainder of its equipment and vehicles would come up MSR NEW MARKET with TF CITADEL. MAJ Chappell, the Battalion XO, would lead the 1-327 Infantry's part of TF CITADEL.

> I remember the mission we had—to support the heavy PZ which deployed the vehicles and equipment necessary to support the air assault of the main and supporting efforts. Afterwards, convoys were formed, and we moved northward along MSR New Market to linkup in the rear of the air assaulted forces—with our battalion having taken numerous EPWs from the bunker complex they overtook. The support platoon then assumed guard on these EPWs until they were removed for additional handling.
>
> We had little to no chance of stopping along the way, so everyone did their maintenance. That sounds trivial, but with a real-world threat looming all around us, driving into hostile territory in thin-skinned vehicles, the soldiers did what their training dictated. They did not want to have their vehicle break down and for them to become a liability, so they did the best maintenance they had ever done before we drove north. And when the "SCUD Overhead" call came out, the soldiers spread out in a herringbone formation, stopped their

> vehicles, immediately put on their protective NBC mask and gloves (quicker than the Army standard), and started digging foxholes beside their vehicles. They did this without having to be "hounded" to do so.
>
> The mindset of how the logistical tail was going to perform was crystalized by MAJ John Chappell, or "The Duke." He was revered by all in our unit as the no-nonsense, "get 'er dun," Soldier-Leader. And let me tell you how he set that tone.
>
> The Duke had this "southern drawl" way about him that, at a quick-glance, you could mistake for a push-over type. But you would make that mistake only once, because when he spoke with that soft, out-of-the-corner of his mouth way, it was for a reason. He didn't mince words and he gave thought to each one coming at you. And he would follow any misunderstanding or thought of not doing exactly what he said with a glance and a scowl that gave you an immediate reorganization of the priorities in your life.
>
> *1LT George Glaze*
> *Support Platoon Leader*

To prepare for the air assault, the battalion tried to concentrate on: (1) Making sure that all the troops were well-informed and prepared for the air assault; (2) Ensuring that the intelligence picture of the landing area was as clear and accurate as possible; (3) Making sure that all the leaders understood the plan and contingencies if something went wrong. To keep the soldiers well informed, I personally tried to talk to all the companies at least every other day with CSM Riley. Because our positions were spread out over an 8-kilometer line, I would talk to individual platoons one at a time.

At these talks, I would update everyone on the enemy strength in our landing area, talk through the overall plan, answer any questions or rumors, and tell them again how proud I was of them. Of particular interest to the troops was the timing of the air assault. On G-Day, the overall plan called for only the 101st and the French 6th Division to attack into Iraq. The remainder of XVIII Airborne Corps and VII Corps would not attack until G+l. The fact that we would be 90 miles inside Iraq and waiting for units to link up on G+2 was something that I had to convince the soldiers was doable. As always, I took CSM Riley with me to help keep the soldiers motivated and answer questions. CSM Riley was the best motivator I ever knew in the Army, so his talents were greatly appreciated.

> A day or two before the attack, LTC Hancock and CSM Riley went to each company to brief all soldiers on the outline of the plan and give the pre-battle "pep-talk." It was a moment I will never forget.

LTC Hancock was his usual humorous and good-natured self. He explained in a down-to-earth way that we were well trained and would do well, which boosted our confidence. He also promised to "hit the enemy with the most impersonal weapons first." He would use artillery, bombs and attack helicopters before he risked our lives in an Infantry assault. Next CSM Riley stepped forward. "Rock" Riley was a legend. He stepped forward and stared at the assembled company. He was quiet for a second and then said "Combat Soldiers! I know you will all do your duty! And remember dying can't be all that bad because a lot of people have done it!" I am not sure it's the technique I would have used, but it seemed to break the tension. Hearing from the battalion command team the balance of expressing confidence and being prepared for reality was what we needed.

CPT Chris Reed
Battalion Assistant S3

After some additional adjustments on positioning the division, our unit eventually took the position at TAA Campbell in mid-January 1991, about 10km south of the Iraqi border. Our unit was on the extreme western flank of the division and my platoon, 1st Platoon, was positioned as the last infantry platoon that connected with the French 6th Division to the west of the division.

At some point in mid-February, it became clear that the ground war was approaching. The occasional mail calls stopped, and no mail was allowed to be sent. The initial plans for FOB COBRA were exactly as we had rehearsed during the walk-through exercise in December. We were all preparing for the air assault.

2LT Dave Esposito
1st Platoon Leader, A Company

Of some interest was a female first lieutenant that was in 1st Brigade's Intel Section. At the time, US Army policy was that women could not go past the Forward Edge of the Battle Area (FEBA). The brigade was air assaulting 100 miles past the FEBA, so whether the lieutenant should go on the first lift as part of the Brigade Jump TOC was questioned. After much consideration, our Brigade Commander (COL Hill) said, more or less, "the hell with it," and let her go. Turns out she was Patty George, the wife of the present Chief of Staff of the Army, General Randy George.

CSM Robert Nichols
1st Brigade Command Sergeant Major

I was working in the 1st Brigade TOC as an Intel Officer and I remember four things: 1. The "water cooler gossip" was that all the women in forward positions were going to be moved back. I was surprised to hear this and then frustrated that this would happen so close to the mission. It made no sense to me, and I remember saying to another female LT that I was sure COL Hill would not move me because I was a Soldier and that was my job, and he'd definitely think it made no sense! 2. I remember COL Hill calling me over for a private conversation where he asked me if I felt like I would be able to continue to do my job if my husband, who was in 3-327 (I believe serving as a Company XO), was wounded or killed. COL Hill explained that I would likely hear first-hand over the TOC Comms if his battalion was taking fire and who was KIA. I remember saying that while I couldn't know how I would respond, I hoped that I would do my job as a Soldier no matter what. 3. Practicing exiting from a Black Hawk with an NCO and a Soldier that were part of the EWO Team. I had coordinated with a pilot who allowed us to use his parked aircraft to practice jumping out with our gear on and a big wooden chest of supplies that we were going to carry to where the new TOC was going to set up. We practiced over and over to be sure we could exit quickly. 4. I remember a time in the TOC when we thought we were shortly going to be engaging the enemy. I felt a deep panic rising up in me. I looked over at COL Hill and will never forget his calm and steady demeanor and I suddenly felt steadier. It was an object lesson in leadership for me; how goes the leader, so goes the team.

1LT Patty George
Intelligence Officer, 311th MI Battalion

At the company level we rehearsed all phases of the upcoming air assault operation. Our battalion and brigade leadership ensured we had all the resources we needed to rehearse, to include static loading of the Blackhawks. LZs and PZs were numbered higher and kept simple. Soldiers headed to LZ 1 would load on PZ 1—it doesn't get simpler than that. A lot of extra gear was directed to go on each Blackhawk load. We had to squeeze an extra Dragon missile onboard, as well as 5-gallon water cans for extra water, sheets of plywood for overhead cover for fighting positions, extra MREs, and a myriad of other things. We finally found a load plan that would allow for all of this extra equipment along with fifteen

> ABU soldiers and rucksacks. It wasn't comfortable and it sure wasn't in any SOP anywhere, but it worked.
>
> *CPT Ken Russell*
> *A Company Commander*

The equipment that would go on the helicopter and on the soldier was extensive. The seats on the Black Hawks were taken out so that there would be more room to jam the soldiers in. On the air assault, soldiers would be sitting between the legs of another soldier, so if you were prone to claustrophobia you had to mentally steel yourself for the flight.

On the floor of the Black Hawk was a Kevlar blanket for ballistic protection, five sections of 4ft by 6ft plywood for overhead cover, steel pickets for overhead cover, extra shovels for digging, and five 5-gallon water containers for extra water. Soldiers and leaders worked hard on the individual soldier's load but were not successful in getting it under 100 pounds per man.

Each soldier had his individual MOPP gear of gloves, boots, mask, coat, and pants. Each soldier had his basic load of ammunition, at least one grenade, food for three days, two 1-quart canteens of water, one 2-quart canteen of water, his web gear, individual weapon, helmet, flak vest, and a bayonet or a knife. Each soldier would also bring in fifty folded sandbags for fighting positions. Each squad would have their M60 machine gun and AT4 anti-tank weapon. The 81mm mortar platoon would bring their mortar rounds and tubes with them.

The CH47 Chinooks would either have internal loads or external "sling-loaded" equipment, carried under the belly of the helicopter. Our anti-tank TOW missile HMMWVs were internally loaded on the Chinooks. For the flight, drivers were allowed to sit in the HMMWVs of the internally loaded TOW vehicles. This technique is something that, in training, would never be allowed because the driver would have great difficulty getting out of the vehicle in an emergency, but was necessary to get the vehicles quickly out of the helicopter.

> Once up north, we spent countless hours and days training for the air assault that was soon to come. We initially tried to sling load the HMMWVs the traditional way, back-to-back. We very quickly learned because of the rotor wash with the sand that this would never work. We were told that we would sling load them side-by-side. The trick to this was trying to figure out how to keep them from banging together during flight and not damage the HMMWV's. We came up with the idea to use the cargo net bags on the front fender driver side of one vehicle and the passenger back fender of the other vehicle. This would also allow us to drive the HMMWV out of the LZ with

> the bags attached until we could get to a place and time to remove them. Doing it this way was much better as far as the rotor wash was concerned, but still wasn't ideal. But at least we had a plan. It was time to put the training to the test.
>
> *PFC Bruce Dittfield*
> *Battalion Commander's Driver*

On the Chinooks were also placed six logistics carts that were made by our Maintenance Warrant Officer out of helicopter tires and tent poles. The carts resembled rickshaws that you would find in Bangkok. Most of the battalion's vehicles were coming with TF CITADEL at G+1, so the line companies—Alpha, Bravo, and Charlie—had no vehicles to shuttle supplies and men around their part of the perimeter. The battalion's trace would be about 15 kilometers (9 miles) so each line company would have a section of the perimeter that was about 5 kilometers, or 3 miles, long. The carts could be loaded and pushed/pulled by two soldiers, giving each of the line companies some flexibility in resupplying their positions.

> The mission for Charlie Company was to land in FOB Cobra and push out the perimeter upon landing. We knew where we were supposed to land, and where the objective was and what the front trace was supposed to be. Second Platoon was on the right flank of Charlie Company, and I was to conduct a friendly linkup in combat with First Lieutenant Joe Gammon from Bravo Company once both elements were in place. Joe and I met and spoke well before the invasion and felt very confident with our plan for that daylight linkup. My Forward Observer, Sergeant Juan Rosado, also prepared the platoon well using the tools at their disposal.
>
> *2LT Matt Karres*
> *2d Platoon Leader, C Company*

The battalion ultimately conducted three full-scale rehearsals, numerous Tactical Exercises Without Troops (TEWT), one brigade rehearsal, and the exchange visit with the French division to help prepare the soldiers to recognize the French vehicles. In the various dress rehearsals, we would pack all our equipment on the helicopters and time ourselves in getting off and getting the helicopter airborne as quickly as possible. Because of all the different pieces of equipment, especially the plywood sheets, all the soldiers, upon exiting the helicopter, were responsible for holding on to a piece equipment to make sure the helicopter blades didn't suck it up into their rotor wash.

Observations

The bottom line for us was that, wherever we landed, we were not prepared for an attack when we were exiting the helicopters. The Landing Zone had to be distant from any enemy forces. The equipment we brought was extensive and heavy but was the minimum necessary to seize and hold FOB COBRA, which would be 90 miles behind enemy lines. There was no water, no trees, no camouflage, and, potentially, a chemically contaminated environment. In practice, we found we did not assault off the helicopters but rolled off and then made sure the helicopters got off the ground as quickly and as safely as possible for the next lift of soldiers.

Note

1. Priest. “Chemical Alarms Rang, But Desert Location Is Lost.”

CHAPTER 10

GOD BLESS THINKING SOLDIERS

TAA CAMPBELL
21 February 1991

One of the things I learned early in my military career was that the most important part of preparing for an air assault was getting a good intelligence picture of the landing area. From corps, division, and brigade intelligence reports, there was one Iraqi division, the 45th, in the area that comprised the 6th French zone and the 101st sector around FOB COBRA. The 45th was an infantry division that had some towed artillery and a tank battalion in its order of battle.

> During most of the battalion's deployment, my intelligence section and I were focused on learning about the enemy, reading and archiving reports (there was no computer support back then), and manually staying abreast of and recording the operational and intelligence picture. LTC Hancock had frequently told me that the most important part of preparing for any air assault operation was getting a good intelligence picture of our landing area. All the intelligence reports we had received reported that there was one Iraqi Division, the 45th, in the area which ostensibly occupied portions of the 6th French Division's zone and the 101st sector around FOB Cobra. However, the reporting was spotty and inconsistent; an issue that made me very uncomfortable.
>
> *CPT Jose Delgado*
> *Battalion S2*

Division intelligence estimates said there were two potential enemy locations within FOB COBRA, and both were in my assigned sector. One was a reported logistical site that was supposedly occupied by fifteen to thirty people. The second area was characterized as an "unoccupied" trench line that could ostensibly hold up to 100 enemy soldiers. This trench line was near my lead company's landing zone.

> The Iraqi 45th Infantry Division did have some towed artillery and a tank battalion in its order of battle. Notably (and of great relief to all of us), the division did not (ostensibly) possess any capability for offensive chemical warfare. Inside FOB Cobra, division intelligence estimates said there were two possible enemy locations, and both were in our battalion's sector. One was an occupied logistical site that appeared to have approximately thirty people. The logistical site was in the very northern part of our operational sector and about 6 kilometers from the battalion's most northern landing zone. The second area was a reportedly unoccupied trench line that could potentially support about 100 enemy soldiers. The trench line was located about 500 meters from the landing zone of the battalion's lead company.
>
> *CPT Jose Delgado*
> *Battalion S2*

Intel Section and the Discovery

The Battalion S2 (Intel) section consisted of CPT Delgado (Intel Officer), 1LT Bowman (Intel Officer), MSG Riley (Infantry Senior NCO assigned to the section) and SGT Gonzalez (Intel Specialist). During our prep time in TAA CAMPBELL, the section was very busy generating our intelligence requirements and posting the enemy spot reports that we received from Brigade and Division, as well as helping the company commanders and staff get ready for the air assault.

One such task was to acquire more maps for the area we were air assaulting into. The entire battalion was allocated a total of five maps for the area where the battalion would be conducting its operation. The shortage of maps was due to a distribution error at XVIII Airborne Corps. Company Commanders, platoon leaders, and squad leaders were forced to copy parts of the limited number of maps on sketch paper so that they would have a facsimile of a map to work from during the operation.

To remedy this, I called in CPT Delgado and told him, "Take my HMMWV and go find some maps." I didn't know where the maps could be found or who to contact, but I did know that CPT Delgado was smart and resourceful and if anyone could acquire more maps, it would be him.

At the end of the day, CPT Delgado walked into the HQ tent and told me he had found hundreds of maps. He had taken with him 2LT Tom Evans, our NBC Officer, and my driver, PFC Bruce Dittfield. Delgado and his crew retrieved maps from 5th Special Forces Group, the 82d Airborne Division, and XVIII Airborne Corps Main HQ. He also bartered with the French 6th Division for spot imagery of the area we

Commander and Battalion Staff, 1-327 Infantry, October 1990, Camp Eagle II.

(Left to Right) CPT Tom Guleff, S1; CSM Johnnie Riley; LTC Frank Hancock, Battalion Commander; MAJ John Chappell, XO; MAJ Tom Dempsey, S3; CPT Jose Delgado, S2; CPT Chris Reed, Assistant S3.

Division, Brigade, and Battalion Commanders of the 101st Airborne, October 1990

First Row left to right: COL Joe Bolt, Division Chief of Staff; BG Hugh Shelton, ADC-Operations; MG Binnie Peay, Commanding General; BG Ron Adams, ADC-Support; CSM Steven Weiss, Division Command Sergeant Major

Second Row, 2d from the right: COL Tom Hill, 1st Brigade Commander

Last row, 3d from the left: LTC Frank Hancock, Battalion Commander, 1-327 Infantry. (Author)

Maureen Hancock with her three sons, Frank Jr., Mike, Brian and husband Frank.

Maureen would run the 1-327 Infantry's Family Support Group (FSG) and be the chief problem-solver for the 600 (+) battalion family members remaining at Fort Campbell. The FSG alleviated much pressure on the deployed soldiers.

Linda Artavia from San Mateo, California on her "unauthorized" visit to South Vietnam in December 1968 to bring Embossed Adopted Sons Medallions to her brother Joe's unit -"ABU" Company, 1-327 Infantry.

South Vietnam 1968.

Linda Artavia being escorted by 1LT Steve Patterson, Platoon Leader in "ABU" Company, 1-327 Infantry. They would later marry and support "ABU" and 1-327 Infantry for the next fifty-six years. Their support during DS/DS was extraordinary.

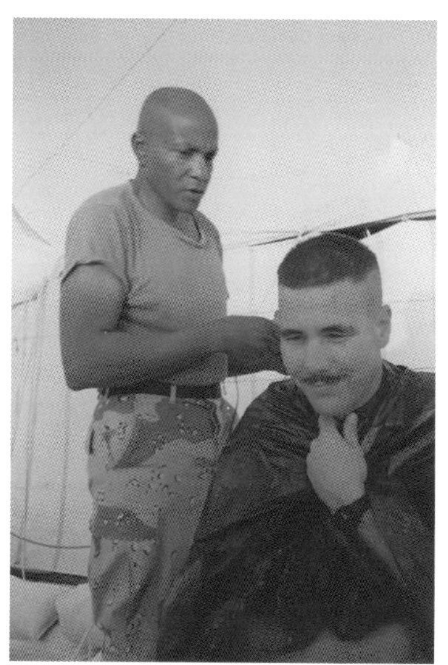

Above left: CSM Riley giving a haircut to SPC Dave Moyers in Camp Eagle II. CSM Riley could do anything, including giving haircuts.

Above right: SFC Tom Levesque, 81mm Mortar Platoon Sergeant, at Camp Eagle II. Tom was deeply respected by his platoon.

Covering Force Area, November 1990.

Bleak and barren – an ocean of sand and brutal sun.

MAJ John Chappell, Battalion XO, and CPT Darcy Brewer, C Company Commander, on aerial reconnaissance of the Covering Force Area.

Above: CPT Jose Delgado, Battalion S2, and LTC Hancock – Covering Force Area, December 1990. Jose's analysis would be critical in getting the A Company LZ moved.

Right: SGT Jesus Gonzalez, Battalion Intelligence Analyst. Jesus started the ball rolling on discovering enemy troops in FOB COBRA.

(Left to Right) SGT Joe Lepion (2nd Squad Leader), SPC John Sokolik, SPC Chris Hunt, PFC Richard Hagedorn, PFC Aarron Clark – 81 mm Mortar Platoon in the Covering Force Area. The mortar platoon was a very close-knit unit, even after the war.

PFC Larry Maroto, D Company, observing vehicles from the 6th French Division in an exchange visit to prevent fratricide when the two units linked up in Iraq.

Above left: CPT Tom Guleff, Battalion S1, Camp Eagle II. A smart and hard officer.

Above right: 1LT Gerry Tertychny, ABU Company XO, boarding C130 aircraft to go to TAA CAMPBELL. Gerry would "create" a POW enclosure out of thin air and then be the official "counter" of enemy POWs.

CPT Chris Reed, Assistant S3

Went "AWOL" from Fort Benning to go to war with his old battalion; did not get paid for nine months by the Army for his efforts.

RULES OF ENGAGEMENT

!THE RIGHT TO USE DEADLY FORCE IN SELF DEFENSE IS NEVER DENIED!

1. USE ONLY NECESSARY FORCE TO ACCOMPLISH THE MISSION; MINIMIZE DAMAGE TO CIVILIANS AND PROPERTY.

2. DEADLY FORCE MAY BE USED FOR PROTECTION OF LIFE, TO PREVENT DESTRUCTION OF PROPERTY, EQUIPMENT, AIRCRAFT, OR AGAINST A DECLARED HOSTILE FORCE. BN CDRS OR HIGHER HAVE AUTHORITY TO DECLARE A FORCE HOSTILE.

3. CHEMICAL WEAPONS AND/OR RIOT CONTROL AGENTS WILL NOT BE USED UNLESS AUTHORIZED BY HIGHER HEADQUARTERS. VERIFICATION IS REQUIRED.

4. UNOBSERVED INDIRECT FIRE, CLOSE AIR SUPPORT, AND HELICOPTER FIRES MAY BE EMPLOYED CONSISTENT WITH MILITARY NECESSITY AND THE PREVENTION OF UNNECESSARY SUFFERING.

5. HOSPITALS, RELIGIOUS FACILITIES, MONUMENTS, AND HISTORIC STRUCTURES WILL NOT BE TARGETED UNLESS APPROVED BY HIGHER HEADQUARTERS.

6. TAKING OF WAR TROPHIES AND LOOTING IS PROHIBITED. CIVILIAN PROPERTY MAY ONLY BE USED IF CLEAR MILITARY NECESSITY EXISTS. ENEMY MILITARY PROPERTY MAY BE DESTROYED OR USED IF ENEMY MARKINGS ARE REMOVED.

7. ENEMY PRISONERS OF WAR, CAPTURED/DETAINED PERSONS, AND NONCOMBATANTS WILL BE TREATED HUMANELY AND GIVEN ALL PROTECTIONS UNDER THE HAGUE AND GENEVA CONVENTIONS.

8. SOLDIERS WILL OBSERVE GEOGRAPHIC CONSTRAINTS AS DIRECTED BY HIGHER HEADQUARTERS.

9. USE OR WEAR OF ENEMY INSIGNIA OR UNIFORMS IS PROHIBITED.

10. THE MUTILATION OR MALTREATMENT OF A DEAD BODY IS A SERIOUS WAR CRIME.

11. CHAIN OF COMMAND WILL BRIEF CHANGES TO ROE TO ALL SOLDIERS AS THEY OCCUR. DETAILED GUIDANCE WILL BE PROVIDED TO AIRCREWS, AIR DEFENSE, AND INDIRECT FIRE PERSONNEL AS PART OF MISSION BRIEFINGS.

12. REPORT LAW OF WAR VIOLATIONS THROUGH CHANNELS.

Above: Rules of Engagement (ROE) Card for the 101st Airborne.

Left: Left to right – 1LT Brian Bedell, Scout Platoon Leader; PFC Richie Hagedorn, Mortar Platoon; 1LT Eric Valentzas, 81mm Mortar Platoon Leader, at Camp Eagle II.

ABU Company on 500-mile C130 flight from Camp Eagle II to TAA CAMPBELL, late January 1991. The flight was nap of the earth, making the ride close to a roller coaster experience.

Captain Bill Reister, Air Force Liaison Officer, 23 February 1991, the day before air assault into FOB COBRA. Bill would be instrumental in getting the Iraqis to surrender.

23 February 1991 – the night before air assault. Packing up and making sure the Black Hawks could carry the weight…a power check was done to see if the helicopters could get off the ground.

Tactical CP the night before air assault into Iraq.

Left to right (Kneeling) CPT Jerome Hawkins (Fire Support Officer) and SPC Booze.

(Standing) 2LT Tom Evans, SFC Ernie Wright, "Doc" Siegel (Battalion Surgeon), CPT Jim Knickrehm, LTC Hancock, Unknown soldier.

23 February 1991, the day before air assault into FOB COBRA.

LTC Hancock and CSM Riley using a soldier's sign saying, "Next Stop Iraq." The wind was already blowing and would delay the air assault the next morning.

LTC Hancock and MAJ Chappell the night before the Air Assault into FOB COBRA.

The two would linkup in FOB COBRA on G+1.

Aerial view of part of the trench line with its bunkers. The trench line was more than a kilometer long.

Painting by SPC Mike Kloppenburg of the air assault into FOB COBRA.

SPC Kloppenburg flew in with ABU Company.

Searching Iraqi POWs in FOB COBRA.

SAW Gunner from ABU Company covers the searching of enemy POWs at the trench line.

Left: MAJ Dempsey and LTC Hancock immediately after the surrender, with 344 POWs in the background. LTC Hancock said, "Take pictures, no one is going to believe what was here."

Below: An estimated 8 tons of ammunition was stockpiled at the trench line.

Destroyed ZPU4 anti-aircraft gun. There were 4 ZPU4s at the trench line. Three were destroyed and one was taken back to the Fort Campbell Museum.

Captured weapons at the trench line.

SFC Ernie Wright and PFC Bruce Dittfield in UH1 enroute to assist with the surrender of enemy soldiers at the logistic site.

SPC Robert Lipker and PFC Brandon Copeland, ABU Company, searching an enemy bunker at the trench line.

Tactical CP, FOB COBRA, late afternoon of 24 February 1991.

(Left to Right) CPT Sung Lee, SFC Ernie Wright (reclining), CPT Jim Knickrehm, LTC Hancock (on bucket).

CSM Nichols placing units into FOB COBRA from TF Citadel. CSM Nichols would use scouts on motorcycles as guides. The vehicles were so overloaded they were alternately described as the "Beverly Hillbillies" and "Mad Max Beyond Thunderdome."

Left: COL Hill, LTC Hancock, and MG Peay inspect the weapons at the "unoccupied" trench line on G +1.

Below: Trench line on G+1 with members of Alpha Company and Headquarters and Headquarters Company. 2LT Mike Huebner is kneeling, holding a picture of Saddam Hussein. LTC Hancock kneeling on Huebner's right; CPT Delgado kneeling to LTC Hancock's right; CPT Ken Russell, ABU Company Commander, standing behind LTC Hancock, slightly to his right.

ABU Company Leaders after takedown of trench line

Kneeling – SSG Charles Miller (Squad Leader), SGT Sean Green (Squad Leader), 2LT Mike Huebner (3d Platoon Leader)

Standing – SGT Tom Craig (3d Platoon FIST NCO), CPT Ken Russell (ABU Company Commander), SSG Jose Fierros (Squad Leader), SFC John Volanos (3d Platoon Sergeant)

This photo sits on the bookshelf of the Secretary of Defense in the movie, *Without Remorse*.

LTC Dick Cody, "No Mercy Six," briefing his pilots of 1-101 Aviation Battalion (Apaches) on G+2. LTC Cody's battalion was instrumental in the takedown of FOB COBRA. On G+2 his helicopters would attack into the Euphrates Valley.

2LT Matt Karres and SSG Stuart Rice, C Company, defending in FOB COBRA. 2LT Karres signed into the battalion one week before the air assault.

PFC Stan Banach, 81 mm Mortar Platoon, in fighting position in FOB COBRA. At the end of the stay in FOB COBRA, Stan would make a gigantic Screaming Eagle out of rocks on the desert floor.

Above: 2LT Dave Esposito, ABU Company, in a fighting position. Dave came to the battalion in December 1990. MAJ Chappell and LTC Hancock chose him and his 1st Platoon to provide security for TF CITADEL because they knew he would get it done.

Right: SPC Mike Kloppenburg, A Company, (left) and PFC Dan Conyers hold a handmade flag that SPC Kloppenburg made and carried during Desert Storm. He would, thirty years later, donate it to the Fort Campbell Museum.

Above: 1LT George Glaze, Support Platoon Leader, sees his son for the first time Campbell Army Airfield.

Left: CPT John Santini reunited with his daughter, Samantha.

A wreath is laid at Artavia's grave site. The ceremony was held July 5 in San Bruno.

Lt. Col. Frank Hancock, commander, 1st Bn., 327th Inf. Rgt., enjoyed spending time with his desert pen pal Genevieve Mahrheinke.

The "Abus" proudly wore their "Adopted Sons" medals above

"Above the Rest" soldiers, led by Hancock, walked proudly down the streets that their brother Eagles had

San Mateo Parade, July 4, 1991. 101 members of 1-327 Infantry attended the parade. Over 50,000 people attended the parade. There were no dry eyes.

Officers and CSM of 1-327 Infantry, along with supporting personnel and battalion mascot, "Bastogne," July 1991. Everyone came home.

May 2021. 1-327 Infantry contingent at the thirty-year Desert Storm reunion at Fort Campbell.

March, 2023. 1st Brigade Bastogne Bulldog Ball in Nashville. Supporting the deployment of 1st Brigade to Eastern Europe. Right to Left – Linda Patterson, Frank Hancock, Frank Bills, Gerry Tertychny, Rich Hagedorn, Joanna Hagedorn, LeAnn Thornton (Americans Supporting America Representative).

were air assaulting into. For the spot imagery, he paid for it with MREs...a lot of MREs. The French bargained hard. In retrospect, I should have given all three of them, Delgado, Evans, and Dittfield, an on-the-spot Army Commendation Medal for going above and beyond duty.

As time was closing toward G-Day, there was a dearth of intelligence reporting. This bothered both CPT Delgado and SGT Gonzales. Lack of intelligence reporting forced them to fill in needed information with their own assessments. Both Delgado and Gonzalez were concerned with a kilometer-long trench line that was 500 meters from where CPT Ken Russell's Alpha Company was going to land. Six Black Hawks with fourteen soldiers and four crewmen each were going into that LZ on the critical first lift of the operation. The analysis that had come down from XVIII Airborne Corps, Division, and Brigade stated that the trench line was unoccupied.

SGT Gonzalez was not buying the assessment that there were no enemy troops in this kilometer-long trench line. On his own volition, he decided to do a deep dive into the 45th Iraqi Division Order of Battle (ORBAT). He templated the 45th Division by using the Iraqi/Soviet doctrine of placing infantry battalions in triangular configurations with standard distances between the triangles. By doing this, SGT Gonzalez found that an Iraqi battalion was unaccounted for, and that the likely location of this missing battalion was the "unoccupied" trench line.

> In looking at the estimates, my Intelligence Sergeant, SGT Jesus Gonzalez, and I could not believe that the Iraqis would have constructed such an elaborate trench line without some plan for occupying it or an intention to cover it with defensive fires. Earlier imagery reports also seemed to corroborate our assessments and indicated potential activity and occupation of the sites during the previous thirty days.
>
> *CPT Jose Delgado*
> *Battalion S2*

SGT Gonzalez knew that his personal estimate exposed the Corps/Division/Brigade intelligence assessments as fatally flawed. He also knew that higher headquarters would have to be convinced of what he, a 26-year-old sergeant, had found. SGT Gonzalez told CPT Delgado of his discovery. CPT Delgado and SGT Gonzalez subsequently went through the entire templating exercise multiple times with the enemy infantry battalions. They came up with the same result every time. In their minds, the evidence (or lack thereof) was solid—the trench line was occupied. To get further proof, they sifted through months of enemy sighting reports from multiple sources that included overhead imagery and intercepted communications. To their credit, they found several reports that matched the coordinates of the trench line.

> Three nights prior to G-Day, I read the order and plotted the grid coordinates. I built a new plastic overlay on top of my situation overlay. I was seriously concerned about what I saw. Our units will land right on top of Iraqi's 45th Infantry Division, that I had knowledge of from the beginning of my journey into Iraq. I was very familiar with my situation overlay and noticed that this Iraqi unit had many months to dig in and fortify their defensive positions. I also knew that intelligence reporting indicated some vehicle movement and dug-in positions in the locations south of the Euphrates River. The unit in question was a light infantry brigade-sized element, at least, with multiple ZSUs—Soviet air defense guns. Not good news for helicopters.
>
> *SGT Jesus Gonzalez*
> *Battalion S2 NCO*

CPT Delgado now brought in MAJ Dempsey, MAJ Chappell, and CSM Riley and briefed them on what SGT Gonzalez had uncovered. My staff was convinced that the trench line was occupied with what could potentially be a large number of enemy soldiers. MAJ Chappell sent a runner to my tent to "wake up the Old Man" and have him come to the HQ tent.

> I informed my S2, CPT Delgado, explained my findings, and told him that, if the coordinates were right, we are in big trouble. Lives will be lost in the initial onset of the air assault mission, and we will also lose men on the ground as they attempt to fight back and regroup. CPT Delgado informed the S3, MAJ Dempsey, and he initially did not believe it. He told the S2 section to prove it and let him see the reporting and the intelligence map board. So, we did. MAJ Dempsey was shocked. He said to grab all the reports, re-plot everything, and reassess our findings.
>
> It was all hands-on deck and the S2 section, with the help from several S3 members, replotted the entire map all over again. Hours later, we showed our new re-plotted map and MAJ Dempsey himself checked the grid coordinates. MAJ Dempsey was one of the smartest S3 officers I have ever met in my twenty-year intelligence career as an NCO.
>
> MAJ Dempsey triple checked the work with CPT Delgado and me. He told us, "I hate to say this but let's wake up the old man. Jesus, go wake up the boss." I guess I had to deliver the news and wake up the commander. He was very tired, and I knew how hard he had worked in the last six months in Saudi Arabia and currently

near the border of Iraq. I knew this man was passionate and he loved our soldiers.

We woke up our battalion commander and told him that we had some bad news and that we would never wake him up otherwise. LTC Hancock said to me, "Gonzo, this better be good."

SGT Jesus Gonzalez
Battalion S2 NCO

When I walked into the tent, my first thought was that my mother had died. In front of me were five professional soldiers—CPT Delgado, SGT Gonzalez, MAJ Chappell, MAJ Dempsey, and CSM Riley—with the most somber looks I think I had ever seen. MAJ Chappell kicked off the briefing and said SGT Gonzalez and CPT Delgado needed to update me on the enemy situation. SGT Gonzalez showed me his work and how he and CPT Delgado had meticulously deduced where the missing battalion was by templating the infantry battalions and then plotting where the satellite photos and other reports indicated enemy activity near the trench line. CPT Delgado then came to the impeccable, and logical, deduction, "Why would the Iraqis build a kilometer-long trench line without putting someone in it?"

We urged the battalion commander to change the landing zone to the south to allow a measure of reaction for our assaulting forces. Once we briefed the S3 and XO on our assessment, they also agreed. The staff and I were so insistent and convincing that the battalion commander opted to go in the middle of the night to the brigade headquarters (two days before the operation) to convince the brigade commander to move the landing zone.

CPT Jose Delgado
Battalion S2

At that time, our S-2 Section consisted of two highly intelligent young men, Captain Delgado and Sergeant Gonzalez. These two analyzed every Iraqi military unit's position and were able to account for all but one battalion. After extensive searching, they found what they believed to be the missing battalion dug in at where A Company was supposed to land. Both division and brigade intelligence reports revealed no one on or near the proposed LZ.

While in Vietnam, I learned many valuable lessons and shared them with LTC Hancock. The Vietnam War took too many of our young men's lives, too many lives were lost on both sides. I remember the dead bodies turning green, the smell, the maggots eating the dead flesh. The cracking of the AK-47, the whistling of

> bullets by the ear, and the fragments of your own mortar rounds hitting your mortar tubes because the enemy was so close. We could have fought that war smarter; the fight should have been in the North and not the South. We had to fight this war smarter; we had to kill the enemy in his territory. Even today, I still have a lot of respect for the North Vietnamese soldiers, they were great warriors, and it was too bad we had to kill them. Now that the time had come to fight and kill again, we had to fight and kill the Iraqis before they could kill us because war is hell, and if we do not want to end up there, we had to fight smarter.
>
> *CSM Johnny Riley*
> *Battalion Command Sergeant Major*

After the briefing, I was convinced that the trench line was occupied. These five soldiers were extremely competent, had done their due diligence, and had deduced critical information. Also, in the back of my mind was the article "Vietnam Stories" by Joe Galloway. It concerned the Battle of the Ia Drang in November 1965, and we had all read it back in October. Why did LTC Hal Moore's battalion sustain 49 per cent casualties and nearly get overrun? Faulty intelligence, that's why. I told my driver, PFC Bruce Dittfield, to get H6, my HMMWV, ready as I was going to brigade headquarters to talk to COL Hill. I told CPT Delgado and MAJ Dempsey to get in the vehicle and come with me.

It was around 2100 when we headed out for Brigade Headquarters. During the thirty-minute drive, my thoughts were focused on how I was going to present this information to COL Hill. The operation would be the most massive air assault in military history with nearly 300 helicopters participating. It was scheduled to go in two days and my battalion was the tip of the spear. The battalion must secure the area where the division's aviation brigade was going to set up its critical rearm and refuel points.

The air assault was going to be executed at night which increased the chances of mishaps. The air mission brief where pilots, commanders, and operation officers checked call signs, coordinates, and coordinating measures had already taken place. How do you explain to the brigade commander that his intelligence estimate is "screwed-up" and the battalion's lead company is in jeopardy of taking heavy casualties? The basis for my assessment is the hard thinking of a 26-year-old sergeant and a 29-year-old captain. If my battalion fails, the Aviation Brigade's timeline slips, and this has a domino effect on the larger campaign; specifically, the division's ability to set up its logistics base, which endangers the conduct of the air assault to the Euphrates on G+1.

When I walked into the Brigade Tactical Operations Center (TOC) tent, the Brigade Commander (COL Hill), the Brigade S3 (MAJ Clawson), the Brigade

CSM (CSM Nichols), and the Brigade S2 (MAJ Chenoweth) were all there, as well as about ten other brigade soldiers. I brought MAJ Dempsey and CPT Delgado with me, and I asked COL Hill if I could talk to him. COL Hill was a little surprised, given the time of the evening, but he agreed to the discussion. I told him that I would like him to hear what CPT Delgado and his intelligence team had discovered. CPT Delgado did an excellent job of explaining how he and SGT Gonzalez went about discovering that there were enemy troops in the "unoccupied" trench line within our battalion's AO. I believed at that time that this was a "slam dunk" and that the LZ would certainly be relocated.

However, after CPT Delgado finished his presentation COL Hill went about assuring me that there were no enemy troops in that trench line. He showed me gun camera footage from an Apache helicopter of the LZ and the area where the trench line was located that showed a lack of enemy personnel present. I remember not seeing anything in the footage because it was so dark. He then said the aviation brigade commander had personally conducted a reconnaissance of the area and had landed near the trench line. According to COL Hill, no one was there. The Brigade S2 also, as I remember, chimed in telling us that it was "unoccupied."

The more COL Hill and his staff talked about there being no enemy troops in the trench line, the more that CPT Delgado and I got agitated. Although I knew that this was a BIG DEAL, and that I was asking at the last moment to change coordinates for a major night air assault, I also knew what happens when a battalion "accidentally" lands on a large enemy force. LTC Hal Moore's experience in the Ia Drang Valley proved to me that it was not only tragic but also stupid.

About thirty or forty minutes into this discussion, my demeanor went from agitation to stone-cold anger. I did not see COL Hill (who was tremendously courteous to me) bending on this. I also did not believe his staff had any inclination to reconsider their estimate, despite what CPT Delgado had shown them. I was beginning to believe that they may not give a shit about what I said, and that Alpha Company's LZ was staying put regardless of anything I or CPT Delgado showed them.

I do not clearly remember what transpired next, but others who were present tell me that for the next five to ten minutes I was totally unprofessional and insubordinate (I prefer to characterize it as passionate) in my loud discussion with COL Hill. I remember taking my helmet off, throwing it on the tent floor, and saying words to the effect of "this is fucking bullshit," along with other colorful characterizations. CPT Delgado later related to me that he thought I was going to be relieved right there.

> The resultant "discussion" was very heated and expletive-laden, as COL Hill was unwilling to move the Landing Zone (LZ) because of the short reaction time and the fact that it was very close to

where the aviation brigade was planning to establish a refuel point. For a moment I believed that LTC Hancock would be relieved of his command, as the heated discussion unfolded in the brigade commander's tent.

COL Hill was convinced that it would cost us time to move the extra distance and additionally he had personally been assured that there was no one in the trench line by the aviation brigade commander, who had flown reconnaissance flights over the area.

CPT Jose Delgado
Battalion S2

LTC Hancock took the S2 Intel report to COL Hill at brigade headquarters. The Brigade Commander was COL Hill, a fellow Texan with some gray hair, and his CSM was Robert Nichols, who was a lot younger than me with fewer years of service, but smart.

Our companies would be spread so far apart it would have been almost impossible to block the enemy's tanks from penetrating our lines if there was also an enemy force on the A Company LZ we had to deal with.

CSM Johnny Riley
Battalion Command Sergeant Major

When I was through with my venting, I looked around and saw that everyone had left the tent except for me and COL Hill. I was so invested in the "spirited conversation", I had failed to notice that our discussion had cleared the tent. There was, at this point, nothing left to say. I thought for a nanosecond to ask COL Hill to put it in writing, and then dismissed that as "Hollywood" talk, since it was already written down in the Operations Order (OPORD) and it seemed like a ridiculous request to make. I left the Brigade TOC and went out to my HMMWV, where CPT Delgado and MAJ Dempsey were waiting quietly for me. According to CPT Delgado (and for good measure), I threw my helmet again at my HMMWV when I walked out. I then simply told both CPT Delgado and MAJ Dempsey, "They're not changing it," and we headed back to the battalion in silence.

Sure enough, LTC Hancock got the news, and he decided to inform the brigade commander. I waited for several hours later that day. I tried to go to sleep but my nerves got the best of me. I didn't sleep much, and I arrived on shift earlier than usual. I noticed that the battalion commander was not happy, and the TOC was a cold silence throughout. CPT Delgado told me to prepare the enemy situation

> brief, to be conducted for the entire battalion staff. We briefed the enemy situation, and you could hear a pin drop. No one said much after receiving the awful news. We all knew what was at stake and we needed to prepare for the worst. It was time for the company commanders to brief their troops now.
>
> I knew one thing though. We had one of the best infantry battalions in the whole XVIII Airborne Corps. But landing on top of an enemy brigade on their home turf is another type of warfare. We would be conducting the largest air-assault in Army history. Lives will be lost, but how many? How will the enemy react to this type of offensive operation? Will we lose the element of surprise? How can we gain the initiative? So many questions and doubts. But my intelligence was accurate, I knew that and my superior officer, CPT Delgado, trusted my judgment. Enough so that the S3 and my commander had to inform our higher, COL Hill. This is going to be tough because this was a Division Operation Order. I prayed, couldn't sleep, and did not eat. My heartbeat was slow, and I felt for our infantry soldiers. We received an imagery report of a dug-in trench line and movement in the sector that coincided with the area plotted on the S2 map board, the enemy situation overlay. That helped but we needed to hear from higher on what they thought about it.
>
> *SGT Jesus Gonzalez*
> *Battalion S2 NCO*

That night, in my head, I dissected courses of action that could be done to lessen the danger to Alpha Company. However, there was little I could think of. The nearest company to Alpha during the operation would be CPT Bill Simril's Bravo Company, which was landing 5 kilometers (3 miles) away. My other line company was Charlie Company, under CPT Darcy Brewer, which was landing 10 kilometers away from Alpha Company. Since this was being done at night, and we were landing with so much defensive equipment, any quick relief of an engaged Alpha Company was going to be complicated and difficult. Moreover, while we would have Apaches in immediate support when we landed, the command and control of those aviation assets was going to be transient and difficult.

In my mind, the brigade leadership's "unoccupied trench line" assumption for the landing scenario made perfect sense to them. No enemy troops meant no need to change the LZ and no need to change any of the aviation flow. At the battalion level, with our assessment that there were troops in the trench line, the air assault looked like sheer folly. My thoughts kept returning to 1-7 Cavalry in the Ia Drang Valley.

Observations

When I think of my spirited conversation with COL Hill, which I often do, I believe it truly had a touch of divine intervention. Two young soldiers, CPT Delgado and SGT Gonzales, on their own initiative, figured out a complicated and tremendously significant intelligence puzzle. Their assessment was verified, briefed, understood, and forwarded to me by my staff of seasoned professionals. Based on my belief in CPT Delgado and in my staff, I took this information to my boss, COL Hill. He courteously listened to me, and, despite my "passionate" argumentation, did not fire me for insubordination.

It is hard to overstate the importance of what SGT Gonzalez and CPT Delgado found. The fact that they made all this effort on their own—with no direction—is even more incredible. It is also hard to overstate what MAJ Chappell, MAJ Dempsey and CSM Riley did in listening to the sergeant and captain and believing in them. It would have been much easier to say, "Don't worry—if Brigade and Division say it's unoccupied, with our overhead flight capability, it must be." No one knew at the time, but this information of an occupied trench line would be the essential factor that allowed the 101st to successfully complete its mission.

CHAPTER 11

G-2 TO G-1

TAA CAMPBELL

22–23 February 1991

The following morning brought with it a telephone call from Brigade. I cannot recall who from Brigade made the call, but they said that COL Hill had changed his mind and that Alpha Company's LZ was going to be shifted 2 kilometers to the south. That shift would move the LZ about 3 kilometers from the trench line. Although I do not know why COL Hill changed his mind, I always assumed it was Brigade CSM Nichols who convinced him that shifting south 2 kilometers in a desert setting would not be a major event. Regardless of why the decision was made, the battalion was blessed with the best of all gifts for my soldiers … LUCK.

> After some heated arguments, COL Hill moved the A Company LZ about 2 kilometers south of the Iraqi battalion's dug-in potion. The hard work of the S2 and LTC Hancock's intuition prevented us from landing on top of a dug-in enemy, where we would have suffered heavy casualties.
>
> *CSM Johnny Riley*
> *Battalion Command Sergeant Major*

> The next day, we finally received news that our LZ would be moved a few kilometers south. I felt a little relieved, but the fun would begin in the next twenty-four hours. I will be approximately 90 miles deep into enemy territory. God have mercy and look after us...please.
>
> *SGT Jesus Gonzalez*
> *Battalion S2 NCO*

> LTC Hancock got the brigade commander, COL Tom Hill, to move the LZ about a mile to the south. Down in A Company, we weren't privy to the conversation/argument between LTC Hancock and

> COL Hill that resulted in the adjustment to the LZ—we were just told that there was possibly an enemy force on the original LZ, that the LZ had been moved south, and that we were still the battalion's main effort. No problem—we figured that one piece of desert was the same as any other. Additionally, this new LZ was better because it was south of a low ridge that would be between us and the Iraqi force. This would allow us to come in low to the LZ, dismount, and move up to a location where we could see the enemy position—all behind the cover of the ridge. Besides, we would be coming in before first light, in darkness, so that would help us stay concealed.
>
> *1LT Gerry Tertychny*
> *A Company XO*

As the hours ticked away toward G-Day, I concentrated on ensuring that every officer in the battalion knew how I wanted to synchronize the battle and why I was doing it that way. In talking to my officers, I emphasized the firepower that we were taking in with us: mortars, TOW missiles, 105mm artillery, attack helicopters, and tactical air support would all be available to us. I told my officers that if we ran into trouble, I wanted them to use all our firepower before we tried to take some position by ground attack. This would minimize our losses and would maximize our capability to put accurate and massed fires on a target. When I was a major in the 25th Infantry Division, my brigade commander, COL Tom Vaughn, had made this point to me in a Division CPX, saying bombs were better than bayonets.

I also reminded everyone to concentrate on knowing where everybody was to avoid casualties from fratricide. There would be many moving parts during the assault—Black Hawks, Apaches, Cobras, Chinooks, close air support, artillery, mortars, and infantry on the ground—and I didn't want us to accidentally kill each other in the process of securing FOB COBRA. When we finally air assaulted, the emphasis on using combined fire, while avoiding fratricidal fire, was to pay big dividends.

> Staff Sergeant Murphy, S-1 Section NCO, finished creating the battalion manifests for the air assault and ground convoy. He had spent the last couple of days working late into the night with the company first sergeants, executive officers, and battalion staff to update, finalize, check, re-check, and confirm the manifests, making sure that the battalion had accurately accounted for every soldier. Developing these manifests was an incredibly tedious and thankless task, but it was also a very necessary and critical function within the

> S-1 Section. SSG Murphy was the right man for the job…competent, dedicated, and professional.
>
> As we worked at breaking down our positions, soldiers who had been in denial that the U.S. would actually attack into Iraq finally began to accept the reality of the pending mission and that they would be in combat within the next 36 hours.
>
> *CPT John Santini*
> *Battalion Assistant S1*

As 22 February arrived, it seemed inevitable that the ground attack on Iraq and Kuwait was going to go forward. The Iraqis seemed as intransigent as ever and President Bush and the Coalition leaders were completely united. From our perspective, the battalion was as ready as it could be. We rehearsed and then rehearsed again. We were confident that we could get into FOB COBRA, secure it, and hold on until we were relieved. The fact that Alpha Company's initial LZ was moved south increased our belief that the battalion would be successful.

> On 22 February, two days before the start of the ground war, I was called to the CO's Humvee to receive an unanticipated change in orders. I was informed that the battalion needed two platoons to secure the ground convoy that would support the air assault and my platoon was chosen to secure the rear of the convoy that would eventually linkup with the rest of the battalion at FOB Cobra. He wished me well and said be prepared to move out to the staging area in the morning.
>
> When I spoke to my platoon, I could see and hear the initial disappointment. However, the professionalism of the NCOs and soldiers was inspiring as they quickly turned to solving the new problem and preparing for the new mission. We began to prepare our equipment and be ready to move out in the morning. Incidentally, about thirty years later when I reconnected with then COL (retired) Hancock at a retirement ceremony for then COL Tertychny, he told me that he personally chose me for that mission as he was confident that I could lead well in a very uncertain element of the overall mission. That made me feel a lot better after all those years of wondering how that decision came about.
>
> *2LT Dave Esposito*
> *1st Platoon Leader, A Company*

On the night of 22 February, an MLRS unit of XVIII Airborne Corps came forward to about 200 meters of our Battalion CP and fired several salvoes of rockets into

Iraq. After being rocked in my sleeping bag, I realized that our time in Saudi Arabia was drawing to a close. On the morning of 23 February, the battalion broke down its equipment and tents and headed out to its Pickup Zones (PZ). The UH60 Black Hawks and the CH47 Chinooks were prepositioned on the morning of the 23rd in preparation for the assault on the 24th.

The companies walked out to their PZs, which were close to the company positions, and linked up with their helicopters. The battalion elements that were going with the ground convoy also linked up with the Task Force CITADEL personnel. My XO, MAJ Chappell, would head our contingent of some 250 soldiers and fifty-eight vehicles in the convoy. During the day, the companies went over last-minute preparations and practiced unloading procedures for the helicopters. Each of the helicopters did a power check to make sure that they weren't overloaded.

The final load on each of the Black Hawks was: fourteen combat loaded soldiers with rucksacks, three 5-gallon water cans for a one-day resupply of water, eight 4x4 sheets of plywood for overhead cover, eight long pickets for overhead cover, fifty sandbags per person for overhead cover, and four picks/shovels for digging. The Chinooks were to carry internally two HMMWVS and crews on the first lift and two vehicles sling-loaded (hooked underneath the helicopter) on the second lift. Eight of the eleven HMMWVS were TOW vehicles, one was a medical evacuation vehicle, and two were command and control vehicles. We also had the six pull carts for ammunition resupply that went on the second lift of Chinooks.

> The afternoon before G-Day, the helicopters that would fly us in were spotted at our locations and we got ourselves and our gear ready. Platoon leaders, platoon sergeants, squad leaders, and team leaders conducted final inspections of weapons, ammunition, and equipment. We did have a bit of an issue with the UH60 load plans. Finally, another chalk figured it out and showed the rest of us how they had done it. That night, we did a final check of our gear and slept next to our helicopters. I was on Chalk 4.
>
> *1LT Gerry Tertychny*
> *A Company XO*

> Soon enough it was time for ABU to gear up and move out for PZ 1. We arrived late afternoon and scattered out near the Blackhawk platoon that would be flying us into Iraq. We did some last-minute rehearsals, made sure everyone understood the company plan, packed all the additional gear in the Blackhawks, and waited. For me, as for most of ABU, it would be a long sleepless night as we waited to load

> up and go. Mike Huebner, my 3d platoon leader, would be in the lead Blackhawk while I would be in the Number 3 Blackhawk. My XO would be on Blackhawk Number 4. MAJ Dempsey, the Battalion S3 and his RTO soon joined us, since they were part of our air assault lift to LZ 1. I remember that one of the Blackhawks crews had a female crew chief, which was a surprise for ABU. At this time, no women were supposed to be in helicopter crews going across the forward line of troops. ABU didn't care one way or the other. We all spent the night quietly talking, smoking, and mentally getting ourselves ready. All of us expected Iraqi air defenses enroute, and we knew there was a possibility of a hot LZ as we arrived.
>
> *CPT Ken Russell*
> *A Company Commander*

On the 23rd, I attended one last coordination meeting at the Brigade TOC. At the meeting were all the infantry, artillery, support, and aviation battalion commanders that would take part in the seizure of FOB COBRA. COL Hill went over again the timing of the air assault, the communication lash-up, and the expected arrival time of TF CITADEL on G+l. The Brigade S-2 went over the latest intelligence estimates and said that, in his opinion, there were no enemy forces in FOB COBRA. The S-2 had also received a large aerial photo of FOB COBRA that we went over, but unfortunately its information was over a month old.

After the meeting broke-up, I returned to the battalion area and went to see the company commanders one more time. Each of the commanders seemed optimistic, and I wished them well for the next day's mission. The troops were enthusiastic and wished me and CSM Riley good luck. That evening, we sat by our helicopters and mentally prepared ourselves for the morning liftoff. At that time, I felt the battalion had done as much as it could to get ready for the mission and I personally was ready to get on with it. Dr. Siegel, our Battalion Medical Officer who was on my helicopter, wanted to say a collective prayer for our helicopter before we went to bed. I told him to "make it a good-one" and we all held hands and prayed for everything to go right the next day.

> On our last evening together with the full A Company, our platoon received a visit from our Company 1SG, MacArthur Fountain. He wanted to speak to our platoon before we headed out to the staging area for the ground convoy and would be separated from our unit. 1SG Fountain gave one of the most motivating speeches I had heard in my time as a soldier. He spoke directly to the fight we were anticipating facing in the days to come and how it was courageous men like us that are always called upon to fight the tough fight

while others choose to sit back in comfort under our protection. His comments hit home for all of us and gave us another extra boost of motivation for the mission ahead.

In the staging area I met with MAJ John Chappell who was the XO from our battalion and who was now leading the entire ground convoy. In the short time I knew him, I felt confident in his leadership as he was well-known as a straight shooter and a leader who we would all be ready to follow anywhere. I also met with CPT Kaiser who was the 1st Brigade HHC Company Commander and was my new commander for this part of the mission. 2LT Steve Caro from B Company was the other platoon leader that was assigned to the group convoy, and we had a chance to connect before we received the operations order.

2LT Dave Esposito
1st Platoon Leader, A Company

SGT Walker and I were assigned to a Chinook on the first lift that would have a battalion aid station cargo HMMWV internally loaded. We would be riding in that vehicle when we landed. I was the senior person assigned to the Chinook, and therefore was the Chalk Leader. In addition to the aid station vehicle, there were about six soldiers and a great deal of other equipment and supplies that would be loaded onto the Chinook, such as crates of Stinger missiles, boxes of ammunition, 5-gallon water cans, and a lot of other "ash and trash."

The eight Chinooks landed in the pickup zone at about 1400hrs. We linked up with the crews, listened to their instructions, and familiarized ourselves with the helicopter. The crew chief told us that we couldn't load the Chinook until early in the morning in case something happened that required the helicopter to leave in a hurry.

Naturally, the helicopter crews were better supplied than the infantry units and they shared with us hot coffee, hard-boiled eggs, apples, and oranges, which we gladly accepted. The crew played heavy metal music to get us psyched up for what lay ahead in the morning. After eating an MRE for dinner, we took our PB pills (anti-nerve agent pills) and tried to get some sleep, knowing that we would have an early first call to load the vehicles and equipment onto the Chinook and begin the invasion before sunrise.

CPT John Santini
Battalion Assistant S1

Our scheduled lift-off time was 0525 hours, so I went to sleep around 2200 hours. I personally may have gotten two hours of sleep. The French 6th Division was to kick off their attack around 0400 hours, so they started to fire artillery around 0100 hours. The French artillery units were not many kilometers from our PZs and provided us a serenade throughout the night.

> The day before we started the ground war, we were all issued more ammo, mortar rounds, along with what we already had plus water containers, three days of MREs. We all weighed ourselves and our rucks—I don't remember the exact weight of my ruck. I have it written down in my journal. I would write the daily activities, but it was close if not over 100 pounds. The speech from CSM Riley was inspiring and made all of us feel bulletproof but his closing speech brought us all back to reality.
>
> *PFC Jesse Hernandez*
> *3d Platoon, A Company*

> I remember the night before the air assault checking over and over to make sure everything was good to go before I tried to wind down and get some rest. However, rest never happened for me. I was a 19-year-old kid who was about to go to war. The only thing I could think about was how I promised my mom when I joined the infantry not to worry, the world was peaceful and there wouldn't be a war. Well, I guess that's the one promise in my life that I broke to her. I also reflected on my namesake, Bruce A Yoder, who died in Vietnam jumping on a hand grenade to save his fellow Marines. I was hoping to have just an ounce of his courage the next morning.
>
> *PFC Bruce Dittfield*
> *Battalion Commander's Driver*

SUBJECT: MESSSAGE TO ALL SCREAMING EAGLES

1. DIVISION OPORD 91-1 IS EFFECTIVE FOR EXECUTION UPON RECEIPT OF THIS MESSAGE. G-DAY IS 240600C FEB 91.
2. THE DIVISION'S NEXT RENDEZVOUS WITH DESTINY IS NORTH TO THE EUPHRATES RIVER. GOD SPEED AND GOOD LUCK.
3. AIR ASSAULT. SIGNED MG PEAY

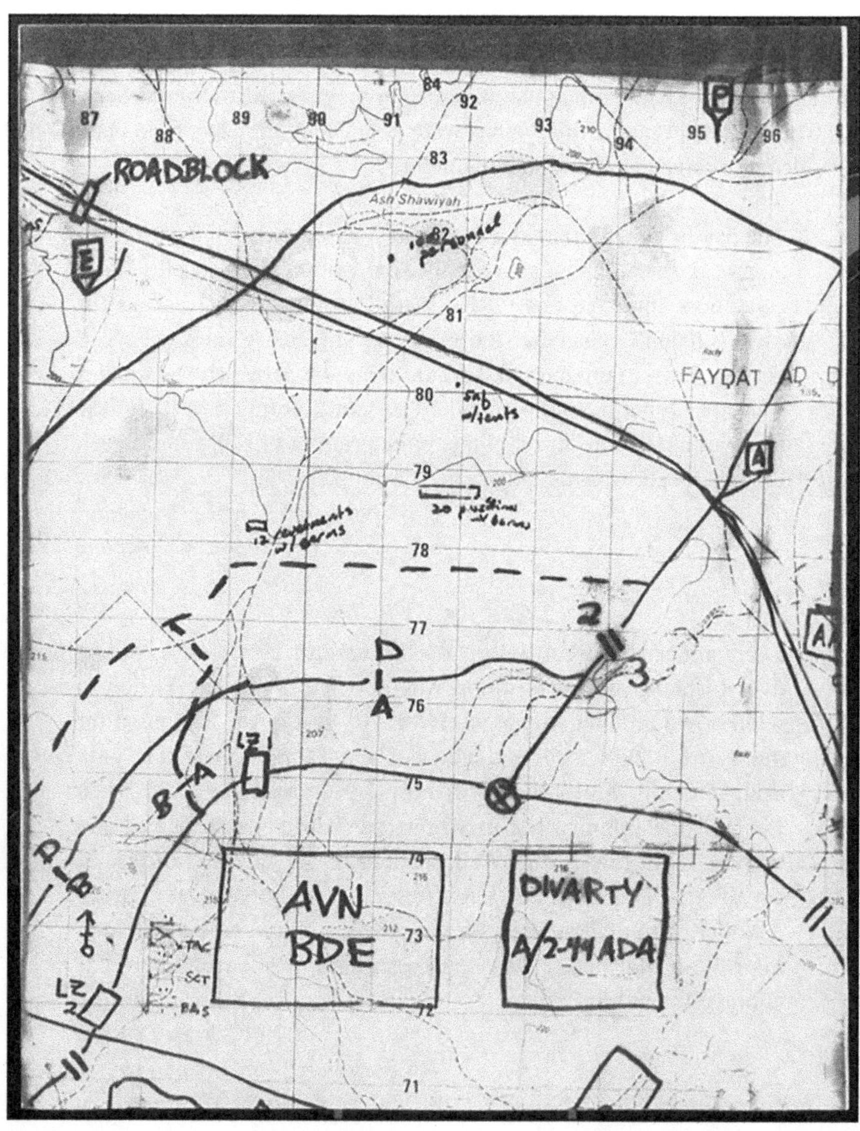

Image of LTC Hancock's Map he carried into Iraq. Grid coordinate 918788 was the center of the "Unoccupied" Iraqi trench line.

CHAPTER 12

G-DAY

Air Assault into FOB COBRA

24 February 1991

After we were awakened at 0330 hours, we loaded our rucksacks and waited for the liftoff. Around 0430 hours we received notice that the PZ time had been moved back one hour because of bad weather. This was not a good omen, because we would now be landing in daylight. The flight time was fifty-five minutes, and we had planned on landing at 0625 hours, which was just before daylight.

> On the night before our assault, we sat by our helicopters and mentally prepared ourselves for the morning liftoff. 2LT Tom Evans, the Battalion Chemical Officer, and I smoked and talked to while away the time while we waited for our scheduled lift-off time (0525 hours). The 6th French Division was scheduled to kick off their attack around 0400 hours, so the arrayed artillery support started a prep around 0100 hours—it added a surreal element to our evening. Around 0330 we finished loading the helicopters with our rucksacks and waited for the liftoff. Unfortunately, an hour later we received notice that the Pickup Zone (PZ) time had been moved back one hour because of a bad sandstorm that made flying close to impossible. This increased our apprehension because we would now be flying and landing in daylight.
>
> *CPT Jose Delgado*
> *Battalion S2*

> Finally, the time had come. We were approaching the ground war. Leadership had strategized how we were going to do it. We practiced maneuvers a few times. We were ready. We were tasked with being on the first air lift. We loaded up ready to go—but then we didn't go. This happened a few times. Finally, we were heading out. We loaded up on the birds. We were all frightened about the uncertainty but

there was this camaraderie and brotherhood that made us all feel like badass motherfuckers. As far as we were told it should be a smooth insertion, however rumor had it to be prepared for something. I know we mixed up and dispersed our platoon talent over different choppers as a precaution.

PFC Stan Banach
Mortar Platoon

While in TAA Campbell, we fine-tuned the plan for the Air Assault to secure FOB Cobra. My vehicles would be internally loaded on CH-47 helicopters, two per aircraft. Because of limited CH-47 aircraft, I was not able to take my HMMWV, D-6, or my driver, Jon Nordin—meaning I didn't have the two good radios in D-6, which always worked because Nordin maintained them well. Only 4 platoons of gun trucks, sixteen TOWs, were in the AA to Cobra, and those gun trucks had one vehicle radio, smaller and less powerful than those installed in D-6. I did the Air Assault with one of the gun vehicles from a platoon.

CPT Al Gill
D Company Commander

The G-Day plan was for 1-101 Aviation to escort in three UH60s with the Pathfinders and beacons for the ensuing air assaults. CPT Doug Gabram, my B Company commander, took off at 0238hrs on G-Day with three Apaches and three UH60s, heading north along the air route into FOB Cobra. I also had two Kiowa's from CPT Tim Gowen's "Stingrays" doing a screen along the ridgeline just south of the Iraqi border. I was following in an Apache with CW2 Greg Gilman.

As soon as CPT Gabram's flight got to the ridgeline, they ran into thick fog and had to slow their flight to 30–40 knots, but they pressed on. About that time, around 0300, I got a radio call from CPT Gowen, saying he had punched into the fog bank and had to climb high and fly south to get out of it. He also said he had lost his wingman. Gabram saw flashes that looked like a crash and circled back. He confirmed the site, passed the coordinates to me, and I told him to press on and I would get to the crash site.

I had CW2 Gilman land close to the burning Kiowa and as we landed, I saw two figures through my NVGs. I quickly exited my Apache with my first aid kit and linked up with the crew, LT Gary Stephens and LT Mike Klee. Remarkably, they only had minor injuries and I told them this was the best crash site I have been to because both of my crew members were alive.

About that time, I heard vehicles approaching from the south, which ended up being FSOs from the 502d Infantry. I asked the NCO if he could get my crew back to TAA Campbell, and he said no problem, so I jumped back into my Apache and Gilman and I continued to fly north, only to hit more heavy fog. I knew that our air assault into Cobra was based on our helicopters maintaining roughly 100 knots in order to have enough fuel to drop off the initial loads and get back to TAA Campbell for their next lifts until we were able to establish the FARPs at Cobra. CPT Gabram reported he had inserted the first beacon but going was slow. I told him to return to TAA Campbell and refuel.

I started flying south and radioed COL Hill, the 1st BDE CDR, gave him the weather sitrep, and recommended at least an hour's delay. MG Peay was monitoring the net and pushed H-Hour from 0600 to 0700. He asked where I was, and I said headed back to TAA Campbell to refuel. He said OK, but that he needed me to get back up and keep him posted on the fog. While refueling, I "reshuffled" 1-101st Apache rotations and told my A Company commander, CPT Newman Shufflebarger, that he was now going to cover 1st Brigade's delayed air assault and CPT Gabram's B Company would rotate in behind him.

I went back around 0500 and flew north. The fog was still thick but had started to rise off the ridgeline. At 0630, I radioed back to DMAIN that the fog was lifting. MG Peay then reset the H-Hour to 0800 for 1st Brigade. I quickly flew back to TAA Campbell, refueled, and met with my four company commanders and reissued the new Air Assault Security mission to them.

LTC Dick Cody
Commander, 1-101 Aviation

On the morning of 24 February 1991, I was in the battalion's TAC/C2 assault helicopter with LTC Hancock and CSM Riley, along with the Battalion S2 (Delgado), Assistant S3 (Knickrehm), Fire Support Officer (Hawkins), and Air Liaison Officer (Reister). I recall there were approximately eleven to fourteen personnel loaded in the aircraft, with boxes of water at the bottom layer, plywood for overhead protection at the second layer, rucksacks at the third layer and personnel were at the top layer. The aircraft was fully packed with stuff, including TAC communications equipment, such as PRC-77 radios and batteries for several days of operations, an OE-254 broadband, omni-directional ground-based antenna, and a multiplexer communications device that allowed us to switch to different nets.

Somehow, all the personnel were packed/squeezed into the aircraft. The aircraft barely lifted off from the ground and flew into Iraq.

CPT Sung Lee
Battalion Communications Officer

Iraqi Position at Trench Line

0500 Hours
24 February 1991 – G-Day

Major Khadir was fairly certain that his battalion was still undetected. So far, no airstrikes or reconnaissance flights had been noticed near his positions. Outside his trench line, the wind was blustering, and visibility was poor. There had been reports of artillery fire many miles to his south during the night. That might be the beginning of the French advance. If so, his defensive position would, in all likelihood, be attacked in the next few days. Thinking of his extensive defense and the amount of munitions he had, he hoped that his battalion could stop or at least slow down the French advance. His superiors would not understand a quick surrender.

At around 0600 hours we received word that the liftoff would be delayed further until 0725 hours because the weather was still too bad. At 0700 hours we received the final word that the mission was a go. We loaded the helicopters and waited for the liftoff. Before lifting off the crew chief wanted to know if I wanted the Black Hawk doors open or closed on our lift. Because we were jammed in the helicopter like sardines with no restraints, I said I wanted all our doors closed so that no one would fall out en-route. There was zero chance we would be firing our weapons from a flying helicopter at anyone on the ground, so we shut the doors on all of the Black Hawks carrying 1-327 soldiers.

> I spoke with our Black Hawk platoon leader, and he told me that our flight time from PZ 1 to LZ 1 would be approximately fifty minutes. We talked and got to know each other a bit better. He was the platoon leader and also the pilot of Black Hawk 3, so I would be flying into Iraq in his Black Hawk. We had done the pre-air assault crew briefings to ABU at last light the previous evening, so now it was just waiting. It would not be quick to load ABU into the helicopters since our load

plan was so tight. We started loading about forty-five minutes prior to take-off. After making sure the rest of the sixty ABU soldiers were loaded up, I crawled into Black Hawk 3 and the crew started the birds up. I remember laying on my back on top of rucksacks with my face about 6 inches from the ceiling and thinking that this sure isn't how I thought we would ride helicopters into battle. We all crossed our fingers and hoped for the best.

CPT Ken Russell
A Company Commander

As the men woke, they automatically started completing their priorities of work—weapons maintenance, checking equipment, personal hygiene, etc. The reality of the situation had set in, and the training and discipline instilled into them over the past months and years were now paying dividends. I was extremely pleased to see the soldiers working so professionally.

When the crew chief directed, we carefully loaded the vehicle and equipment onto the Chinook. The driver was trapped in the vehicle due to its tight fit inside the Chinook and the need to quickly unload the vehicle from the helicopter when we landed in Iraq.

With the vehicle loaded and the Chinook's engines turning, we waited outside the helicopter for word to get ready to launch. The crew again played loud heavy metal music. This time they played "Hells Bells" by AC/DC, and a surreal image came to life. The rising sun was just beginning to illuminate the desert sky and the sounds of bells tolling and the guitar riff playing at the beginning of the song rose above the noise of the helicopter's two massive propellers spinning. I felt like I had been transported into a scene from a war movie…but this was real! To this day, whenever I hear the opening of that song, my mind automatically brings me back to the desert and I have the vision of the last few moments before we loaded onto the Chinook to air assault into Iraq!

CPT John Santini
Battalion Assistant S1

At 0725 hours the Black Hawks started to hover and then we were off. Looking out on the ground we could see the troops that were coming on the second lift yelling at us and giving us the thumbs up. We could also see out the window the fifty-some-odd helicopters that were carrying the other three battalions backed up behind us. All in all, it was a very impressive and moving moment. You could almost imagine the emotions of what the Second World War 101st paratroopers felt like who took off from England and jumped into Normandy on D-Day in 1944.

> We got up on G-Day well before sunrise and got ourselves ready. We were supposed to launch shortly after 0500 and hit the LZ at 0600. However, the weather that morning was appalling, lots of fog and mist. The launch time slid an hour. Then, when the fog still didn't clear, it slid another hour. None of us were happy about going in daylight, and there was a lot of bitching, but we figured we'd be OK if we came in low, behind that ridge. Finally, the fog lifted, and the mist cleared. We got off the ground at about 0720, which would put us on the LZ at about 0800—two hours late. Sure. Whatever.
>
> *1LT Gerry Tertychny*
> *A Company XO*

> As our Blackhawk platoon struggled to lift off from PZ 1, I heard our co-pilot say to our Blackhawk platoon leader that the Blackhawk was red-lining. The platoon leader/pilot replied that he thought that was great information but that it just didn't matter, we were going in anyway. You could feel the helicopter struggle but eventually once the Blackhawk was able to dig into the air a bit it took off just fine.
>
> *CPT Ken Russell*
> *A Company Commander*

> At close to 0725 we started our fifty-five-minute flight to FOB Cobra; as our lift took off, we could clearly see the over fifty helicopters that were carrying the three battalions in our task force backed up behind us. It was an impressive and terrifying moment that I will never forget. As we closed the doors of the Blackhawk helicopters and we flew off, the troops from the second lift cheered us on and gave us the thumbs up as encouragement. We flew in formation—nap of the earth—at about 20 meters off the ground. Although it was daytime and we were clearly visible, the pilots wanted to evade radar and any potential handheld Surface to Air Missiles (SAMs) along the insertion route.
>
> *CPT Jose Delgado*
> *Battalion S2*

> At about 0730, the first lifts of UH 60s and CH47s took off with soldiers of 1-327th Infantry headed towards Cobra. Once the

> flights neared their LZs, my Apaches sighted Iraqi troops dug in an escarpment just north of LTC Frank Hancock's troops' LZ. Our Apaches started covering the escarpment with fire along with LTC Mark Curran's AH1 Cobras. Soon, we had flights of CH47s carrying refuel blivets into Cobra. A little later, I was in a flight of two Apaches headed towards Cobra along with the rest of CPT Gabram's B Company to guard forward of 1st Brigade's positions.
>
> *LTC Dick Cody*
> *Commander, 1-101 Aviation*

Iraqi Position at Trench Line

0745 Hours

24 February 1991 – G-Day

At the trench line the weather had calmed down after the stormy night. There was clearing visibility with no rain, fog, or heavy winds. However, Major Khadir could now see numerous helicopters approaching from the south of his position. Not French Gazelle helicopters but American Apache attack helicopters. Khadir could not believe that he had been discovered after all these months, but it appeared that the helicopters were coming straight at his position. Major Khadir passed the word and made sure his soldiers and his anti-aircraft weapons, four 14.5 mm ZPU4 machine guns, were on station and prepared to engage. With the ZPU4s maximum range of 8,000 meters, his forces could engage at a decent distance. Khadir knew his ZPUs could penetrate and bring down the American helicopters.

Within five minutes of flight, we were in Iraqi airspace. Our altitude was about 15–20 meters off the ground as the helicopters were trying to evade radar and avoid any hand-held SAMs. The low altitude made the flight very close to a carnival ride. The flight was uneventful, and we reached the landing zone with no incidents. During the flight, I had heard no reports of any problems at the LZ and expected to move quickly into our perimeter.

> We backed the vehicles into the aircraft the evening before the Air Assault into Cobra so we could drive them out more quickly on the LZ. It was a very tight fit, just an inch or two on each side and not much on the top either. Because we needed to get unloaded quickly when we hit the LZ, and because the vehicles were so tight inside the aircraft, drivers stayed inside the vehicles, and had empty 1.5-liter plastic water bottles to piss in during the night. All other crew members, including me, sat on the hoods of the HMMWVs inside the aircraft. That's the way I flew into Iraq, with the ramp

of the CH-47 partially down, sitting on the hood of a HMMWV looking backwards at the desert floor, flying low at maybe 50 or 60-feet altitude.

CPT Al Gill
D Company Commander

We had crammed ourselves, our rucks, and our weapons into the birds. It was uncomfortable but we knew that the flight wouldn't be too long—about fifty minutes. I was sitting between the two door gunner seats, facing backwards, and looking at SGT Rich Purdy, who was in our company mortar section. He and I had known each other for a couple of years, and he was a solid NCO. He just looked at me and said, "Shit, sir—looks like we're really going." It also hit me that it was Sunday and, back in Maryland, my family would be attending the baptism of my nephew, who had been born a few weeks before. Right now, however, it was still the middle of the night in the States, and they had no idea what I was doing.

1LT Gerry Tertychny
A Company XO

During the flight, I remember looking at the men in the helicopter. We all had our "game faces" on. I remember looking at their name tags and connecting those names to the countries of origin—where their ancestors came from. Wondering if, when their ancestors came to America, did they think that someday their grandchildren or great-grandchildren would be fighting alongside a friend or foe from the old world they left behind?

2LT Mike Huebner
3d Platoon Leader, A Company

I was sitting in the left door of the UH-60 to lead my platoon from the front into combat. On my right was my RTO, SPC Kevin Stack, and on my left was SPC Vance Fraley, an M-60 gunner. There was lingering sand and haze as we flew into Iraq. As we looked out the doors of the UH-60, was every single aircraft in the 101st Airborne Division, as far as the eye could see, flying 1st Brigade into combat in one lift to seize FOB Cobra. Passing only 20 feet off the ground, they flew over a few Long Range Surveillance and Pathfinder teams marking the route to Cobra.

2LT Matt Karres
2d Platoon Leader, C Company

A few minutes into the flight, we passed over the "Convoy from Hell." We saw well over 100 vehicles moving slowly. All the vehicles looked like something out of "The Beverly Hillbillies," loaded down with as much equipment and supplies as they could carry.

A few minutes after passing over the convoy, one of the Chinook crew members test-fired the machine gun from the window hatch. All the men looked at each other and nodded approvingly with a slight smile.

CPT John Santini
Battalion Assistant S1

Upon landing, we exited the aircraft and held our equipment down as the Black Hawks left the area. I personally was holding down a plywood sheet. When the Black Hawks had gone, the first sound I heard was gunfire coming from the battalion's northern sector, which was my Alpha Company's area. A portion of the gunfire was from a heavy machine gun(s) that I had never heard before. The machine gun(s) had a slow cyclic rate which contrasted greatly with the rapid fire of the 30mm on the Apache attack helicopter.

Our Black Hawk hit the desert hard, and the doors slid open. ABU literally tumbled out of the Black Hawks and started getting our bearings while frantically off-loading the helicopters. My RTOs were getting the SLGR readings, and I was monitoring the radio nets as I made sure everyone was off the birds. Sand was blowing, men were screaming at each other to hurry up, and we were all trying to do everything at once. Then we heard the Black Hawk rotors change pitch, blowing sand increased, and our Black Hawk platoon was gone, headed back to PZ 1 for the next ABU lift. For better or worse, we were on the ground deep in Iraq. It feels very lonely to be one of just sixty young men almost a hundred miles into enemy territory.

As our Black Hawks descended, two things happened very quickly. First, my RTOs showed me the SLGR readout, which had us on LZ 1 accurately to eight digits. Second, we saw an AH-64 Apache hit by enemy automatic weapon fire. The firing came from a position about a kilometer away from LZ 1. We saw the Apache hit, and we also saw an AH-1 Cobra move into position firing a TOW missile at the Iraqi gun position that hit the Apache. As all this happened, the men of ABU spread out on the LZ and established security, as well as ensuring we had everyone and everything on the LZ and that we were prepared to execute the ground tactical plan. ABU mortars were setting up, A10s were flying overhead, AH-1 Cobra gunships were transitioning with the AH-64 Apache gunships, OH-58 reconnaissance helicopters were flitting around, and reports were starting to come in about the Iraqi positions nearby. I monitored all the radio traffic and tried to make sense of it.

CPT Ken Russell
A Company Commander

The helicopter touched down and we piled out and dragged out our rucks and all the other stuff, faced out, and looked for any threats. No incoming fire—good. After the helicopters took off, I went to see CPT Russell. He was sitting about 30 meters away with his field artillery Fire Support Team (FIST), led by 2LT Kevin Nikodym, and was getting a fix on our position with an early model GPS that we had. He looked at me and said, "T, you ain't gonna believe this—they put us down exactly where we're supposed to be." That WAS amazing, since there were no terrain features out there to navigate from. We made comms with battalion and got ourselves sorted out.

Fortunately, we did not land on a hot LZ, but there was clearly some action north of the ridge, where our attack helicopters were pounding someone or something. One of our AH64 Apache gunships was damaged by Iraqi ground fire and flew away trailing smoke, and an AH1 Cobra came in and fired a TOW missile at the Iraqi position. CPT Russell got the word from LTC Hancock to move out to the north to see what was going on and to put eyes on the enemy position, so he, 3d Platoon under Mike Huebner, and the FIST got ready to go. The Battalion TAC, with MAJ Dempsey, was co-located with them and the battalion Scout Platoon was in the area, as well. A bit south was the TOC, where LTC Hancock was, and the battalion Mortar Platoon. Additionally, there were some D Company HMMWVs with TOW missiles up with our 3d Platoon.

1LT Gerry Tertychny
A Company XO

As the helicopters left and we maintained noise discipline, there was a calming silence in the air as we moved into a perimeter position just as we'd rehearsed. It was a short time after this brief moment of silence when we would hear what sounded like an engagement out to our front. I remember meeting with Captain Russell on the LZ after the helicopters left and we could hear some enemy contact off to our front. Eventually our platoon was ordered to move forward up to a ridge line about ¼ to ½ mile away.

2LT Mike Huebner
3d Platoon Leader, A Company

We were supposed to lift off before dawn but due to weather conditions we were delayed a few hours, when we did take off, I looked around at my fellow platoon buddies—everyone sat in silence, some in muffled prayer, all of us knowing what we were about to do. When our birds landed, I was the first one out to set up a defensive position with my SAW (Squad Automatic Weapon) while the helicopter was being unloaded. Once it took off, we gathered our rucks and began our movement. I remember dropping off the mortar rounds and someone calling in a fire mission.

PFC Jesse Hernandez
3d Platoon, A Company

On the lift into Iraq, it was one hell of ride. I was sitting near the edge of the chopper's doorway. We loaded in the wrong sequence. Our 2nd Squad base gunner, Sokolik, was in the rear. He should have been outside edge, first out. Just as we got close, I went to jump out. I had a full ruck and parts of a mortar gun system. Well, the chopper raised up and I dropped and hit the dirt like a rock. My left leg knee and hip were crushed badly. I was in pain, but I was on the ground. Everyone else was just getting out as well. The chopper behind me did a pendulum maneuver and swung hard. They dumped gear and supplies which, I believe, landed all over one of our guys from 2nd Squad—Clark. Now Sokolik was on my chopper, the 2nd Squad base gunner. He heads out to help dig out his Assistant Gunner from the pile of rubble. Their whole squad was tied up trying to get things back in order.

While all this was going on LTC Cody was taking out the quad guns. I was trying to scurry to the rendezvous point. I looked back and my squad member, Tom Hite, fell to the ground. He had the mortar baseplate, so I ran back to get it and to check on him. I was already overloaded with my ruck, the gun tube, two mortar rounds, plus rifle ammo. I lifted Hite's headgear up and I saw a little blood trickle down. He was limp so I let go of his head thinking he was smoked. I wasn't quite sure what to do. Should I stay and help him, or should I get the gun line? I chose to strip his gear and move out.

I felt like shit because I left him there. I grabbed the baseplate and his weapons, leaving him behind.

I wound up next to SGT Lepien. I will never forget his face. He told me, "You did the right thing, Banach, you did the right thing." That made me feel a lot better. Then suddenly I hear, "that's fucked up Banach!" I thought someone was calling me out from behind for leaving my squad member there. Nope. It was Tom Hite himself who was now alert and standing on his own two feet. For a moment I thought I saw his ghost. Apparently, he tripped and fell and hit his head on a rock or something. It briefly knocked him out with a small cut. What was fucked up was I had his weapons, and he was a distance behind at this point.

PFC Stan Banach
Mortar Platoon

As the Outlaws (2nd Platoon, C Company) neared the LZ, the crew chief gave me the "one minute out" signal and Kevin Stack reached to open the door handle. With so much adrenaline running, Kevin grabbed the door handle and pulled it so hard that the handle broke off in his hand. We looked at each other wondering how they were going to get the door open as they rolled into the landing zone. We both reached the door and fortunately the latch had unhooked so we could get our fingers in the door and slide it open.

As the helicopter landed it was so heavy that we rolled 20–30 feet in the soft sand of a dried-up lakebed that they were templated to land in, leaving tire marks deep in the sand. The Outlaws' SOP for unloading such a packed aircraft was for the M-60s and half of the rest of the lift to push out and pull security while the remaining Outlaws unloaded the rucks, ammo, water, and barrier material. The SOP was also for each Outlaw to keep twenty empty sandbags under the top flap of his ruck. I recall a smooth effort unloading the aircraft until someone grabbed the top of a ruck and the empty sandbags came loose. As I looked on I saw twenty empty sandbags get pulled up into the rotor wash and I wondered if it would possibly cause a catastrophic mishap while we were sitting on a landing zone in enemy territory. Fortunately, the only harm done was a scare.

When the Outlaws landed and the aircraft took off, the noise of the rotor blades and engines spinning was replaced with the clear noise of gunfire and bombs being dropped nearby. I quickly took a knee to pull out my map and compass to confirm our location. I could confirm with map and compass exactly where we were, sitting in the dry lakebed with a single-track dirt trail running through it, and then one single length of higher terrain in front of the Outlaws represented by a contour line on the map. I knew exactly where we were and what specific direction and distance the Outlaws needed to go to accomplish our mission.

2LT Matt Karres
2d Platoon Leader, C Company

We touched down at 0840hrs, the ramp lowered, and we ran out the back of the Chinook, onto the desert sand about 20 feet from the helicopter, dropped our rucks and hit the ground. When I hit the ground, I instinctively turned the selector switch on my rifle from "Safe" to "Semi" and scanned all around for signs of enemy soldiers. When I turned the selector switch to "Semi," time seemed to stand still for a moment as I realized that of the hundreds of times that I did that simple act in training, this is the first time that I've done it and meant "business." I thought about that for a quick second and acknowledged to myself that I was okay with it…on with the mission.

Realizing that there was no enemy present, we ran back onto the Chinook to begin unloading. It was truly "assholes and elbows" as we quickly unloaded the Stinger crates, ammo boxes, water cans, and other gear to make way for the vehicle to drive down the ramp. Amazingly, and much to my surprise, we completely unloaded the Chinook in about two and a half minutes…much faster than I ever thought possible.

CPT John Santini
Battalion Assistant S1

The Apaches firing on the trench line were from LTC Dick Cody's 1-101 Aviation. This sound was obviously not what I had expected when we landed nor was the sight of the machine gun duel between the Apaches and the Iraq's gun(s) on the trench line. Additionally, the trench line was on this huge plateau that surprised me.

As we neared the FARP LZs, I noticed three CH47s on the right and continuing to fly north towards the escarpment where there were still some Iraqi positions with ZPU4 anti-aircraft guns. I chased after them, called them on the air battle net, and told them to immediately fly south. I guess they heard the urgency in my voice and quickly banked hard and headed south.

As I rolled out my aircraft, I came under fire from the escarpment. Gilman banked hard and low, and we headed south. My Apache wingmen (never leave your wingman), CW3 Dave Jones and CW2 Tip "Gadgetman" O'Neal saw the tracers and immediately fired two Hellfires into the escarpment, taking out the remaining ZPU4s. Jones' radio call to me was something like, "You're taking fire, don't worry we have you covered!" Later, when we got to the FARP to refuel and rearm, I went over to Jones' and Oneal's Apache, and they played back their Hellfire engagement. I said, "I owe you boys big time."

LTC Dick Cody
Commander, 1-101 Aviation

Our prayers were answered, and our insertion was uneventful. When we reached our objective, we unloaded the aircraft and held our equipment down as the Black Hawks left the area. As soon as the aircraft had lifted off, gunfire erupted from the battalion's northern sector. Alpha Company was under fire from what sounded like a heavy machine gun. Within seconds, Apache attack helicopters returned fire and all hell broke loose.

CPT Jose Delgado
Battalion S2

When we got close to the LZ, there was a lot of comms going on between the pilots and crew chiefs—I did not have a headset and could not monitor what was being said. I found out later that the pilots were getting real time reports from the ground from the first units from 1-327 on their LZ's and that there was enemy in the bunker/trench complex as LTC Hancock and our S-2 had predicted. Because they were engaging those enemy positions with all kinds of munitions, the CH-47s decided to put us down about 8 KM/5 miles away from our planned LZ.

That's not far, but when you're in a desert with very few terrain features, it makes things harder. When we hit the ground and one of the pilots told me we weren't at the planned LZ—that there was firing in the vicinity of the planned LZ that would put the CH-47s at risk. I just looked at him and said "well, where the hell are we?" This conversation happened over the rotor wash of the CH-47s as the vehicles were being unstrapped and driven off the aircraft. He just pointed at a place on the map I was holding and said, "I think we're about right here."

CPT Al Gill
D Company Commander

My CH-47 Chinook pilot informed me that we needed to cut sling-load because one of the chains broke. We had the commander's HMMWV dangling sideways. I told him to cut sling-load to avoid any issues with the crew and all aboard.

I landed in FOB Cobra via Chinook, with PFC Dittfield, the Medical Officer, and the Air Force Liaison, and my mission was to deliver the CDRs HMMWV to the TOC location. Our Air Force Liaison was just a young Airmen First Class. He was so young, scared shitless, that I had to snap him out of it. I told him he was in good hands, and nothing is going to happen to him on my watch.

PFC Dittfield said to me when we landed, "Which way are we going, Sergeant?" I said, "Let's follow the bombs and bullets and head in that direction, wherever the enemy is shooting, friendlies are there." We had to find the HMMWV first, I informed the team. Twenty to thirty minutes later, we found the hummer about 2–3 kilometers away or so. We stayed low the whole time to avoid any bullets coming our way.

SGT Jesus Gonzalez
Battalion S2 NCO

I remember flying with SGT Gonzales and being told that we had a problem, we had a broken chain, and the HMMWV was hanging by three chains. The decision was made that they would have to cut the load early to avoid all of us crashing. Doing so meant that we were going to have to find the vehicles and then hope we could drive them. Through the sounds of bombs and bullets, we went a few kilometers from where we were supposed to be, and we soon found the HMMWVs. Upon inspection, I quickly realized I had a problem. My HMMWV's front tire was on top of the other HMMWV's hood. Only having a few seconds to try and figure out a solution, there was only one—drive it off and hope I didn't cause too much damage that I would be required to have to answer for later.

With minimal damage from a bent bumper and a cracked hood, we were off to find LTC Hancock. I remember thinking to this point, nothing had gone right for me. I was hoping it wasn't an omen of how the rest of the war would play out. We finally made it to the TOC about thirty minutes later.

Originally, LTC Hancock told me I wasn't going because he promised my mom that I would come home alive. As a PFC, I knew better than to put my foot in my mouth, but I did it anyway and I told him, "Too fucking bad I was going."

Later, I joked with LTC Hancock, and I told him he wasn't going anywhere without me because he had a malfunctioning one shot .45 pistol and he may have needed me. In conclusion, it was a scary but rewarding experience, especially for a teenager to have so much responsibility as I had been given.

PFC Bruce Dittfield
Battalion Commander's Driver

At this moment, I had three very brief thoughts in quick succession: 1. The machine gun I am hearing is not an Apache but a large caliber Iraqi gun. 2. The Army might replace its 1980s' motto of "No More Task Force Smiths" with "No More Task Force Hancocks." 3. If I got out of this mess, I was going to punch in the mouth every S2 (Intel) officer from Brigade to Corps who said the trench line was "unoccupied." As I was picking up my gear, one of the young soldiers who came in with us asked me, "LTC Hancock—what are we going to do?" I thought for a second to myself, "That is a damn good question," and then gave my first order in Iraq: "Go up there about 20 meters, lie down, and face north."

Iraqi Position at Trench Line

0805 Hours
24 February 1991 – G-Day

The gunfire exchange between Major Khadir's ZPUs and the American attack helicopters was not going well for the Iraqi soldiers at the trench line. Two of the four ZPUs had already been taken out, one had been destroyed by a missile and the other had been split in two by a helicopter's 30mm machine gun. Some of Khadir's troops exited their bunkers to fire their individual weapons, but this was very difficult to do. In this action, one of the helicopters was hit and had smoke coming out of it as it left the battlefield. To make matters worse, troop-carrying helicopters were now landing south of his position. Unfortunately for Major Khadir, his troops were positioned on the north side of a hill. This was optimum for defending against a French armored column coming along the road to his north, but not for this helicopter attack from the south. To engage the landing troops, 3 kilometers away, his men would have to leave their bunkers and go over the lip of the hill in order to fire south, impossible to do with the attack helicopters shooting at the trench line and at anyone who showed himself.

CHAPTER 13

FOB COBRA

0805 Hours
24 February 1991

After securing our gear, my TAC CP moved about 300 meters from the landing zone and set up our radios. I had come in with CPT Bill Simril's Bravo Company, so I was about 6 kilometers from the trench line. My first call was to my S3, MAJ Dempsey, who was with A Company in the north. He said that he saw the Apache helicopters, which had preceded us into the area, firing at something on the trench

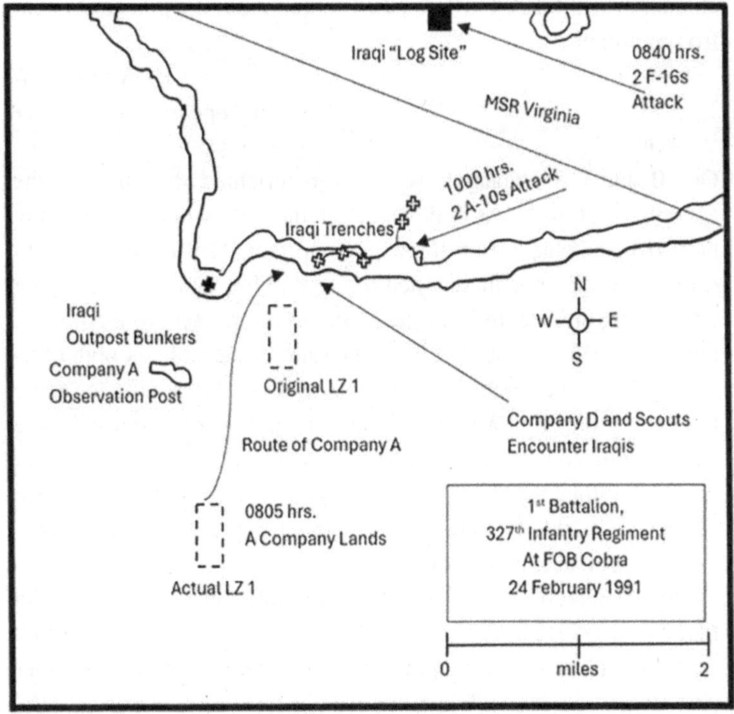

Schematic of the Trench Line Fight.

line that we had been told was unoccupied. He said he couldn't see exactly what they were firing at, but said he and the A Company Commander, CPT Ken Russell, would move closer to the trench line to get a better look.

> As the situation stabilized, my perception was that we landed near a fairly large Iraqi force equipped with air defense guns—we hadn't seen any missiles or rockets at this point, just automatic weapons fire at the Apache. Aviation was sporadically reporting on enemy activity on the high ground where the automatic weapons fire came from, and LTC Hancock was directing A10s to a position just on the other side of the high ground, where trucks had been spotted. ABU wasn't receiving fire, direct or indirect, so we just continued to expand our security perimeter as I tried to make sense of the radio traffic and intelligence reporting. I was monitoring a pilot named Blue Max on the fires net. He was calling in artillery on the enemy positions on the high ground, but the spotting rounds were going all over the place. I ordered 3d Platoon to move with me to a position where we could better observe the enemy positions, and I ordered 2d Platoon to start moving into their planned defensive position. I needed to react to the contact near the LZ, but I couldn't forget about the potential threat from our flank.
>
> *CPT Ken Russell*
> *A Company Commander*

Our B and C Companies, which were oriented west to face the enemy threat from As Salman, held the line while A Company moved against the enemy force to the north. CPT Russell told me to stay on the LZ to be there when the second lift, which was carrying 2d Platoon, arrived, to brief them, and to orient them to the fight—that way, he and I wouldn't be in the same place and risk both of us getting hit at the same time. He also told me, "Be ready for some Enemy Prisoners of War (EPW) and, if I get hit, Huebner will take charge until you can get up and take over the company." It might seem a bit dramatic now but, at the time, it made perfect sense. He also said, "If 2d Platoon needs to be committed against a threat from the west, you take charge of that."

As 3d Platoon moved out, I heard SSG Charles Miller, a 3d Platoon squad leader, say over the radio, "OK—let's go kick some ass." For some reason, that struck me as extremely funny—Miller was always saying stuff like that. CPT Russell, the Company HQ, and 3d Platoon moved off to the north and we kept up with what was going on over the radio. It was high adventure up there. As they made their way up to the ridge, the second lift came in with 2d Platoon and the rest of the Company HQ. I told 2LT Kipp and SFC Juhnke what was happening, and then sent them out to their defensive position to the northwest, after first contacting CPT Russell to let him know that they were on their way.

1LT Gerry Tertychny
A Company XO

I got the gun to the front and had it set up. I can't remember what happened after that, but bullets were whizzing by and CSM Riley was yelling at us to keep our asses down. Someone yelled out, "What about you, CSM Riley?" Riley was practically standing straight up. CSM Riley replied (if I remember correctly), "I am so mean these bullets are scared of me." That was fucking awesome.

PFC Stan Banach
Mortar Platoon

I had the honor of flying on the first Blackhawk along with LTC Hancock and CPT Delgado. We did not encounter any chemical threat and for the next four or so days my role changed from Chemical Officer to bodyguard. I went where the battalion commander went and was poised to act if he came under threat. I learned more about combat operations in those four days than at any point before or after in my career.

2LT Tom Evans
Battalion NBC Officer

We found the TOC after maybe driving fifteen to twenty minutes. I got there and saw the S2 and S3 personnel. Moments later, though it felt like forever, we were having communications problems with A Company, and we needed to establish a relay point. They asked for a volunteer and the chopper was ready to lift…I volunteered…I was a radio operator on the O/I net…I said, "Sir, I'll go." I was gathering my ruck, he said that we had no time, get on the chopper.

I flew in the chopper and landed a few kilometers from A Company, set up my radio and antenna, and proceeded to do a commo check with HQs (MAJ Dempsey and CPT Delgado).

I tried the best I could to hide behind some rocks, though there was not much cover and concealment in the desert, so if the enemy decided to leave the compound, I was dead meat. I was there in

> my location for hours. I don't remember how long but it felt like a lifetime.
>
> I could hear the shooting, loud bombings, commotion, and the chaos of war. I thought the HQs forgot about me. I was trying to keep as quiet as possible; I knew the communications was working because I could hear the A Company commander and The Warlord on the radio.
>
> *SGT Jesus Gonzalez*
> *Battalion S2 NCO*

I called my two other company commanders, CPT Bill Simril and CPT Darcy Brewer, and they both said they had no enemy in their area and that all their personnel had landed with no problems. Finally, I called the Brigade S3, MAJ Clawson, who had flown in and told him that we had landed but had contact in the northern sector. He told me in return that the Apaches that were covering that trench line had reported one helicopter had been hit and had to land.

> I was monitoring the Aviation Combat Network at the start of the ground war. The Apache engaging the Iraq plateau, the pilot said, "I'm hit with small arms fire and broke a hydraulic line. I'm pulling back."
>
> *PFC Steve McFarland*
> *Battalion S3's Driver*

At this time, when I received this report that the Apache got shot down, I pretty much knew that everything that the Brigade/Division/Corps Intelligence folks had assumed/deduced about that trench line was wrong. In the CPXs and computer-run exercises that I had participated in over the past five years, Apache helicopters never got shot down because of their lethality and their survivability. The fact that the first situation report I received was that one was shot down did not shake me but came close to it. I now assumed there were at least fifty enemy soldiers in that trench line. I later found out I was being entirely too optimistic. I called the B and C Company commanders back and told them to move their troops out to their designated areas, which were about one kilometer from their LZs, and set up their perimeter.

> As the Outlaws moved to their positions out of the haze came an AH-64 flying left to right and clearly noticed movement off to its right in the direction of the Outlaws. The helicopter turned toward the Outlaws and started flying towards us in a nose-down approach as if interrogating friendly or enemy. The Outlaws made sure the AH-64

could identify us as friendlies and then the aircraft dipped left and right to give its greetings and then moved on towards the gunfight. Situational awareness on the battlefield for both units moving in the haze of battle avoided any blue-on-blue incidents in Cobra that morning.

Once the Outlaws got to their objective, the squad leaders went to work setting their men in until the rest of the platoon arrived on the second lift. The skies cleared and the sun got high in the sky, and I then moved to my right flank as planned to linkup with Joe Gammon from Bravo Company. As planned prior to the combat operation, we met on the battlefield to effect linkup of the two rifle companies. We exchanged pleasantries and the usual gallows humor, talked a bit about how the day had gone for each, and then ensured the respective squad leaders were connected. This went as well as it could have based on good planning, keeping it simple, and both units being tactically proficient.

2LT Matt Karres
2d Platoon Leader, C Company

As all this was swirling around, my Air Force Liaison Officer (ALO), Captain Bill Reister, was trying to get us air support. He was running into some bureaucracy from the Division ALO who wanted to make sure I could visually see the Iraqis. Since the Iraqis were on the reverse side of a big hill I could only see and hear their anti-aircraft guns. Captain Reister asked me in a slow and methodical voice, "Can you see the enemy?" I looked and him and said, "Yes." He then relayed my answer to the Division ALO and the bureaucratic roadblock was lifted.

Around 0830 hours, Captain Reister said that he had contacted two F16s and that they were inbound to our location. He said, "Boss, we got bombs." I called the air battle captain (a CPT Jones in an OH58 Scout Helicopter) and told him that I wanted to hit the logistic site that was across the highway and for him to clear the area. The logistic site was about 6 kilometers from my A Company and was easily identifiable from the air because it was near the highway and had the only trees in the area around it. I knew our aircraft had big bombs and did not want to have a fratricide incident, so I picked the logistic site.

CPT Jones had the Cobras (1-101 Aviation had left the area and LTC Mark Curran's 3-101 Cobra attack helicopters were now providing cover) move out of the area and my ALO then brought the F16s in. When the F16s arrived, they identified the target and then each dropped two 2,000-pound bombs. The air battle captain monitored the strike and said both bombs hit inside the logistic site. A side note—the OH58 was too close to the bomb blasts (which looked like mini-atomic bombs) and got caught up in them. The OH58 made it out of the blast cloud but, in my opinion, barely.

Iraqi Position at Trench Line

0840 Hours.

24 February 1991 – G-Day

Stay in the bunkers! Major Khadir was uncertain how long the attack helicopters could loiter over the trench line. No one was manning the remaining ZPU or shooting back. Everyone was hunkering down inside the bunkers. The first wave of attack helicopters had gone and had been replaced by a smaller type of helicopter. Khadir believed these helicopters were what the Americans called Cobras. How appropriate. BOOM...BOOM! Four kilometers north of the trench line, two F16s, each loaded with two 2,000-pound bombs, attacked his logistic site. The size of the bombs and the shock waves were horrific. Mercifully, he thought, the bombs did not hit the trench line.

After the helicopter strike, CPT Jones flew to my CP and landed, and we talked over how we were going to continue to attack the enemy. I told him I was proud of him, and put my arm around him, but told him he was going to have to go back up and call in more fire. I also told him to give himself more distance between his helicopter and any more helicopter or CAS strikes, something I'm sure, in retrospect, I didn't need to say. He reported that the trench line was occupied and stretched for about 3 kilometers. He said there were also two vehicles and some personnel in the logistic site. I told him that an artillery battery had landed by Chinook and was moving up to support us, as Brigade Headquarters had diverted them to my sector. After discussing our options, I told him that we would alternate using his gunships and artillery to hit the trench line and the logistic site. I told him that I wanted him to call the artillery strikes back to me and that my FSO, CPT Hawkins, would relay the data to the battery as, at this time, CPT Russell still could not see the enemy in the trench line and was unable to call in the artillery.

When we were finished, I patted CPT Jones on the back, told him he was doing a great job, and told him not to get shot down. Around 0900 hours, the 105mm artillery battery, C/2-320 Field Artillery, had moved into position and CPT Jones started the calls for fire. He passed the calls to me over the battalion command net, and I gave the info to CPT Hawkins, who was standing next to me. CPT Hawkins then called the information to the firing battery. Although this was awkward, it was the best way at the time to get the calls for fire executed. After we had fired one mission on the logistic site and one mission on the trench line, CPT Jones brought back his Cobras and started to rake the trench line again.

At around 0830 hours, my second lift of troops and vehicles started to come in. The Chinook lift, for reasons I did not understand at the time, landed my TOW vehicles 8 kilometers from their LZ. The LZ was planned 500 meters from my position. When CPT Gill, the D Company commander, said he had landed I knew something was wrong. You could see seemingly forever, but I couldn't see where the Chinooks had put down. CPT Gill got his navigational aide out and could not initially get the three satellites he needed to navigate. I told him just to stay put and wait till he got his SLGR, the navigational aide, up and running and then come to our location. Eventually, he got his SLGR working, found his position, and then headed to our location.

> I had a slugger. I kept trying to get a grid coordinate but couldn't get a signal. When I tried to get the BN CDR on the radio, I initially couldn't talk to anyone. I finally got through to the BN Commander, and told him we were on the ground, but not on the planned LZ. I was frustrated, understood there was a fight going on and that the battalion might need the TOWs, and the helicopters were leaving just as quickly as they could get the hell out of there. Finally, I used the old compass and pencil, hoping that pilot was right about where they put us down—I shot an azimuth in the direction I thought we needed to go to link up with LTC Hancock and the rest of the battalion. We also had these fabricated two-wheel carts, loaded with crates of extra ammunition, that we had to tie to the back of the HMMWVs before we could start moving. LTC Hancock loved those things, and they worked, but they were a pain in the ass on the LZ and limited the speed we could drive once we got them attached. All of this had been rehearsed, but that didn't make it go faster!
>
> Finally, we got our shit together and started driving, with me in the lead and an NCO still trying to get coordinates, holding the slugger out the window. Every time we crested a small rise, of what looked like a lunar landscape, and I didn't see the rest of the battalion in front of us, my heart sank. But soon, we could hear explosions in the far distance, in the direction we were headed, so I figured we were headed in the right direction.
>
> Maybe forty minutes after we hit the LZ, we crested a small hill and could see the makeshift BN TAC in the distance. I was greatly relieved.
>
> *CPT Al Gill*
> *D Company Commander*

I retrieved my rucksack, headed to the vehicle, and due to the adrenaline running through my body, easily lifted the incredibly heavy ruck over my head and threw it on top of the load of supplies and equipment in the cargo bed. Like I did with the selector switch, I paused for a split second to realize what had just happened.

As SGT Walker and the other men finished loading the supplies onto the vehicle, I looked around to get my bearings on where CPT Gill and his TOW vehicles had landed. I spotted them nearby and saw the TOW crews instinctively performing their crew drills as they had been trained—assembling the missile launchers, calibrating the TOWs, and completing their functions checks. So far, so good. Next, I scanned to determine where the battalion staff and the infantrymen from the line companies who air assaulted twenty minutes ahead of us on the Blackhawks had landed. Their landing zone should be only a kilometer away, which in the desert would seem like a stone's throw distance. I scanned 360 degrees and didn't see any sign of them…wonderful!

With our vehicle fully loaded, I instructed the driver to head to Delta Company's location. I linked up with CPT Gill and told him that we were "Up!" CPT Gill was holding the Slugger (GPS) to the sky, trying to get satellite reception and determine our grid location. He said that it would take a few minutes before his crews finished establishing radio communications across the company and with battalion, assembled their TOWs, and completed their functions checks. I told him that I intended to go a kilometer in each direction to try to find the infantrymen.

CPT Gill approved my course of action and my driver quickly headed off in the direction we were facing. We drove for about a kilometer, stopped and looked around. Nothing! We turned and headed to another point about a kilometer away from the Delta Company vehicles. Again, nothing! We turned and headed to a third point about a kilometer away from Delta Company.

In the distance I saw a soldier standing in the desert, it was obviously an American soldier, so we drove toward him. After driving about another 500 meters, I got out of the vehicle, ran up to the soldier and the first thing I noticed was the rank of Command Sergeant Major (CSM) on his helmet. I got a lump in my throat and thought to myself, "Great! I'm in a combat situation and am about to live the classic Army scenario of a lost lieutenant asking a senior NCO for directions." Recognizing that the man wasn't CSM Johnnie Riley, the Command Sergeant Major for 1st Battalion, I approached him and asked, "Do you know where 1st Battalion is located?" He responded "Nope! This is 1st Brigade, not 1st Battalion!" With the man identifying himself as part of 1st Brigade, that meant he was CSM Nichols, the Brigade Command Sergeant Major. Knowing there was nothing more he could do for me, I thanked him, got back in the vehicle, and headed off to the fourth point about a kilometer away from Delta Company. Again, nothing. I thought to myself, "What the Hell is going on? We are nowhere near where we are supposed to be!"

We would have to carefully navigate our way the five miles to the rest of the battalion, without knowing what lay between us and them. I told the driver to fall in line toward the rear of the convoy, with CPT Gill's TOW vehicles providing front and rear security. Wanting to be able to react to anything as quickly as possible and knowing that we would be moving very slowly through the desert, I told SGT Walker to get into the front passenger seat, and that I would ride on the hood of the vehicle to keep guard. We slowly and carefully began our convoy, looking like a ragtag band of wanderers in the desert.

After moving for about an hour, we drove up a dune. As we crested the top, we saw the battalion a little way off. We also saw Army attack helicopters and Air Force fast-movers (jets) working over known enemy locations in our battalion sector.

CPT John Santini
Battalion Assistant S1

Iraqi Position at Trench Line
0910 Hours
24 February 1991 – G-Day

Another flight of troop-carrying helicopters had just landed south of the trench line. There was nothing that Khadir's troops could do. As long as the attack helicopters were circling, no one would leave their bunkers. THUMP! THUMP! THUMP! THUMP! THUMP! THUMP! Artillery, and accurate. The day had just gotten much worse. Where did the artillery come from and how did they get this far north? Rounds started to crash into the bunkers' overhead cover.

Right around this time, I believe 0945, I received a radio call from COL Hill, the Brigade Commander, asking for a SITREP. He had been over watching the various lifts come into FOB COBRA and wanted to know what I was doing with the trench line. I explained my actions, and he said that I needed to expedite what was going on and take the trench line. Since he was not in the area, I don't believe COL Hill had seen the trench line or knew, as neither did I, what was in the enemy position. I said, "Roger," and got back to my business. CPT Reister, who was right next to me and had overheard the conversation asked me, "Are we attacking up that hill?" According to him, I replied, "Fuck no." Looking back, there was zero chance I was sending any soldiers up that hill until I had expended every bit of mortar, artillery, helicopter, and fast-mover ammunition first. I was soon to do just that.

> We (the battalion command group) landed at the LZ in daytime (not night). The attack helos were engaged with a battalion of the enemy on a hilltop—the hilltop we would have landed on in the dark. We started walking generally in the direction of the fighting, about 3 kilometers away. The sound of weapons had everyone on the high edge of excitement, and the radio chatter was loud. After a while I asked Sgt. Rock, "Now?" "Not yet" was all he said. I didn't know his reasoning, because the entire area up to the mesa was as flat as a board and no place was different from any other, but I trusted his experience.
>
> After asking two more times, he finally said, "this will do" and so I approached the command staff and said, "Hey, Warlord—would this be a good place to set up operations?" "Great idea, Air Force!"—and so they stopped walking and set up a small table of operations. Sgt Rock and I started digging foxholes, an impossible task as the entire ground was an ancient coral seabed and hard as cement. I worked out that the reason he had let them walk so long was just to let them work off some of the nervous energy—a smart decision. After a bit, they called me over to the command group and asked me, "do you have any air assets." The atmosphere was tense, and everyone was talking loudly, so I said, "No, but I have something better"—and pulled out that silly coffee pot. It became dead silent, and the Warlord finally said, "G..D...mit. You're right, Air Force. Everyone take a deep breath and calm down." So, I asked if the enemy was attacking down from the hilltop. No. Were we going to attack up the hilltop? H... no! OK, so do you want them dead, or do you want them to surrender? So, we talked about how we might use an air strike to convince them to surrender.
>
> At this point, I should mention a bit of dysfunction in my own chain of command. I will not name names, but anyone who was there knows them and knows it is all true. Our Division ALO was, to be blunt, a careerist unprepared for actual war. Shortly after we arrived in theater, he shaved his head and started listening to whale music "to help with the stress." Seven of the other ALOs filed IG (Inspector General) reports against him, prompting an investigation. He had been overheard saying he was going to "kill

as many Iraqis as he could." The officer they sent acting as the IG was a full colonel who was also the theater ALO commander. He was a piece of work, too, and was eventually relieved and sent home—but that's another story.

Capt Bill Reister
Air Liaison Officer/Forward Air Controller

By this time, CPT Russell, his fire support officer, 2LT Nikodym, and MAJ Dempsey had worked their way to a point from where they could oversee the trench line. MAJ Dempsey said they could see the trench line clearly and wanted the Fire Support Officer to start calling in the fire missions. Using their navigational aid and a laser range finder, they brought the artillery fire in more accurately than when CPT Jones and I were calling in the fire.

Upon reaching our forward position, I talked with LTC Hancock and persuaded him that since we had eyes on the area to let us take over the fire mission. We could see the spotting rounds getting further away from the Iraqi positions. Blue Max flew his OH-58 to our location and landed so that we could talk. I went over to him as he sat in his helicopter, and we exchanged information. He made sure I knew the location and he relayed to me that there were a lot of individual soldier positions and a white pickup truck located up on the high ground. He verified that this was the location of the air defense gun that attacked the AH-64 previously. At the time, based on radio traffic and the intelligence provided by Blue Max, this sounded like a reinforced company sized position to me, but the presence of the air defense gun suggested it was larger, possibly a battalion. Blue Max and I finished up our coordination and he took off to get back into action.

My FSO, 2LT Kevin Nikodym, and the 3d platoon Fire Support NCO, SGT Craig, moved forward to a position where we could see and call in artillery. We checked the range to target but from LZ 1 our company 60mm mortars were just outside of their range to engage the enemy positions. As part of the first lift of the 1st Brigade, artillery in the form of a 105mm field artillery battery was brought in. They were limited on artillery ammunition, but it would have to do. We bracketed the high ground, and in three rounds had a round on target. Once we were on target, we called a "fire for effect." Since Blue Max had previous eyes on and he reported dug-in Iraqi positions, we called for high explosive, delayed penetrating fuse (HEDP). This shell-fuse combination was designed to collapse dug-in positions.

In hindsight, if I had known how poorly the Iraqi positions were constructed, I would have called for a mix of HE and HE-VT (high explosive-variable time or an airburst). After three fire for effect missions, we had fired all the ammunition the artillery battery had or would have until the next lift arrived in a little over an hour.

CPT Ken Russell
A Company Commander

Upon getting word we were to move out towards the sound of the gunfire, I have this memory of telling the NCOs about bringing every weapon, grenade, every bullet, bayonet, water, etc., but I also remember stressing bringing every first aid kit. One of our men PFC Jesse Hernandez, Jr., remembers being told to bring ammo, water, his AT-4, and remembers wearing his butt pack.

It was stressed to us as officers, though we were focused on mission accomplishment, that we should let the men know that, should we have casualties, we would do everything possible to get them out alive. We owed them that. This is why I specifically remember stressing the first aid kits—I want to say we dropped our rucks at or near the LZ and took "weapons and water" to prepare for a fight. I remember that alone was pretty heavy…we could never have enough ammunition and water.

As we moved forward from the LZ to the ridgeline, I remember off to my right seeing an Apache helicopter idle on the ground. I learned later it was disabled from an Iraqi anti-aircraft gun.

As we crouched low to the peak of the ridgeline, we tried to lay as low to the ground as possible. I remember our platoon RTO, Jason Hardin, was always by my side. Also with us was SGT Tom Craig—our platoon artillery FO and he had an RTO whose name I can't remember. We couldn't pronounce his name so we all just called him "Eddie" and he was originally from the Philippines.

Off straight ahead about ¼ mile away was a higher, much larger ridgeline. At the base of this ridgeline there were two anti-aircraft guns, about 150–200 yards apart. To my left there was a Cobra attack helicopter that was hovering—moving up, down, forward, backwards—like a skittish wild animal. Then it settled in position and fired a missile right into one of the anti-aircraft guns. Both guns appeared unmanned at the time. But having heard some gunfire exchange we knew they withdrew.

Captain Russell and his RTO SPC Gallup were just to our left. Sometimes I could hear some of his radio transmissions.

We were told by Captain Russell to put some artillery on that ridgeline—so our PLT FO Tom Craig went to work. I remember SGT Craig had a "GLID," a Ground/Vehicular Laser Locator Designator; a handheld instrument the artillerymen used for fire missions. SGT Craig was talking to his artillery unit, and I remember Captain Russell verifying (double checking) the grid coordinates, so we were all on the same sheet of music.

I remember SGT Craig saying, "Lasing!" as he used this GLID device to calculate the direction and distance for the artillery's fire missions. The first rounds flew off to our left and hit the upper left portion of that higher ground ridgeline to our front. Then I remember SGT Craig working with his GLID as there was a pause—like resetting or adjusting? We were just quietly letting him and the artillery do their thing. Then he'd say "Lasing!" and then send coordinates back and then a second round of 105mm rounds flew above—this time hitting more to the right of what would be an Iraqi bunker complex.

I also remember overhearing the artillery only had enough rounds for one more fire mission. So, SGT Craig went back to "Lasing" and the third set of 105mm rounds flew above and then hit the center portion of the enemy bunker complex. It looked like great shooting to us. Keep in mind we weren't sure what was out there. The Iraqis did a great job concealing their position. All we saw was higher ground and two anti-aircraft guns!

Then came the A10. We watched with amazement as it flew above. It did some maneuvers above the enemy bunker complex then we saw it drop some flares. Then it dropped munitions on the target. It somewhat reminded me of the beginning of the movie "Apocalypse Now," but with a little faster motion. It was honestly a "holy shit" moment watching some of the firepower. It may have fired some rounds before or after dropping munitions. Honestly, I can't remember if it did. But I do remember the bombing. After it flew away, that Cobra moved back in. As we faced the target, the Cobra was to our front left.

As per doctrine, I was anticipating what we were going to do next. You start with your indirect fire weapons then move the ground forces in. I couldn't have imagined being on the receiving end just thinking this was coming at you before ground forces. However, I remember seeing an individual reappearing from the target area. He was unarmed waving his arms towards the Cobra attack helicopter. I believe he was waving some white cloth, if I remember correctly.

2LT Mike Huebner
3d Platoon Leader, A Company

As soon as we rolled up to the TAC, I jumped out and found LTC Hancock. He briefed me on what had happened, and what was happening, just a few kilometers away on the ridge where the enemy trench was, maybe 4–5 kilometers from the TAC. If memory serves, when I arrived the Air Force had already dropped ordnance, 105 artillery was coming in, and attack helicopters were engaging—either Apaches or Cobras or both. LTC Hancock instructed me to take my TOW platoons (I believe one platoon stayed at the TAC) and move out in the direction of the enemy positions.

And that's what we did. After a short movement, we linked up with the A Company Commander, Ken Russell, and Major Dempsey, the BN S-3, who gave me more details about what was happening on the enemy position. We were on a small rise, looking at the enemy position through binos. I'd estimate, today, we were maybe a kilometer or 1,500 meters away. The battalion Scout Platoon was also there, near us. We could see helicopters firing on the enemy, and 105 rounds impacting, as well.

CPT Al Gill
D Company Commander

Shortly, the howitzer battery finished setting up and began firing on the bunker system, as directed by the forward observers with the line companies. With the sounds of the howitzers firing, the attack helicopters in the distance, and the radios from the CP blaring, SGT Walker and I looked at each other as if to say, "Wow! This shit is real!"

We continued to dig our fighting position and soon we were sweating. I took off my helmet and put it on the ground to allow me to cool down and move more freely. A few minutes later I heard the battalion commander, Lieutenant Colonel Frank Hancock's voice boom, "SANTINI! Put your helmet on! This is war, goddamn it!" I immediately complied but felt like a child who had been scolded by a parent. I had never heard the battalion commander swear before and wasn't proud that the first time was at me.

As the sound of the battle continued to rage, we heard that the howitzer battery was running low on ammunition. That didn't give us a feeling of confidence.

CPT John Santini
Battalion Assistant S1

Around 1000 hours, CPT Reister had contacted two A10 Warthog ground attack aircraft, who said they had 500-pound bombs and cluster bombs and were coming to our location. I told CPT Reister to tell them that we wanted the 500-pound bombs but not the cluster bombs. Cluster bombs had a reported 10 per cent dud rate, and I did not want to "mine" the plateau with unexploded cluster bomblets. We contacted CPT Jones and told him to guide in the two A10s because we were going to drop the bombs on the trench line near our troops.

> With a Division ALO intent on a body count, I was not going to be allowed to control any airstrikes (giving them a chance to surrender) unless we were willing to be a bit flexible. The rules of engagement stated that the on-scene commander (me) could commandeer control of any flight if we had eyes on the enemy. So, when we had air inbound, I asked the Warlord, "sir, is that the enemy on that hill?" He started to answer, and I interrupted him, "…because, if we have eyes on the enemy, we get to control the air—otherwise our Division ALO is going to kill them all." Taking a second look, he agreed we could "see the enemy" and so I directed a flight of F-16s to drop their four 2,000 lb. Mk 84 bombs about 200 yards north of the enemy position.
>
> When Sgt Rock heard me giving clearance to strike, he came over and stood by me, took off his helmet, and stood arms outstretched facing the strike zone and leaning towards it. I laughed and followed suit—and we watched the shock wave approach us across the sand at the speed of sound. THUMP! At 3km, the impact was about like a beefy bouncer thumping you on the chest with an open palm—enough to know that those closer to the blast were having second thoughts about continuing to fight. That was followed a bit later with another strike by two A10s each dropping six 500 lb. Mk 82 bombs close by.
>
> *Captain Bill Reister*
> *Air Liaison Officer/Forward Air Controller*

> Upon landing in FOB Cobra, LTC Hancock quickly got oriented and immediately started to direct the companies to conduct maneuver to find, fix, and destroy Iraqi forces. He also integrated both artillery fires and air strikes to support the companies' maneuver and to destroy the dug-in Iraqi battalion. He always had his Fire Support Officer and his Air Liaison Officer close to him at the battalion TAC location for any fire support requests. I recall LTC Hancock wanted to pound the Iraqi positions with artillery fires and air strikes until they could no longer take it and eventually surrender. I recall, him requesting the ALO to use bombs on the Iraqi position that had the most devastating effects to force the Iraqi soldiers to surrender.
>
> *CPT Sung Lee*
> *Battalion Communications Officer*

After the A10 strike, and two more fire missions of artillery, MAJ Dempsey called and said that he saw white flags coming from the trench line. This was fortunate, as we had only six more rounds of 105mm left to fire. Additionally, the Cobra helicopters were given a new mission, and there were no more close air support missions in the area.

Iraqi Position at Trench Line

1015 Hours

24 February 1991 – G-Day

THUMP! THUMP! THUMP! THUMP! THUMP! THUMP! For the past hour, the artillery fire had been pounding Khadir's positions. In between the artillery barrages, the attack helicopters would spray the trench line. Many of his soldiers were suffering from concussions. Some could not stand up, and some were bleeding from their ears from the overpressure of the explosions. BOOM...BOOM! BOOM... BOOM! Two American A10 aircraft just dropped twelve 500-pound bombs on the trench line. That's it. Khadir now believed he could not hold out without having his battalion destroyed. Nothing in the war with the Iranians prepared him for this. Khadir passed the word...we are surrendering.

> We watched, and listened, as CPT Russell, 2LT Nikodym, the Battalion TAC, and LTC Hancock orchestrated a bombardment of the enemy position that included artillery, attack helicopters, and, at one point, USAF A10 ground attack aircraft and F16 fighters. Though the enemy position was over a mile away, when the Air Force aircraft rolled in and dropped their bombs it sounded, and felt, like they were right on top of us. Shortly, we heard over the radio that there were white flags all over the enemy position—they were surrendering. These would be the EPWs CPT Russell had told me to prepare for.
>
> *1LT Gerry Tertychny*
> *A Company XO*

Observations

Some plans go right from the beginning, and some go sideways like an unguided missile. This one was a little of both. For 95 per cent of what went on in FOB COBRA, it went off with atomic-clock precision and just as planned. However, what happened at the trench line came off as well as it did because

of the professionalism of the soldiers and airmen who were there. Air Force Captain Bill Reister was a total professional during the entire time. CPT Jones, MAJ Dempsey, CPT Russell, CPT Gill, CPT Hawkins, and the soldiers of C/2-320th Field Artillery were superb. Without the support of the aviation battalions of 1-101 with LTC Dick Cody and 3-101 with LTC Mark Curran, my battalion would have been in very, very serious trouble. Finally, thank you United States Air Force. With a little bit of serendipity, one of the F16 pilots, I later discovered, had been the roommate of my younger brother, Tom, at the Air Force Academy.

CHAPTER 14

SURRENDER

1015 Hours
24 February 1991

At the time of the surrender, my closest unit to the trench line was my scout platoon, under 1LT Brian Bedell, who had moved to within 2 kilometers of the plateau. 1LT Bedell had also reported the emergence of white flags and said on a radio transmission to me, "There are white flags going up…a LOT of white flags." When I heard that transmission, my inclination to punch people in the mouth rose in me again. I just could not imagine the number of enemy troops that I was going to actually find on the plateau.

> I was on the radio with LTC Hancock when he gave me a Warning Order that the 1-327 Infantry would have to prepare to attack the Iraqi positions early the next morning and to start planning for that operation. ABU would be the main effort with a lot of battalion and aviation support. Screaming Eagle aviation continued to keep an eye on the Iraqi positions and then suddenly we heard radio traffic indicating something was happening on the objective. Screaming Eagle gunships had spotted a white flag on the high ground. The gunships were calling for ground forces to go up to the top and see what the situation was while they maintained overwatch. In response to LTC Hancock's orders, I ordered 3d Platoon to go forward. LTC Hancock also sent some of our D Company TOW vehicles that recently arrived from the heavy LZ, accompanied by the Scout Platoon. As CPT Gill, our D company commander, arrived with the various elements from 1-327 Infantry, he accepted the surrender of an Iraqi battalion commander and his battalion.
>
> *CPT Ken Russell*
> *A Company Commander*

Since the scouts were still a good distance away from the trench line, I called CPT Gill, the D Company Commander, and told him to load the scouts on his TOW HMMWVs and ride forward to accept the surrender. After putting as many of the scouts on his HMMWVs as possible, CPT Gill went forward. The Scouts would later refer to themselves as the "reactive armor" for the TOW HMMWVs, as they sat on the hoods of the vehicles and went forward to the trench line.

At the trench line an Iraqi major, the battalion commander, came out and said that he wanted to surrender his command. During this time, there were some shots fired out that were either from the Iraqis or the Cobras that were supporting us. CPT Gill told the Iraqi major that there would be no more firing or there were going to be dire consequences. The Scout Platoon began to organize the prisoners who were coming out of their holes and bunkers, and CPT Gill radioed back that he had an Iraqi battalion commander under his control.

> After twenty or thirty minutes, the sounds of the firing started to diminish, and the rate of fire was not nearly as intense as it had been. We saw what appeared to be white flags being waved from the enemy positions. It appeared they'd had enough and were attempting to surrender.
>
> All of this was relayed to the TAC, and soon, LTC Hancock called and asked me to mount as many of the Scout Platoon soldiers on my vehicles as possible and move forward to accept the surrender—if that's in fact what they were doing. I was only about 50 per cent sure that's what they were doing, and I was also worried that this might be a ruse to get us to expose our men and vehicles. Once we left the hill we were on, there was absolutely no cover or concealment between my vehicles and the enemy. Now, my vehicles were occupied by the Delta company crews, covered in equipment and rucks, and there wasn't a lot of space available, so the Scouts had to hang onto the hood and roofs of my vehicles. If someone was to start firing at us, people were going to die, no doubt about it.
>
> When we got to the base of the ridge that held the enemy position, there were already about twenty to thirty Iraqis there, unarmed, and holding white flags or their hands in the air. We quickly identified the Iraqi Battalion commander and I moved to talk to him. I can't remember who translated, but we began communicating and I had a list of questions to ask the man. At some point, he said he spoke English, and we began talking in English. He immediately said he had wounded soldiers and asked me to evacuate them and get them first aid. I told him I'd do that as soon as the situation allowed, but

I needed information—was there any Iraqi Armor in the area, were we within range of any Iraqi artillery? He said no. I'd ask a couple more questions and he'd again remind me of his wounded men needing evacuation.

Within that first five to ten minutes, we heard a sustained burst of automatic weapons' fire that seemed to come from the top or backside of the enemy position. I know I flinched, and so did several soldiers around me. But there was nowhere to go and nowhere to take cover. It's a damn desert. So, I pulled out my .45 (which was old, and I mean *old*), and told the Iraqi Commander that if his troops fired on us, after waving white flags, the first person to die would be him—or words to that effect. And I've got to give the guy credit. He did not look scared, and he assured me that what we were hearing was not fire coming from his soldiers. And it turned out he was right—I believe it was a burst from an attack helicopter a kilometer or so on the other side of the ridge, which we could not see from where we were.

We had a few more minutes to talk as more and more Iraqis came off the escarpment and surrendered, Scouts and Alpha Company soldiers began to move them towards the rear. I don't remember any of them having weapons with them—we later found they'd left their weapons on the ridge, inside their dugout fighting positions or the trench. Some of the positions had overhead cover and others did not. I asked the Iraqi Commander how he came to speak English and be out here in the middle of the desert without support or other units. He told me he'd been to college and law school where he learned English. He said he'd been an Infantry Captain in the Iran-Iraq war, had been wounded and spent a while in the hospital. After his release, he went back to his law practice which I believe he said was in Baghdad. He said something like six weeks earlier he had received a letter stating he was now a battalion commander, and he was to move to our current location and assume command of an Iraqi reserve battalion. He had driven his family car to the site—we found it later on the back side of the ridge, where he had attempted to hide it in a draw. The attack helicopters made a real mess of his family wagon. It wouldn't be driving away from that ridge. Probably still out there today.

The Iraqi soldiers I observed ranged in age from fairly young to pretty old—I'd say somewhere in their fifties, and even maybe sixties. Saddam was hurting for manpower. Some of them looked scared, some looked resigned, and honestly some of them looked relieved that their war was over. Their battalion commander also had some concerns about how his surrender would be reported, and I didn't think until later that he was probably concerned for his safety and the safety of his family.

I have to say I kind of admired the Iraqi Battalion Commander. He was not flustered by his ordeal. He tried to ensure his wounded were cared for as soon as possible. He did not strike me as a coward or as stupid. So, I had to wonder why he'd surrendered relatively quickly.

Honestly, I can no longer remember if I heard this from the Iraqi Battalion Commander or whether I came to the conclusions myself; I think it is a combination of both. First, I don't think the Iraqi soldiers, or this guy, were strong supporters of Saddam. Most people know a tyrant when they see one. Second, the man's soldiers had been pounded with artillery, attack helicopters, and Air Force ordnance, including 2,000-pound bombs, for a couple hours straight, taking several casualties, a few of them badly wounded. He had no artillery, no armor support, no way to evacuate casualties, no comms with his higher headquarters, and I think his ADA weapons were taken out early by Apache pilots. Last, he really had not seen any American ground forces to fire at with his organic small arms. A Company, Major Dempsey, me, and the scouts stayed behind cover until the white flags appeared.

So, what was he going to do? I think he cared about the lives of his soldiers and saw that any further resistance was futile and would produce nothing except lots of dead Iraqis. And when you think about it, that's exactly the mindset you want to put your enemy in—and that's what 1-327 had done in a very short period of time. So, he opted to call it a day and keep his men alive.

CPT Al Gill
D Company Commander

About this time, COL Hill landed, and I apprised him of the situation. COL Hill listened to my appreciation of the situation and then gave me a UH1 helicopter to help me get around the battlefield. After COL Hill left, I took the UH1 forward to assess what was going on at the trench line. When I landed, I was taken to where the Iraqi battalion commander was being held. This was a new experience for me, as I wasn't exactly sure how to act—magnanimous or like a mean bastard. Since I was not sure that we had captured all the Iraqis in the area, I chose the latter demeanor.

As I walked toward the battalion commander, I was formulating in about fifteen seconds what I was going to say. When I got in front of him, I told the interpreter, "Tell him that if everyone doesn't surrender, I am going to bring back the helicopters and aircraft and kill everybody." While this seems pretty dramatic, I was out of cards to play. I knew that there were six 105mm rounds left, that the Cobras had just left because they were ordered out of the area to prevent an Iraqi tank counterattack that was supposedly forming further to the west, that there was no more close air support, and that there were at least twenty more Iraqis in the logistic site some 5 or 6 kilometers away. I also knew that division was way behind their timeline of setting up their refuel points. I later found out they were waiting on me and had already started looking for alternate locations for the refueling operation.

After telling the battalion commander that I wanted all the Iraqis in the area to surrender, he agreed to go over to the logistic site, where we hoped to get the remaining Iraqi personnel to surrender. I didn't know who these Iraqi soldiers at the logistic site were, or if they even belonged to this battalion. The Iraqi battalion commander asked if he could return to the trench line and get his wallet. I said yes, but added one more caveat—after we went to the logistic site, he would take us through the trenches and remove any booby traps.

MAJ Dempsey had arrived at the trench line and recommended that he take the battalion commander in a HMMWV, with a bullhorn, and go to the logistic site to talk the Iraqis into surrendering. As you remember, MAJ Dempsey was an Arab linguist and could translate anything that was said. I told MAJ Dempsey that we would use the UH1 I was in to cover him. The Iraqis had seen so many different types of helicopters that day that I believed they would also think the UH1 was an attack helicopter. We added an M60 machine gun, hung it out the door, and myself, CPT Sung Lee, the Battalion Communications Officer, SFC Ernie Wright, and my driver, PFC Bruce Dittfield, went in the UH1 to provide cover.

Before we moved out, there was one more wrinkle to take care of. Over the radio, we received a SITREP that an Iraqi tank unit was being pushed to the east by the French 6th Division. Their path appeared to be headed toward our perimeter. CSM Riley had heard the same transmission and said to me, "Commander, I will take care of it." CSM Riley rounded up four TOW vehicles and headed to the west to set up an early-warning screen line for our perimeter. Problem solved…there was a reason CSM Riley's nickname was "Combat."

As we were taking off, CPT Delgado, the S2, contacted me by radio and asked me what my destination was. I replied I was going to go and "habla with these motherfuckers and see if they will surrender." Since CPT Delgado was of Hispanic extraction, he chuckled, and I remember it was the first and last time (almost) I ever used profanity on the radio, which was an Army no-no.

MAJ Dempsey arrived at the logistic site and found the Iraqi soldiers more than willing to surrender. I landed in the helicopter and found we had fifteen prisoners. We loaded four of the prisoners in the UH1 and put the other prisoners in and on the two HMMWVs and headed back to the trench line. In a side note, to make a weird day even more bizarre, because of the number of Iraqis and our few soldiers, CPT Lee was searching two of the POWs and I was his guard. The trouble was that my .45 pistol had come back from maintenance two days before G-Day. I sent it out because it would fire one round and would jam. When it came back, it still would fire one round and jam. Too late to get another weapon, so here I was guarding POWs with a one-shot .45. Some type of a day.

When we arrived back at the trench line, the 3d Platoon of A Company had arrived and, along with the Scout Platoon, was processing the prisoners. At the time, I thought the process was taking too long, as I thought the Iraqis' higher command would surely know that the trench line had fallen and that they would fire artillery on the plateau to kill the Americans who were on it, just like the Soviets would have. So, I told the platoon leader, 2LT Mike Huebner, to speed it up. In response, 2LT Huebner got right in my face and said, "LTC Hancock, we have to do this right." He was, of course, correct so I said, "OK," and told him to do it right.

> After the Iraqi surrender, ABU soldiers and the Scouts rounded up the Iraqis on the objective, searched them, organized them into a walking column, and started the long trek back to LZ 1. As it turned out, ABU had over 340 Iraqi EPWs, so I ordered Gerry, my XO, to take charge of the EPW operation on the LZ with the ABU 3d platoon. I gave him a heads up that they were coming and hoped we would be able to get division MPs to come forward from FOB COBRA and take charge of our EPWs. I was running out of ABU soldiers to manage the tasks we had before us, and I was still very concerned about Iraqi forces that might come from our flank.
>
> To this day I don't know how Gerry managed to get concertina wire and establish a fairly decent holding area for all our EPWs, but like the good XO he was, he made it happen. As the sun was getting low, I looked out towards the column of EPWs and 3d Platoon strung out across the desert as they made their way to LZ 1. To me, it looked like something out of the movies, specifically a scene in "Bridge Over the River Kwai." On LZ 1, Gerry had a holding area established and was stocking up on MREs and water sufficient for the number of EPWs we had to control. Between the ongoing actions on the Iraqi positions and the threat of potential Iraqi forces from our west, I had my hands full…and then the ABU soldiers in the ground convoy arrived. Honestly, I didn't expect to see them until Day 2, but the best news I think I ever received was when I got that radio call from 2LT Esposito that 1st Platoon had arrived at the Battalion release point and was heading our way. As darkness closed in, and

the winds and sand picked up, ABU was once again all together, in defensive positions, and ready for whatever came next.

CPT Ken Russell
A Company Commander

I have a memory of the Scout Platoon moving past us in vehicles. I can't remember if they were in Humvees or with some of the Delta Company TOW vehicles. But I do have a memory of thinking to myself "You're fucking shitting me! We hump all this equipment/ammo and these guys get a ride!" Seriously, I wasn't mad, but it made me wonder if mechanized infantry was the way to go in the future.

Sometime later as we approached what would be a bunker complex, we saw about well over a hundred Iraqis' who had surrendered. They were lying on their stomachs in a long line guarded by some of our scouts. So, we sort of did a "relief in place" with the scouts and they rejoined the others in searching the bunker complex for more Iraqis.

I remember when Captain Russell told me and our Platoon Sergeant, SFC Volanos, we had to process these POWs, I was proud to remember from past training and said to SFC Volanos, "The 5 S's! (Search, Silence, Segregate, Speed and Safeguard)" but suddenly realized that, in what training I went through in the past, we never "played out" processing POWs. We had always trained from the planning phase to the actions on the objective, and then stopped. Then we'd be told to "consolidate and reorganize." Plus, add the large number of them. SFC Volanos—a Vietnam veteran of a "Blues Platoon" with an Air Cavalry unit, told me he knew a good way to do this, and we called the squad leaders in. Here's where the NCO leadership went to work.

The beauty of being surrounded by outstanding NCOs was they made missions much easier for us officers. We put out the mission and the NCOs "made it happen." All we had to do was facilitate, supervise, and follow up. I'd been told repeatedly by some of our NCOs within the platoon, "Sir, all you should care about is 'mission accomplishment!' We'll see it gets done." I guess I crossed the line into their business a few times. Captain Russell really was a good mentor for us platoon leaders. He'd always say, "Make sure to tell (or have) your guys (fill in the blank for the mission)." He just wanted things done right. Optics were big. So, as always—I put my trust in our NCOs.

I remember as the squad leaders departed our meeting to put the plan into action, SFC Volanos walked up to the Iraqis who were lying on the ground on their stomachs. SFC Volanos looked at them and said, "Is anyone here from Texas?" The Iraqis looked at each other with confusion. Even I was confused as to why he was asking this. Then SFC Volanos said, "Maine? Is anybody here from Maine?" Then I realized this old Vietnam Vet was bullshitting! Then he said, "Chicago? Is anyone here from Chicago?" Then one Iraqi said in broken English, "Chicago? Gangster?" Then another Iraqi said, "Chicago? Bang bang?" SFC Volanos, caught off guard with the response, said, "Yes! Chicago. Gangster! Bang bang!" It kind of broke the tension.

I'm positive there was one Iraqi who spoke good English. The scouts passed him off to us. He was used to explain the "search and silence" part of the operation to their men. From what I remember, we had our M60 and SAW gunners pull security. Some were placed guarding the POWs yet to be searched, while others guarded the new line of POWs who were being searched. We also had security facing up towards the bunker complex—just in case. The squad and team leaders searched the POWs. They worked in two-man teams to search each POW. After the search, the POW would move to the "searched" line. Any item deemed dangerous (potential weapon) was collected and put into a pile. Also, any item beneficial to give to military intelligence was confiscated.

I remember our scouts would randomly come down from the bunker complex with various sized groups of Iraqis who had surrendered. We had enough security so the scouts could hand over the POWs to our platoon. Then our soldiers guided them to the "to be searched" line.

They also had wounded soldiers—I remember our men treated them. I remember our guys made poncho stretchers for some and used our first aid kits to treat them. Some of our men carried their wounded so we could treat them. I was proud to see this.

Though things seemed to be running smoothly, I knew "speed" was important. Our men were searching them as fast and as thoroughly as possible, but I couldn't help but to use caution. I was concerned that, since they couldn't match our military might, some Iraqis might sneak some weapons along to try something later so as to guarantee their place in paradise with seventy-two virgins.

Many of the Iraqis were hand signaling to us for food. I do remember sharing some of my "Gator Gum" with some of them

(Gatorade Gum to help quench thirst.) I also remember one particular Iraqi who was dragged down the hill by one of the scouts. He was dressed a little different in uniform and was more resistant. My first thought was he could be from Saddam's Republican Guard as a "morale officer" but I wasn't sure. The scout had this individual's hands tied behind his back and somewhat threw him down in front of PFC Jesse Hernandez, Jr. who was providing security. Hernandez would recall years later that the scout told him if this uncooperative Iraqi tried anything, that Hernandez was to shoot him.

I remember this individual lying on the ground with his hands tied. He'd continue to yell and scream and kick. As I continued to pace and supervise the Iraqi POW processing, some minutes later SFC Volanos walked up to me and told me about that one Iraqi. He said he seemed a little tired from trying to resist so much—so SFC Volanos says, "Sir, I gave him a pillow so he could rest his head on and feel better." I was confused. So, I looked over to see that SFC Volanos had placed someone's NBC mask under this Iraqi's head.

Early as we started searching the POWs, I also have a memory of the scouts (one being 1LT Bedell, their platoon leader) escorting a couple of the Iraqis' key leadership. One being their battalion commander. I remember being told these officers had been searched. I remember thinking "segregate" and noticed that 1LT Bedell escorted their commander as we would in military courtesy—with the higher-ranking officer to his right. I remember instinctively saluting their commander. I remember him saluting back, as well. I hope I wasn't "aiding the enemy"—but wanted to show him we were a professional, disciplined military with high standards.

Once all the POWs were searched, they were formed up and marched back towards the LZ where our Company XO—1LT Tertychny and 1SG Fountain had built a makeshift POW holding area using a lot of concertina wire.

SSG Charles Miller—one of our Squad Leaders (had been the acting platoon sergeant prior to the Army fully staffing us) led the march back. In all, there were roughly 344 POWs. SSG Miller positioned SAW (M249 Squad Automatic Weapon) gunners on the flanks and M60 gunners to the front and rear. Speed and safeguard. One of the men, PFC Jason Montesanto (who became a 1SG or CSM), remembers some of our soldiers fell out of the march, being so mentally and physically drained. I believe some of those D Company vehicles or Scout Platoon Humvees transported their wounded. Or they were taken by Blackhawk helicopter. I want to say I have a memory that we used a helicopter.

I remember at one time, all of us "had to stop and rest a minute." We hadn't stopped moving all day and suddenly the mental and physical fatigue seemed to hit us all at once. I remember the Iraqis who were with us were tall and took long strides. They had no equipment. It was dark and we had our night vision goggles on. The men tell me back at the POW holding area they would work a rotation plan and guard the prisoners throughout the night. Eventually, they all had to give up their MREs to feed the Iraqis. 1LT Tertychny even screened the MREs to separate which ones had pork.

2LT Mike Huebner
3d Platoon Leader, A Company

A loud cheer erupted from the CP as the infantrymen forward reported over the radios that they saw a white flag being waved from the bunker.

The spot reports started coming in, "ten enemy surrendering…", then it increased, "twenty-five enemy surrendering…", and continued to increase, "More than fifty enemy surrendering…" When the number of surrendering Iraqis climbed to over a hundred, the feeling of elation across the CP turned to concern as we all realized that we may not have the manpower to handle such a large group of prisoners.

Alpha Company radioed the CP saying they were desperately low on water and needed a resupply before they could begin their new mission of moving the prisoners by foot to the brigade holding area.

With everything the battalion had going on, 1st Brigade "sliced" a Huey helicopter to the battalion to use as needed. When Alpha Company's call for the water resupply came in, CPT Knickrehm looked around to see who he had to spare for the mission. SGT Walker and I eagerly volunteered, and CPT Knickrehm instructed us to take the Huey with as many five-gallon water cans as the CP was able to spare to Alpha Company. We were extremely excited to have the chance to see what was happening up close.

We landed near Alpha and coordinated with them about the water and other supplies we were able to provide. We had to wait for them to distribute the water so we could take the empty water cans back to the CP. As we waited, we had the chance to talk with the Alpha soldiers about what happened and how they were processing the prisoners in accordance with the 5-Ss (search, silence, segregate,

> speed, and safeguard) as best as possible. One of the Alpha soldiers told us that an Iraqi prisoner spoke English and said that he had attended college in Chicago. The Iraqi said he knew of the U.S. Army's capabilities and wanted nothing to do with fighting us…he had been forced into service by the Iraqi government.
>
> After about a half hour, the company had returned the empty water cans, and they were ready to start moving the prisoners to the brigade holding area. SGT Walker and I knew it was time to head back to the CP, so we climbed onto the Huey and lifted off. Once again, a surreal image came to life…the sun was going down as we took off in the Huey. As we gained a little altitude, we could see Alpha Company marching more than 300 prisoners in the direction of the setting sun and moving toward the brigade holding area. As had happened earlier in the morning, I felt like I had been transported into a war movie.
>
> This time it was like the final scene as the victorious Americans marched the defeated enemy prisoners to the rear. I almost expected to hear patriotic music start playing and credits start rolling up.
>
> *CPT John Santini*
> *Battalion Assistant S1*

The total number of prisoners was 344. The XO of Alpha Company, 1LT Gerry Tertychny would, thirty years later as COL Tertychny, give me that number, as he and SFC Ray Juhnke did the count. Of these, about twenty-five appeared disoriented from the artillery and close air strikes and were laying on the ground and couldn't walk. Six of the prisoners were badly wounded and had to be evacuated, which we did with the UH1.

> CPT Russell and the rest of the company spent the remainder of the day clearing bunkers and fighting positions, collecting and searching prisoners, and consolidating captured weapons, ammunition, and equipment. There were SVD sniper rifles, mortars, RPGs, pistols, ammunition of all calibers, and over 700 AK47s. There were also four quad-.51 heavy machine guns—these would have caused us serious problems had we landed on this position instead of having moved the LZ south behind the ridge. In addition, there were somewhere in the neighborhood of 350 Iraqi EPWs.
>
> While all this was going on, CSM Riley rolled up in a cloud of dust with a few HMMWVs loaded with concertina wire. In his typical, low-key voice he said, "Hey, sir—looks like you could use some wire." Funny guy—right where he needed to be with what we

needed. We got together the soldiers in the area and made a large, concertina wire pen for the prisoners. We didn't know how many, but we figured on at least a couple hundred because we had heard over the radio that the enemy position had been battalion sized. At the same time, we gathered the 5-gallon water cans and collected up as many MREs as we could spare so we could feed them, and we separated the ones with pork from the ones without.

Just about the time the sun was going down, CPT Russell called me on the radio and told me that there was a bunch of EPWs headed my way. I specifically remember him saying, "T—don't get excited but there's a column of EPWs headed down to you. They're escorted by some of our guys. They should be coming over the ridge in a minute or so and it looks like the opening scene from 'Bridge on the River Kwai.' Are you guys set up to receive them?" He had just said it when I looked north and saw them marching over the ridge looking like, well, the opening scene from "Bridge on the River Kwai." I told him, "Roger—I have them in sight and we're ready." I had to laugh—Russell always had the right movie, TV show, book, or song to describe something.

When they reached us, I directed them over to the concertina pen. They were in one long column of four ranks. SFC Juhnke appeared out of somewhere and we did a quick search of them, four at a time, and counted them into the pen. The final count was 344. When they first showed up, before we started counting them into the pen, one of our soldiers, SPC Glenn Decouir, asked me, "Hey sir—do you think there's any NBC threat here?" The words weren't out of his mouth when a gas mask came sailing out of the Iraqi column and bounced on the sand a few yards away from the two of us. We just looked at each other and I said, "Well, Glenn—there's your answer. They don't seem to be concerned about it, so I guess we're safe." We just shook our heads and laughed.

I got together with the senior Iraqi officer, who spoke limited English and was a major, I think. I showed him the water and the MREs, told him which ones had pork and which ones didn't, and left it to him to distribute the food and water. He thanked me and left to take care of things. Later, he asked me if we had any tents or something for his men to get out of the weather, as it had gotten cold and was a bit rainy. I told him we were both in the same boat. He just nodded. In both exchanges, he would stare at my 101st Airborne patch and point at it. We did have an interpreter there by then, and I asked him what that was all about. The interpreter told me that the guy was afraid

> because they had been told stories about how the Americans with the eagle on their shoulders treated prisoners. Not wanting a riot on our hands, I told him he had nothing to worry about as long as they didn't give us any trouble. He seemed satisfied with that.
>
> *1LT Gerry Tertychny*
> *A Company XO*

In a quick interrogation of the battalion commander, we found that the unit was the reserve battalion of the 45th Division and that it had fought in the Iran-Iraq war. Its mission was to be a blocking force that would cut the highway that ran behind the trench line. The commander said he had been briefed that a French force was in front of him and that when the ground war started, he would have four days to get ready for the attack. He said he couldn't believe how fast and quickly our force moved and that he surrendered because he believed his responsibility was more to bring home Iraq's sons than to do Saddam's work. In retrospect, I believe it was more because the 2,000-pound and 500-pound bombs were collapsing their trench line than anything having to do with Saddam.

> The scout platoon organized the prisoners coming out of the trench line and an Iraqi battalion commander was segregated from his staff for debriefing. In a quick interrogation of the battalion commander, we found that the unit was the reserve battalion of the 45th Division and that it had fought in the Iran-Iraq war. Its mission was to be a blocking force that would cut the highway that ran behind the trench line. The commander said he had been briefed that a French force was in front of him and that when the ground war started, he would have four days to get ready for the attack.
>
> *CPT Jose Delgado*
> *Battalion S2*

> We had quite a few Iraqis in our camp, one of them was a master sergeant and he attended school in the US, University of Utah. We spoke a bit and I gave him and others some crackers and peanut butter, some cheese as well.
>
> When I spoke with the Iraqi master sergeant, he said that their unit was threatened with retaliation against their families by the Republican Guard if they surrendered to the Americans. They had no choice but to hunker down. They did not expect an air assault in their area of operations, let alone a large force. The bombings were devastating and demoralizing. However, the Iraqi battalion was willing to withstand the Air Force bombs, the Apaches and Cobras,

and the artillery, and not surrender. The fear of retaliation drove them to make a stand. Hours later, the MPs rounded up the Iraqi prisoners and started moving these guys to the Prisoner Control Point. Later on, I made my way back to the TOC to find my NCOIC, MSG Smiley. I felt relieved that it was almost over for us. We had to do some cleanup and continue to round up the prisoners.

SGT Jesus Gonzalez
Battalion S2 NCO

After consolidating, we kept the 344 prisoners until the next day when we turned them over to the MPs. The total count of men and equipment in the bunker complex was: 344 prisoners, 775 RPG rounds, 600 rifles, twenty machine guns of different types, thirty-one 9mm pistols, four ZPU4 anti-aircraft guns, eight mortars, eight tons of ammunition, and $5,000 worth of Iraqi money.

Observations

Don't underestimate your enemy or make assumptions about how he is going to fight. This particular Iraqi battalion was dug into the back side of a plateau/ridge, had significant overhead cover and eight tons of ammunition, and had no intention, in my view, of giving up. That is why it took about three hours to dislodge them. The attack helicopters and artillery were keeping them inside of their positions but were not going to destroy those positions because of how fortified they were. The 2,000-pound and 500-pound bombs from the Air Force were the deciding factor. It was too much firepower for their positions to withstand and too much for their bodies to take.

For a defense against a French attack, along the road to their rear, the Iraqis were in a pretty good position. However, with an attack coming from the south, which was where 1-327 Infantry was coming from, they were in a tough position as they were on the wrong side of the hill. They could not shoot at us because the Apaches and Cobras kept them from firing.

In an air assault, the Black Hawks and Chinooks are the "Golden Eggs" and have to be protected at all costs. If there is an enemy position, the lift helicopters must be landed far enough away to avoid a firefight. Each lift helicopter destroyed is a catastrophic loss of men and materiel.

On the trench line, there were a tremendous number of weapons and a lot of ammunition lying around. This equipment and ammunition would have to be rounded up, secured, and ultimately destroyed. This would take most of Alpha Company, the 81mm Mortar Platoon, and the Battalion Scouts to do the collecting.

CPT Bill Simril's Bravo Company was a good 5 kilometers away from the trench line, and CPT Darcy Brewer's Charlie Company was even further, about 10 kilometers away. It was just too far for them to march to assist and then march right back to their fighting positions. Additionally, for G-Day and G+1, we did not know if Iraqi forces, particularly Iraqi armored forces, would try to retreat through our area. The French 6th Division and the 82d Airborne were attacking to the west of FOB COBRA, and I didn't know if there were other unidentified enemy forces that might run into us. After what had just transpired at the trench line, I was not going to weaken the perimeter by diverting more soldiers to the mop-up.

> That night, like all the nights of the 100-hour ground war, we were up all night. While I no longer had to plan for an early morning assault on a fortified position, we all knew things weren't over. We had to make plans for the next day. We knew we needed to go up to the escarpment the Iraqi battalion positions had been on and do a detailed sweep for any remaining enemy soldiers and collect up and consolidate their equipment and ammunition for destruction. That order eventually came down from battalion that evening, and it looked like we might actually get some vehicles to take us up there on the following day. ABU maintained security despite being smoked like a cheap cigar from everything that occurred, and 1SG Fountain, Gerry, and I kept circulating within the company perimeter to check on our platoon leaders, and ABU leadership. Of course, we also had to keep a close eye on the Iraqi EPWs.
>
> *CPT Ken Russell*
> *A Company Commander*

There was one more problem other than the 344 POWs that had just surrendered. The Iraqis had catacombed the entire area with "spider hole" fighting positions. Many of these positions had ammunition in them and we did not know if they were booby-trapped or had stay-behind troops in them. Over the next two days, the battalion would search for these spider holes and destroy them.

> Looking through the bunker complex, I do remember finding drawings of naked American/European women. I had no desire for any war trophies or anything like that. I do remember many of the Iraqi ammunition had wooden boxes that read "Made in Jordan."
>
> SFC Volanos posed with the one undamaged anti-aircraft gun, as he wanted to send his photo to some biker magazine (he was a member of the Vietnam Veterans Motorcycle Club). He made a sign that read "Up your ass Jane Fonda." It was a little payback

for him from the Vietnam War, where Jane Fonda posed with the North Vietnamese looking through an anti-aircraft gun. She aided the enemy and shouldn't be an American in our opinion. But to me it was therapeutic to Vietnam Veterans like SFC John Volanos. This anti-aircraft gun is now at Fort Campbell, Kentucky.

Looking back among our officers, I'm proud of the military courtesy I witnessed from them. Even 1LT Tertychny being respectful as to the Iraqis' religion (identifying pork in the food).

I was also proud of the way the men of ABU conducted themselves. No one got "trigger happy"—their professionalism as well as the humane treatment they gave the Iraqis was a great example. All this while still accomplishing our mission.

2LT Mike Huebner
3d Platoon Leader, A Company

On the afternoon of G-Day, FOB COBRA became one of the busiest airports in the world. 2d Brigade was to be brought forward that afternoon to be staged in the FOB for future operations and the ammunition and fuel that was to support 3d Brigade's air assault to the Euphrates on G+1 was also brought forward. It was some type of organized chaos. In total, the 101st used 370 aircraft, flying 1,046 sorties, to secure and establish FOB COBRA on G-Day. By the end of G-Day, inside of FOB COBRA were five refuel systems with a total of forty refuel points. Rations, fuel, water, and ammunition were also brought forward, as were elements of the other DISCOM units. Much of this logistical magic was performed by LTC John Broderick, commander of the 426th Support Battalion. LTC Broderick air assaulted into FOB COBRA that morning and oversaw the setting up of the logistical sites.

1st Brigade CSM Robert Nichols was in charge of laying out the positions for TF CITADEL's 700+ vehicles and 100,000 gallons of fuel that were coming up on MSR NEW MARKET. CSM Nichols would use scouts from each of the infantry battalions as escorts and guides once the vehicles arrived. The vehicles started arriving in FOB COBRA late that evening. The vehicles for 1-327 Infantry arrived the morning of G+1. Much of the credit for the expertly done organization and layout of FOB COBRA was because of the hard work of CSM Nichols and his cadre of scouts.

Around 2330 on G-Day, I decided to try to get some sleep. One of the soldiers, I never knew who, had dug a hole/fighting position outside the TOC tent for me and put a poncho liner in it. I told the staff officer monitoring the radio to wake me only if we were attacked by tanks, and if we were attacked by infantry, just kill them.

CHAPTER 15

TASK FORCE CITADEL

G-Day to G+1
24–25 February 1991

For the follow-on air assaults by the 2d and 3d Brigades into the Euphrates River Valley to succeed, the resupply convoy, TF CITADEL, would have to make it to FOB COBRA on schedule, not later than G+1. TF CITADEL was led by the 1st Brigade Executive Officer, LTC Jim McGarity, and would be comprised of over 700 vehicles transporting 100,000 gallons of fuel. Each of the infantry battalions in the 1st Brigade would provide their executive officers to serve as the Task Force's leadership, along with two rifle platoons and several TOW platoons to provide security for the convoy.

MAJ John Chappell headed up the 1-327 Infantry section. Because John knew the lieutenants in the battalion well, I told him to pick the platoon leaders he wanted to be on the convoy. The platoon leaders had to be very competent because they would have many responsibilities and, if attacked, would probably have to act independently. The two rifle platoon leaders were 2LT Steve Caro of Bravo Company and 2LT Dave Esposito from Alpha Company. CPT Mike Landers, the Battalion S4; CPT Tom Guleff, the Battalion S1; CPT Chris Reed, the Battalion Assistant S3; and 1LT George Glaze, the Support Platoon Leader, would provide further leadership for the 1-327 Infantry portion of the Task Force.

> Task Force Citadel was commanded by LTC James McGarity, the 1st Brigade XO. The mission was to clear the ground route (MSR New Market) to FOB Cobra and bring in an initial load of 100,000 gallons of fuel for the helicopters. It was also to secure the area for the Division Main Command Post. The entire convoy would consist of 722 vehicles broken into five elements. Team Stein, made up of Company D, 3rd Battalion, 327th Infantry, cleared and secured MSR New Market up to 14 kilometers inside Iraq. Following Team Stein was Team David, consisting of 3rd Battalion, 327th Infantry elements and 1st Brigade staff. Next came Team Oliver and elements

> of 2nd Battalion, 327th Infantry, Team Smith and elements of 1st Battalion, 502nd Infantry, and Team Chappell with elements of 1st Battalion, 327th Infantry. The convoy was supported in the air by Team Rattler—two cobras and two scout helicopters.
>
> *MAJ John Chappell*
> *Battalion XO*

The convoy was directed to make an infiltration movement through 90 miles of Iraqi territory, which made the operation a high adventure movement. There were no armored vehicles accompanying the convoy, so any attack would have to be repulsed by the infantry platoons, the TOW platoons. and any attack helicopters escorting the convoy. There was no artillery in the convoy, so any fire support would have to be from the attack helicopters or from Close Air Support.

> The greatest fear of anyone in a military convoy is losing sight of the driver in front of you. The desert treks were not like planned trips from Clarksville to Nashville. There were no road markings or gas stations on the way. The area looked like a barren, isolated, wasteland, a place for the non-living. The visibility was poor at times, and if a vehicle veered off in the wrong direction the rest of the convoy would follow.
>
> I assumed the aviation units were using the same goat path to navigate that we did, due to all the military debris that appeared to have fallen from the sky during their trips back and forth to FOB COBRA. There were damaged vehicles, one helicopter crushed and broken-up on the desert floor, one artillery piece with the tube stuck in the ground, and all kinds of other junk on the sides of the road.
>
> During our entire time deployed, every logistical movement felt like a scene out of the movie "Mad Max." The story of a wandering soul trying to survive the chaotic world upon its collapse. For the unit, it resembled a band of scarfed and goggled gypsies carrying warfighting supplies. This is the supply line or logistical tail of the infantry unit. Spare tires, concertina wire, pickets, plywood, gas cans, water cans…you name it, it was loaded inside and on the outside of every vehicle on the caravan.
>
> CPT Michael Wright was the commander for the majority of these traveling soldiers. He was always friendly and respectful, no matter the rank. He grew up in the Berlin Brigade as a lieutenant and later found his spot as commander of HHC (Headquarters and

Headquarters Company) of our unit. The organization chart for HHC was more of a Ponzi scheme that wasn't quite developed.

The marshalling and travel of Task Force CITADEL under Chappell looked exactly like a clip from "Mad Max Beyond Thunderdome." In the movie, Tina Turner sang its theme song ("We Don't Need Another Hero") and also starred in it. The movie centered around the search for fuel/methane in a post-apocalyptic world. Desert Storm was "reality imitating art" at its best. CPT Wright would break out in the theme song every time he saw our vehicles, especially our large trucks packed with supplies hanging on every square inch of them. This time was no exception, he sang in perfect pitch. It was definitely an MTV moment. I couldn't stop laughing every time he did it. By the way, the truck that had the most gear draping off of it was called the "Thunderdome."

The lyrics of the song killed me...... *"We don't need another hero, We don't need to know the way home, All we want is life beyond Thunderdome."*

CPT Wright also had the patience of a seasoned kindergarten teacher. He was calm and deliberate, making sure everyone got their turn at pin the tail on the donkey.

CPT Tom Guleff
Battalion S1

The route of TF CITADEL was to be cleared by the division's 326th Engineer Battalion. The convoy moved out the morning of G-Day. Snaking its way through Iraq on 24 February and into 25 February, the 1-327 Infantry contingent was scheduled to link-up in FOB COBRA the morning of G+1.

On G-Day, we started probing through Saddam Hussein's defense line at 0330 with the division's combat engineer battalion punching through the obstacles. By 0600, most of the four combat teams followed Team David through the gap, headed for the site of FOB Cobra. We carved out and mapped our MSR as we went and, by 2300 hours, I had all elements at the outskirts of FOB Cobra. This included the 100,000 gallons of fuel for the FOB that 1st Brigade had set up to pass 3rd Brigade through to air assault further into Iraq so as to isolate Iraqi forces in Kuwait and cut off the Republican Guard escape route.

LTC James McGarity
Brigade Executive Officer

Back in the TAA, communications were sparse with 1-327th Infantry Battalion Headquarters. However, through 1st Brigade and the Division, we were made aware that contact had been made. Our attention turned to making sure our portion of TF Citadel was prepared to execute our ground convoy mission. After the first lift of helicopters took off, TF Citadel was launched.

Originally, Team Chappell was not due to depart along MSR New Market until G+1. However, the flow of air assaults and the movement of convoys to FOB Cobra was going well. Team Chappell received a Warning Order to be prepared to move and was subsequently told to move out at 1630 local. Just prior to crossing the Line of Departure (LD), two soldiers driving a low boy carrying a small bulldozer took off and headed south. Apparently, the two soldiers did not want to go into Iraq. We spent about fifteen to twenty minutes searching the area but to no avail. We turned the incident over to the 101st Airborne Division (Air Assault) MP's and crossed the LD on time.

Movement was slow as the initial ground was rough with large rocks and heavy dust. We reached the top of an escarpment at about 1830 local where a 101st Airborne Division MP Check Point was established. It was dark by then. The Check Point had been set up beside the ruins of an Iraqi outpost—the ruins were the complement of the 101st Airborne Division Attack Aviation. As our convoy was about halfway through the Check Point, I received word from the back of the convoy that the MPs were telling us to halt. I halted the convoy and walked back to the MP position and asked what the problem was. I was informed that Division G-3 ordered a halt to all movement. I told the MPs to get Division G-3 on the radio and, after an exchange of some unpleasantries, told them I was continuing to move.

By the time I reached the front of the convoy, the air was filled with dust and smoke. We were now apparently down wind of the smoke coming off the oil field fires set by the Iraqis coupled with the remnants of dust from a sandstorm. Visibility was low which made movement more difficult. We continued to move slowly forward with intermittent stops to change busted tires on the trucks or drivers falling asleep at the wheel. I believe our men had to change out three tires that night. We closed in on another MP Check Point at about 2300 local, moved to the side of the trail, put out security, and waited for visibility to improve.

Early on G+1, the air began to clear, and we set out again for FOB Cobra. We linked up with 1st Brigade CSM Nichols at about 1330 local. With minimal problems, we closed with the rest of the battalion and set up. At 0300 local, G+5, the President of the United States announced the cessation of hostilities and called for a cease-fire by 0800 local, G+5. The ground war lasted 100 hours.

MAJ John Chappell
Battalion XO

In the early morning of 24 February, we began to get assembled on the HMMWVs to prepare to secure the back of the convoy and move out across the Iraqi border. It seemed like only a few hours and by mid-morning we were pulling rear security and heading out across the border. There was an unimaginable amount of dust being kicked up by all the vehicles plowing through the desert trails. It was difficult to see around us and difficult to breathe. Given the challenges with radio frequencies at the time, a decision was made to keep all radios in vehicles on the same frequency. This created a massive amount of static and difficulty with communicating security issues or observations through the journey. The heat-sensitive sights on the Delta Company TOW missiles were perfect to assess any potential enemy positions on the hillsides surrounding the trails we were following to the various link up sites.

Through Day 1 we had limited observation of enemy positions along the route. Our main issues were avoiding unexploded ordnance along the route and trying to see through the dust to ensure we kept the convoy moving forward safely together. We eventually pulled into a defensive position around nightfall. Our task was to spread out and pull security across the southern end of this massive convoy. We had a squad per vehicle spread out across about 500 meters.

As I proceeded to check in with each of my squads, it was an eerie feeling of quiet, darkness and dust as I navigated to each of their positions. I can remember the green glow of my night vision device and the soft powder-like sand in this part of the desert that made me feel like I was walking on the moon. Each step created a cloud puff of powder that made me feel like I was on another planet.

2LT Dave Esposito
1st Platoon Leader, A Company

The ground war began on 24 February 1991. I was part of the convoy into Iraq with HQ 82. My vehicle had the slings attached with the clevis just in case it was needed for an air assault. I had a full load of 81mm mortar rounds (High Explosive, White Phosphorous, and Illumination). We all were in MOPP Level 1. Brand new chemical suit worn, and mask/gloves/boots carried. I had an AT-4, a Claymore, and multiple hand grenades in my vehicle. I remember that morning well. All drivers were instructed to stay in the tracks of the vehicle in front of you because of landmines or obstacles. If a vehicle was hit, we would drive on to our objective.

We were told by our S-2 that there would be no enemy combatants on our way up to FOB Cobra, but anything could happen. Have your head on a swivel and be alert! As I stated earlier, I was a 20-year-old young adult. I was never scared for my life and the whole experience was like another training mission. We all had extreme confidence in ourselves, our equipment, and our leadership. We drove all day into the night. When we stopped at night there were flashes of bombs going off in the distance to the northwest of our location. I remember seeing green tracers from AK-47's when we got closer to FOB Cobra.

PFC Rich Hagedorn
Mortar Platoon

On the morning of 25 February, the 1-327 Infantry portion of TF CITADEL motored into FOB COBRA. I was extremely happy to see MAJ Chappell and his convoy. Not only did it bring the rest of the battalion's vehicles, supplies, and about 200 troops, but it brought MAJ Chappell back to us. MAJ Chappell was a force in his own right. His competency and force of will made him a superb soldier and leader. When he arrived, he told me about the convoy up (hard business) and then asked me what I wanted him to do. I told him about the spider holes and that we needed to find and destroy them. MAJ Chappell took off and that was the last I worried about the spider holes, as I knew he would take care of it… and he did.

On Day 2, 25 February, we started moving out before daylight. There was a similar amount of dust and grime that made visibility difficult during the remaining part of the convoy. We continued to have some communication challenges within the convoy, but we worked it out throughout the day and found our rhythm on the combined frequency to send up situation reports efficiently.

Beyond the continual avoidance of unexploded ordnance, we eventually made our way to FOB Cobra late in the afternoon without any major incidents. It was a great feeling to be reunited with A Company at the top end of FOB Cobra. We were quickly assigned a defensive position and were updated on the events that took place over the last two days. It was great to reconnect with CPT Russell, 1LT Tertychny, and the other platoon leaders of A Company.

2LT Dave Esposito
1st Platoon Leader, A Company

When I got to the Mortar Platoon, I was relieved that we didn't have any casualties or deaths. SFC Levesque told PFC Sturgill and me to get our vehicles ready to help escort/taxi the Scouts. Our mission was to go through bunkers, take POWs, and kill anything that engages us. We picked up the Scouts in HQ81 and HQ82 and made our way to the Iraqi positions. We drove by the main concentration of Iraqis and headed to the bunkers. We approached every bunker with extreme caution. We didn't know if any enemy combatants were inside ready to fight. I cleared two bunkers with PFC Plata (Scout Platoon). I had a loaded .45 pistol in one hand and a flashlight in the other. At this time, all I can think about was the books I read about Vietnam, and that I can't believe I am doing this. All bunkers were abandoned and no booby traps. Speaking of booby traps, when I was crawling out of a bunker, I heard a metallic click from the ground. I told PFC Plata, "I am on a mine!" He searched around my knee and noticed I was on top of a large "tuna can" of 7.62 X 39 ammo. We were both relieved and kept on going.

PFC Rich Hagedorn
Mortar Platoon

Despite all the jokes in the Army about lost young officers with maps and compasses, my navigation turned out to be dead on. We linked up with the motorcycle mounted scouts from our battalion who guided us toward CSM Nichols, the 1st Brigade Command Sergeant Major, link up man, and head traffic cop for FOB Cobra. I hopped out of my HMMWV and shook his hand, hearing artillery off to the west from the French sector. CSM Nichols gave me a run down on where to go and I followed the scouts who guided us to the position where we would set up the battalion Tactical Operations Center (TOC).

CPT Chris Reed
Battalion Assistant S3

Observations

The supplies on Task Force CITADEL were essential to the completion of the G+1 mission by 3d Brigade of air assaulting and cutting Highway 8 and the Euphrates Valley. To say this operation was a calculated risk is being very conservative. A 90-mile route over uncharted desert terrain with 700 vehicles, 2,000 (+) soldiers, carrying 100,000 gallons of fuel, with no armored vehicles (M1 tanks or Bradley fighting vehicles) for close-in support, with a timeline of eighteen hours to completion could only have been accomplished by very professional soldiers. The Brigade XO, LTC McGarity, provided great leadership in getting this organized and completing the mission. The Battalion Executive Officers—Major Chappell (1-327), Major Oliver (2-327), Major David (3-327), and Major Smith (1-502) were all superb.

CHAPTER 16

G+1 TO G+3 AND CEASEFIRE

FOB COBRA
25–28 February 1991

G+1
25 February 1991

Later that morning, I took the Huey helicopter that COL Hill had loaned me on G-Day and flew to where the Military Police POW collection point was located. When I got there, the site was not set up nor ready for POWs. I walked up to the young sergeant-in-charge and told him that I was bringing 300+ POWs to his location that afternoon and that he needed to get ready. The sergeant said his site would not be ready nor could they hold that many POWs. After what had transpired the day before, I was in no mood to argue and flatly told him, "Well, they're coming, so get ready because we're not keeping them." I assumed that the battalion would conduct another air assault out of FOB COBRA, and we couldn't guard over 300 POWs. Later that morning, the POWs were processed by the MPs and marched away from A Company's sector.

> The following day we saw the helicopters flying over us filled with Rakkasans soldiers on board, so we knew the division had extended the attack all the way up to the Euphrates River valley. MPs from the division MPs arrived and took charge of our EPWs, so 3d Platoon was released from the chore of guarding and taking care of the EPWs. Trucks arrived and my ABU 3d Platoon and the ABU HQ, along with some folks from battalion drove up to the top of the escarpment that had been the location of the Iraqi battalion positions.
>
> Upon arrival, ABU soldiers fanned out and started deliberately going through individual Iraqi positions and the half-hearted attempt they had made at a partial trench line. We even found the Iraqi battalion commander's personal vehicle parked behind the escarpment. ABU soldiers found a live goat that we turned loose,

> and once all the fighting positions were checked we started gathering up weapons, equipment, and ammunition. LTC Hancock and COL Hill sent an engineer platoon to help us, so as ABU gathered things together the engineers figured out the best way to destroy it. For the next two days we worked on gathering equipment together for destruction.
>
> *CPT Ken Russell*
> *A Company Commander*

After leaving the POW site, I had the helicopter crew fly me to Brigade Headquarters to see COL Hill. I gave him a short situation report and then he gave me another mission. Northwest of our perimeter, about 4 kilometers out, was an enemy logistics site that had not been thoroughly checked out. COL Hill told me to get that done, and get it done in as short a time as possible, as enemy troops there could be a threat to helicopter routes in and out of FOB COBRA. Needless to say, I was not pleased about this. The closest unit to the site was my Alpha Company, which had 344 POWS, eight tons of enemy ammunition to collect, and spider holes all over their sector to destroy. My Bravo and Charlie Companies were 10 kilometers and 15 kilometers away, respectively, and in no position to leave their perimeter to help. The only helicopter to lift troops up to the position was the Huey I was in, as every other helicopter was supporting the 3d Brigade's air assault to the Euphrates that day. Doing a quick appreciation in my head, I said to no one in particular, "Screw it, we'll do it," or words to that effect.

To expedite getting the mission done, I told the soldiers in the Huey we were going to clear the logistic site ourselves. In the helicopter were about five other soldiers with me, including Air Force Captain Bill Reister who saw the irony of what we were going to do. When the helicopter landed just short of the location my initial thought was, "This is stupid," but stupid or not, we went through the site and cleared it. There was an abandoned truck there, some other equipment, and a grove of trees. When our small patrol had walked to the end of the site, there were three figures we saw walking/running quickly away. I never knew if they were Iraqis, Bedouins, or someone else. They ran away and that was that. I reported to the Brigade Commander that we had landed and "cleared" the logistics site.

> The highlight of my day was joining LTC Hancock and some other soldiers from the CP on a search for Iraqis that were reported in our area. The battalion still had the Huey from 1st Brigade, so we climbed on and searched the whole 1st Battalion sector area for about thirty minutes, to no avail.
>
> A little while after returning to the CP, the weather deteriorated and started to rain for a long time. Around this time, the "Convoy

from Hell" arrived at the battalion CP. I linked up with CPT Guleff and provided an update of the current situation.

CPT John Santini
Battalion Assistant S1

Later on in the day, I returned to the trench line and MG Peay came to the location. He wanted to know what happened and I explained what actions the battalion had taken to get the Iraqis to surrender. He was pleased and was also impressed by how much arms and ammunition the trench line had. Later on, in the interrogation of the Iraqi battalion commander, we discovered that this battalion was in an ambush position for the French armored column that was expected to drive up the road north of the trench line. While at the trench line, MG Peay told me that he wanted all of the weapons and ammunition destroyed, which in itself would turn out to be a pretty tall order.

As MG Peay was inspecting the equipment on the trench line, one of the more surreal occurrences of this already eventful war came about. Standing on the hill/plateau, the battalion's soldiers were about 100–150 feet above the desert floor. Off to the west of the trench line appeared the 3d Brigade in Black Hawks heading north toward the Euphrates. The helicopters were less than a ¼ of a mile away from us and we could clearly see into them, as their altitude was close to our height on the plateau. The 3d Brigade soldiers were giving us the "thumbs-up" sign and we were waiving our hands and weapons at them. I knew personally the three battalion commanders – LTC Andy Berdy, LTC Hank Kinnison, and LTC Tom Greco. Hank and Tom were my classmates at West Point. COL Bob Clarke was the Brigade Commander. Some moment! MG Peay would later remark that it was the most memorable moment of his time in the Gulf War.

From the *Clarksville, Tennessee Leaf-Chronicle Newspaper* interview with then LTG Binford Peay, May 1992.

One dark, rainy afternoon in particular stands out in Peay's mind. It occurred on the second day of the ground war as he was standing on a hill that had been captured along with a whole battalion of Iraqi soldiers by a battalion in the 101st led by LTC Frank Hancock. As Peay stood there talking to the soldiers, hundreds of Black Hawk helicopters flew overhead heading 165 miles deep into the Euphrates Valley. "I particularly remember the soldiers in the helicopter giving the "V" sign and the soldiers on the hill giving the thumbs up sign as they streamed overhead" Peay said. "It was a very poignant reflection and memory of the hundreds and hundreds of Black Hawk helicopters," he said. "They looked like blackbirds covering the sky you almost felt like you could reach up and touch them as they screamed underneath the air defense umbrella and into the Euphrates for a major part of our mission, which was to cut the Valley."

G+2

26 February 1991

LTG Gary Luck, the XVIII Airborne Corps Commander, came to inspect the trench line on G+2. I briefed him on what actions were taken to get the Iraqis to surrender. LTG Luck was impressed by our ability (infantry, artillery, attack helicopters, and US Air Force assets) to coordinate, "on-the-fly," the attack to force a dug-in enemy battalion to surrender. LTG Luck said it was a "classic operation." When he said that remark, I thought, "Yes, it was a classic combined arms operation that was done fairly seamlessly." However, I also thought it was close to a classic screw-up of epic proportions. Changing the Alpha Company Landing Zone made it possible for it to be a "classic" and not an "infamous" action.

> During one of the bunker clearings that morning, one of my M-60 gunners fired his pistol into a bunker where he thought he heard some movement. It turned out there was no enemy in that bunker.
>
> As we returned that evening back to the A Company perimeter, I was informed by CPT Russell that my platoon was going to take a security post north of FOB Cobra across the highway in the morning. I was starting to get a complex that, for some reason, I was being sent off on these solo one-platoon missions with poor communication and no back-up support…Ha Ha.
>
> *2LT Dave Esposito*
> *1st Platoon Leader, A Company*

> I spent these days acting as a radio relay between the TOC and the companies up near the complex. I eventually went up on the complex to have a look around. This battalion was well equipped and had all the means to put up a stiff fight. A further eye-opener was learning that we had fired artillery and dropped bombs on this complex for several hours yet had managed to wound only seven Iraqis and had killed none. It gave me a great appreciation for how being even just a bit below ground could protect one from indirect fire. I ran into COL Hill, our brigade commander, at the bunker complex and he was shaking his head. As a Vietnam veteran, he understood the implications of what we were seeing. He told me, "If these guys had decided to fight, it would have taken the whole brigade to dig them out." It was then I realized just how lucky we had been.
>
> *CPT Chris Reed*
> *Battalion Assistant S3*

When I woke in the morning, there was a strong wind blowing—the strongest I had experienced since arriving in-country. The wind intensified all morning, preventing us from setting up the tents that would comprise the Field Trains.

Soon, the wind developed into a full-blown "shamal," a severe sandstorm. We couldn't do anything other than sit in the back of the crowded cargo vehicles with the flaps closed and zipped through most of the afternoon to stay out of the sandstorm.

The shamal started to let up around 1600hrs and we were finally able to set up the tents, adjust the perimeter, and dig new positions. As the storm subsided, we once again heard U.S. jets back in the air.

CPT John Santini
Battalion Assistant S1

G+3

27 February 1991

On G+3, a windstorm "shamal" blew into our sector. It was intense. When the windstorm blew in, I had gone out to relieve myself and walked about 500 meters away from our TOC tent. When it blew in, I could not see more than 5 meters away. I ultimately pulled out my compass and shot what I thought was a 180-degree azimuth, as I had walked north. Eventually, I found the TOC tent to the relief of the soldiers in the tent who knew I had walked outside before the shamal started. One of our soldiers from B Company got separated when the shamal hit. We did not find him until the next day, when a French unit that was passing near our sector had picked him up. To say that these shamals are biblical in their power is a good description of what they are like.

On Day 4, February 27, our platoon loaded up on some 5-ton trucks and a few Humvees and were dropped off on the highway north of FOB Cobra. I linked up with a 2LT from 2d Brigade who gave me an update on the situation. We quickly changed responsibility for security of the position and my platoon spread out across about 400 meters of desert and secured the surrounding high ground to establish clear lines of sight on any approaching enemy.

2LT Dave Esposito
1st Platoon Leader, A Company

We had a very uneventful day other than the occasional artillery fire from the French 6th Division which continued to assault the town of As Salman to our west.

We anticipated having some enemy soldiers retreating from west to east and cross our path, but they never came. I made several trips to each of the squads positioned on the hillside and the men were in good spirits and remained ready for action.

After the surrender, we moved into the bunker complex and discovered, literally, tons of ammunition and weapons. Whatever logistical problems the Iraqi Army had, it didn't involve getting small arms and ammo to units, even reserve units in isolated positions.

In the subsequent days, Delta Company established a screen on the northwest side of Cobra, tied in with other Delta companies to our flanks (2-327 to the south and 3-327 to the northeast) who were performing the same mission, and had a couple of other interesting missions. The only 101 assets ahead of the D Companies providing security for Cobra were aviation units that screened forward of us. The huge logistics and aviation units that supported and conducted later missions further north, toward the Euphrates, were in the center of Cobra, secured by an inner band of rifle companies, then Delta company mounted TOWs, then an aviation screen.

North of Cobra ran a good, paved road, MSR Virginia. On the second day, as I remember it, my company went up to MSR Virginia and moved west a few kilometers to establish a roadblock on the MSR to close that high-speed avenue of approach into Cobra. I was issued a couple of anti-armor mines, which were heavy, and huge, as well as some signs saying in Arabic that the road was closed. I honestly don't think we ever employed those mines, which were, in fact, practically useless in a country where one can just drive off the road and around any roadblock because the desert is so wide open. But I do remember I wanted to get those damn things out of my vehicle as soon as possible. If the things can destroy main battle tanks, they'd have had a hard time finding the smallest piece of D-6 had one of them gone off in my vehicle.

We also got the mission to move up to MSR Virginia, again, to meet/pass through elements of the 82nd Airborne Division. They had been transported, in trucks, along the MSR moving from West to East, and needed to continue moving east past Cobra. My soldiers got a huge kick out of that mission, the 101st already on the ground, setting the conditions for the 82nd to arrive by truck! I heard jokes about this from my guys for years, literally.

Among the weapons caches on the escarpment where the Iraqis surrendered, and at other locations, with my consent, we "acquired" serviceable PKM machine guns and thousands of rounds of belted

7.62×54mm ammunition for those guns. I think we had one on each TOW HMMWV. The soldiers and NCOs created mounting systems on the roofs of the HMMWVs using bungee cords and other material. The guns had bipods attached, but no tripods or vehicle mounts.

We rode around with those things for several weeks, covering them with ponchos to avoid "oversight." One day we had a visit from Colonel Hill, I forget the occasion. As I spoke to him, one of my vehicles stopped nearby, and he was looking at it pretty closely. Then he said, "Al, what's under the poncho." The gig was up, so I motioned to the soldier to remove the poncho. That revealed a very clean, well maintained PKM, on a swivel bungee cord setup, with a 100-rd belt installed (but not one in the chamber). I told the brigade commander that I thought having no automatic weapons was a mistake in the Delta Company TO&E, so we'd acquired the PKMs to make up for that deficit.

Colonel Hill looked at me for about ten seconds, then smiled, and said, "good idea Gill. Get rid of them." The PKM/TOW experiment ended that day.

Near the end of our time in Cobra, Jon and I had a very close call. We'd been at some kind of meeting, a good distance away from the company position, and we were headed back. The sun had set so we were driving at night. Jon was wearing NODS, and I was not, which we frequently did because you saw different things with and without NODS. On clear nights in the desert, with a full or near full moon, you didn't need NODS. Moon and starlight made it seem almost like day. This was not one of those nights. It was very damn dark.

The desert around Cobra was mostly flat and hard packed, and you could drive at a good clip. I think we were probably going 40–50 when Jon slammed on the brakes and almost threw me into the windshield, spilling some of that good coffee I acquired at the meeting. When we came to a stop I said, "Jon, WTF??" he simply kept staring out the windshield, then he said, "I think there's something in front of the vehicle." I said "what?" and he replied, "I don't know." So, I got my flashlight (we drove without headlights) and got out to see WTF it was.

When I got to the front of the vehicle, I saw something sticking up out of the desert about 1.5–2 feet high, and maybe 15 feet in front of the bumper, centered on the vehicle. Walking toward it, I saw that what was sticking out were fins. The fins on a bomb that had not exploded. I don't know whether it was a 250 or a 500 pounder, but it was big. I don't know if it would have gone off if we'd hit it going

45 mph. But I do know this; if we had hit it and it did go off, there wouldn't have been enough left of Jon and Al and D-6 to pick up with a spoon.

Jon also got out and had a look. I just looked at him and said, "good call Jon, good eyes. Don't worry about my coffee." Then we marked the thing off with engineer tape and called in a grid to the TOC for EOD to deal with when they had the chance. Those guys stayed pretty busy. I suspect the bomb had been ejected from an aircraft returning to its base that did not want to land with it. Whether that happened way before we established Cobra, or during the assault on the enemy objective, I have no idea.

CPT Al Gill
D Company Commander

As we sorted the letters, one of the S-1 soldiers called my name and threw a letter at me…it was the very first letter I received since arriving in country. It was from my wife, Mary, whom I hadn't been able to communicate with in any manner since deploying in late January. The letter was dated 11 February, so I was sure that there would be other letters she had sent prior to that one that just hadn't arrived yet. I quickly stuffed the letter into my cargo pocket and continued sorting the mail. With the arrival of that first letter, I began to eagerly await every mail call like all the other soldiers in the battalion.

With sorting the mail completed, I headed to my position, read the letter from Mary, and went to sleep in the best mood I had been in quite a while.

CPT John Santini
Battalion Assistant S1

Ceasefire

28 February 1991

On 28 February, the ceasefire was declared, and the battalion would stay in FOB COBRA until 28 March. During that time after the ceasefire, the most memorable of events was the destruction of the Iraqi ammunition and weapons that were captured at the trench line. According to our calculations, there was around 8 tons of ammunition and hundreds of rifles, pistols, mortars, machine guns, rocket propelled grenades, and anti-aircraft weapons. I had been told by MG Peay to destroy everything and that there would be no souvenirs taken. The only weapons that would be saved from the hill were those designated to go to the Fort Campbell Museum. This strict "no souvenirs" guideline was a result of the purported taking of souvenirs during Operation JUST CAUSE in Panama in 1989.

The solution that the staff and I came up with was to pile everything together and blow it up with C4 explosives. Not an elegant solution but one that seemed to meet the intent of what MG Peay wanted done. After the detonation, guards would be posted around the hill to make sure souvenir hunters could not go on top of the hill (which did occur) where there would be possible undetonated ammunition.

The date was set for the detonation, the ammunition and weapons were stacked together and laced with C4, and a notice was put in the Division Bulletin for helicopters to keep clear of the air space over that grid location. All the troops were pulled back, I believe, 3 kilometers for the blast. My engineer platoon leader had set a fuse for ten minutes and then began his descent with his HMMWV off the hill with his driver going at a fast speed. Then began the most bizarre series of events for me in DESERT STORM.

As the HMMWV was speeding off the hill, I looked with my binoculars about 500 meters to the south and there were two dogs. The two dogs were mating. I thought this would be a significant, emotional event for them. As I looked farther to the south, up in the sky there were twelve Chinooks in formation heading north for the hill. I could not believe it! I assumed they were non-divisional aircraft that had not been notified to stay clear of the area. MAJ Chappell, who was standing next to me, blandly said, "They're not going to make it."

For the next two or three minutes, there was a frantic search for a radio frequency to contact them as the formation slowly but surely headed for the hill. Finally, one of the pilots who was with us came up with a frequency that worked. The Chinooks then did as close to a 180 degree turn as you could do. As they were heading south, the C4 exploded, and the hill erupted. Obviously, as a cadet at West Point, I had not studied physics well enough to know that this much ammunition exploding would displace a lot of air. Now coming toward us was a tsunami of air that looked like a bow wave. After a few profanities were exchanged, myself and those soldiers with me jumped into a small depression near us. The bow wave came and blew over our backs like a 30mph wind.

When I got up, I looked through my binoculars to see if everything was OK, meaning no downed helicopters. There were none. Surprisingly the two mating dogs were not only alive but still running south from the hill. Those were some intense minutes of my life causing at least 100 new grey hairs. The soldiers who were near, within 10 kilometers of that explosion, will never forget it.

> One of the more aggravating aspects of our stay in FOB Cobra was stopping sightseers from visiting the scene of the action at

the bunker complex, which was now surrounded by munitions of all sorts. At least once a day, some idiot would drive up there and we would have to run them off before they killed themselves. Unfortunately, this required us to pick our way through the same minefield of unexploded ordnance. CPT Russell and I took turns. One day, almost on schedule, a HMMWV was reported by 2d Platoon as it headed towards the bunkers. CPT Russell looked at me and asked, "Your turn or mine?" I admitted that it was my turn, took our HMMWV and driver, SPC Rodney Stephens, and went to tell them to beat it. On my way, I picked up SGT Kelly Huett and we headed over.

We got out of the vehicle, and I was just about to yell at them when one of them kicked an 82mm mortar round lying on the ground. I jumped into a hole in the ground and landed on top of Kelly—I thought I had moved pretty fast, but he had beaten me into that hole. We looked at each other, waiting for the boom that would turn them both into grease spots, but it never came. We slowly looked over the edge of our hole and saw two aviators staring at us as if we were nuts. I walked over to them and asked, "What kind of a fucking moron are you? Don't you know that's a live mortar round?" When I got closer, I could see that he was a lieutenant colonel, and his partner was a major. Well, now I've done it—I just called a field grade officer a moron. He didn't say anything—his face turned white when he realized what he had done and how close the two of them had come to being turned into hamburger.

One day, after the ceasefire, we were listening to the radio and heard Secretary of Defense Dick Cheney say that there were no more American servicemen in Iraq. This was news to us. We wondered if maybe we had been forgotten.

1LT Gerry Tertychny
A Company XO

The engineers ran det cord freely through air defense guns and water buffalos and planted 40 lb. shape charges and C-4 on top of weapons that were placed into a large trench dug by a bulldozer. Mixed with that was all the ammunition the Iraqis had as well. The day came when we were complete, and it was time for the big bang. We all backed off and let the engineers do their job. It was a gloriously massive explosion. We hadn't quite considered that an explosion that large might scatter sensitized munitions over a large area, but that is what happened. It literally rained destroyed weapons' parts and sensitized ammunition. We didn't care at that point because our battalion and ABU needed to move on and start planning and preparation for our next mission.

CPT Ken Russell
A Company Commander

CPT Wright woke me at 0030hrs and told me that a ceasefire had been declared. As I tried to wake up and comprehend what he said, I thought to myself, "What? So soon? How can that be?"

The excitement about the ceasefire continued to buzz throughout the morning, but there was still work to do. I took advantage of the opportunity to go to the ALOC three times this day. When I arrived the first time with the mail, CPT Guleff was counting money captured in the bunker system. As he completed totaling the amount, we calculated that it was equivalent to $7,000.

The second trip to the ALOC was to attend the first Command & Staff meeting held in about two weeks. During the meeting, I was told that I would be promoted to captain the next day, 1 March. When I returned to the Field Trains, I put in my pocket a set of subdued pin-on captain bars that I had brought with me for this very occasion.

With the ceasefire declared, and word that I would be promoted the next day, I began to think of other things that may be within the realm of the possible but had completely dismissed when I deployed. Finally, I thought to myself "What a great way to run a war. Kick ass, take names and don't mess around!"

CPT John Santini
Battalion Assistant S1

VALOROUS UNIT AWARD

1st Battalion, 327th Infantry distinguished themselves by gallantry in action during Operation DESERT STORM as they captured a large enemy bunker complex which contained a large cache of ammunition, weapons, and soldiers to include a Battalion Commander and his staff, on 24 February 1991. 1st Battalion, 327th Infantry acted with courage, bravery, and dedication to mission accomplishment during combat operations. The actions of the 1st Battalion, 327th Infantry reflect great credit on themselves and the United States.

CHAPTER 17

GOING HOME

Fort Campbell, Kentucky
April 1991

At the end of March, the battalion received orders to leave Iraq and return to Camp Eagle II. If you had canvassed the battalion at that time, no soldier would have voted to stay another second in Iraq. At Camp Eagle II we began our preparations to go home. Standards for the return were very stringent—no dirt, dust, sand, war trophies, or anything from Saudi Arabia or Iraq was to be brought home. Of course, this was violated by troops who had been exemplary over the past nine months and who had endured all types of privations from 130-degree temperatures to scorpions climbing into their boots. One such soldier was my first driver and later driver for CSM Riley. In 2018, MSG (Ret) Dave Moyers told me, during our monthly telephone call, that he had brought a weapon home. I asked him how he did it and he confessed that he had disassembled the weapon and hid the parts in the engine block on my HMMWV. A very smart soldier. Who would look in the engine of the battalion commander's HMMWV?

> My Best Day. The Black Hawk helicopter was flying with its doors open over the Iraqi desert. I was sitting at the prime location next to the opening of the aircraft, staring out at the terrain speeding beneath us. I looked at the other soldiers with the wind whipping around us, and I felt that we were moving in a dream. I was among this new generation of soldiers that understood that our mission was complete. Desert Storm was over, and we were returning home. It was the proudest moment of my life. I am sure others felt vindicated in some way about the US military at the end of Desert Storm. The ghosts of past failures seemed a million years away. The turnaround was remarkable. It is hard to fathom that this was an Army in despair just sixteen years earlier with the fall of Saigon. But it was even harder to understand the faith of those, the true believers, who stayed

the course to fully restore an institution, especially in a time, where a good portion of the citizenry was disillusioned with the military and shared a common ill will toward soldiering.

CPT Tom Guleff
Battalion S1

I was sitting there on my rucksack, when I saw a civilian SUV drive up. I watched with somewhat idle curiosity as the passengers got out—and then I recognized that one of them was the XVIII Airborne Corps Commander, LTG Gary Luck! I went forward to greet him, but he just waved me off after a brief introduction—he wanted to talk to the ABU soldiers without any leadership getting in the way. As I watched him enjoy talking and glad-handing with the soldiers, I turned my head and noticed a figure walking toward ABU from out of the desert. As he got closer, I could swear I recognized the walk…and I did. As it turns out, my old 82d Airborne Division platoon sergeant, SFC Norman McCollum, had been deployed as part of the XVIII Airborne Corps Tactical Operations Center (TOC). I ran out to greet him, and as we hugged each other he told me he had been following my company actions from the TOC since we arrived in theater. He wanted to come out and say hi before we all left, so he did. SFC McCollum had been a 173d Airborne Brigade infantryman during Vietnam. To say I respected him more than any other NCO I had ever worked with up to that time would be putting it lightly.

CPT Ken Russell
A Company Commander

One day, shortly before we redeployed back into Saudi Arabia, my driver and I were on a ridge, and it was a beautiful day. We smelled like goats for lack of showers and decided to take our shirts off and do some sunbathing. I had just settled down on my sleeping mat on the hood of D-6 when I heard the dreaded rotor blades of a Huey coming our way—which normally meant some sort of visit by a senior officer. We could see it in the distance coming straight at us. Both Nordin and I jumped through our asses trying to get our T-shirts, blouses, LCE, Kevlars, and weapons secured & adjusted. I figured whoever it was had seen us fucking off and decided to counsel us.

The helicopter landed at the base of the ridge, and a kind of pudgy looking Major I didn't know got out. I walked down the hill to see what was up, saluted and said, "Can I help you Sir?" hoping he wouldn't say, "Yeah, you can, by staying in fucking uniform."

He did not say that.

He was from one of the aviation brigades, and he said, "Have you guys seen a helicopter? A Black Hawk lost power two days ago and had to land, and we haven't heard from him in over twenty-four hours. His batteries might be dead, we don't know. We're trying to find him and recover the aircraft. I said, "sorry, can't help you there." Yours is the first helicopter we've seen in the last two days." Then I looked around, 360 degrees, and said "big desert out here. Like an ocean." He wanted to bullshit for a while, and finally left, whereupon I walked back up the hill to Nordin who said, "Can we continue now?" I said, "hell yeah." I was asleep five minutes later.

CPT Al Gill
D Company Commander

The war was over in 100 hours, and it was time to clean up and get back to King Fahd. This time was spent taking accountability of everything and getting ready to head south to Saudi Arabia. We were told about "war trophies" and that we needed to turn everything in. I took one thing while we were in the bunkers—an Iraqi eagle off a black beret left from an Iraqi soldier. I still have it to this day and I'm not turning it in. I must bring this up—we didn't take a shower for fifty-seven days and when we took that shower what clothes do you think we put back on? The same shit we had on for the last fifty-seven days. I would do it all over again.

PFC Rich Hagedorn
Mortar Platoon

In early April, GEN Schwarzkopf came to Camp Eagle II to meet and talk to the brigade and battalion commanders of the 101st before the division redeployed to Fort Campbell. GEN Schwarzkopf had served in the 101st in the late 1950s and said that the 101st had been "The Lightning" of DESERT STORM. In the briefing, MG Peay gave his explanation of how the ground operation went and the different key points of it. When MG Peay got to the part of how the "unoccupied" trench line in FOB COBRA was actually occupied, and how 1-327 Infantry had taken it down, he singled me out. GEN Schwarzkopf turned, looked at me and gave me a head nod. When this happened, I felt I like I had just hit the lottery for a million dollars. GEN Schwarzkopf, for legitimate reasons, is considered in the pantheon of US generals, along with Grant, Sherman, Lee, Pershing, Eisenhower, MacArthur, and Patton. To get recognized by him in front of my peers was a very big deal for me.

In mid-April 1991, the battalion started its trip home. On the flight, the movie *Ghost* was playing on the screen and for the first and only time in my life I was in the first-class section of the plane. When we eventually made our way to Campbell Army Airfield, after a short stopover in Boston, the reception was everything and more of what each of us had dreamed about in the desert. Wives, children, cousins, girlfriends, local supporters, the Post Band, and the news media were all arranged at the airfield to greet our arrival. After the welcome at the airfield, the battalion would hand in its equipment and go on thirty-day block leave until May 1991.

> We were at Camp Eagle II for about three weeks. We got our gear sorted, packed up, and ready to load. The guys spent a lot of time getting the vehicles cleaned up, which for A Company wasn't too difficult as we only had the one HMMWV. We flew home in early April and returned to Fort Campbell. On the flight home, I bought George Glaze's 1968 Cougar. Campbell Army Airfield was quite a scene—there were hundreds of family members there to greet us. A few of us who were unmarried were just standing off to the side watching the mayhem when a couple of Vietnam Veterans approached us and said, "Welcome home." I was a little embarrassed because I knew that these guys didn't get any kind of welcome when they came home, and I told them that I was sorry that our country didn't give them the same reception. One of them said, "Don't worry about that—you guys had nothing to do with it. We just want to make sure that shit never happens again." Nice guy. We talked a bit about our experiences before we got on trucks that took us back to our company area.
>
> When we got back to the company area, the first order of business was getting the weapons turned in. I took one look at the young replacement who was in the arms room and knew that he wasn't going to be able to handle this. I turned around and yelled, "KELLY!" I was going to ask SGT Huett, who had been the armorer prior to and during our deployment, to help the guy out. When I turned around, he was standing right in front of me because he had the same idea. He just smiled and said, "I got this, sir." He went into the arms room, took charge, and made sure that everything was turned in and accounted for. When this was completed, CPT Russell gave the guys a short safety briefing and we were released. I slept on the desk in my office that night. The married guys went home, and the single guys went to their barracks rooms. The next day, everyone took off on about a month's leave. It had been about one year since I had gone

up to battalion to be the S3 Air. We returned in May and picked up where we had left off back in August.

1LT Gerry Tertychny
A Company XO

One awful event marked ABU's return after block leave. An ABU soldier who volunteered to be supercargo and escort our vehicles home on the merchant shipping finally arrived back to ABU after completing the voyage with the vehicles. We immediately put him on block leave. He went home to the Boston, Massachusetts, area to be with family. While he was there, he was stabbed through the aorta—he was an innocent bystander in the wrong place at the wrong time who happened to be sitting between two tables that decided to fight in a bar. We got the Red Cross message and I asked for permissive TDY to go to Roxbury, Massachusetts, and see him. Honestly, no one thought he would survive but I wanted to make sure his parents knew how proud I and all of ABU were of his service over in Iraq. I visited his family, talked with them, and visited him in the ICU although he was in a medical coma at the time. I returned to Fort Campbell thinking ABU would never see him again—but I was wrong. He pulled through after many weeks of hospitalization and eventually returned to ABU; however he was medically retired due to his injury.

CPT Ken Russell
A Company Commander

When we got back to the states it was incredible. We were all treated like heroes. We felt so proud to serve our country. We had awards and parades. We left with a bond that no one else could understand. We had the best leadership anyone could possibly want. Being part of the largest air assault mission in history—it was all worth it. Because of our success we are able to grow into successful individuals. To this day I will always remember what we had and what we did. Above The Rest—Honor and Country!

PFC Stan Banach
Mortar Platoon

Let me tell you, those agricultural inspections were no joke, they wanted every piece of sand off those vehicles. Our vehicles returned to the States by ship, and some of my soldiers volunteered to ride with the vehicles on the ship. The rest of us flew commercial contracted flights home.

> When I arrived at the airfield on Campbell, my wife Yon was waiting for me, with our daughter, Andrea. Andrea had not been walking when I left—but she ran into my arms in a pretty sun dress Yon had bought for her when she saw me.
>
> *CPT Al Gill*
> *D Company Commander*

When the block leave was over the battalion went back to work. Because the nation was truly enthusiastic and thankful about the outcome of DESERT STORM, numerous parades were arranged all over the nation. Our battalion would go to two of these parades—one in Nashville and the other in San Mateo, California. In my view, the enthusiastic reaction was part happiness that the war was over and that the troops were coming home, but also a cathartic effort to make amends for the shameful way the Vietnam Veterans were treated upon their return from Vietnam.

The City of San Mateo, California, which had completely and wholeheartedly supported 1-327 Infantry, not only in DESERT STORM but also in the Vietnam War, asked that the battalion support their 4 July 1991 "Welcome Home" parade. After much wheeling and dealing with brigade and division staff, and also receiving supporting "fire" from San Mateo politicians, 101 soldiers from 1-327 Infantry were resourced to go to the parade.

> On 23 April 1991, I wrote to the commander of the 101st Airborne Division, Major General J.H. Binford Peay, requesting his approval for the soldiers of LTC Hancock's battalion to attend a homecoming hosted by San Mateo for the city's Adopted Sons. Once again, LTC Hancock was all-in. San Mateo rolled out the red carpet and the three-day homecoming took place—something I know our Adopted Sons will never forget.
>
> We kept our promise to our Desert Storm troops. The bridge from San Mateo to our Desert Storm warriors—who were the tip of the sword in the fight—was reinforced and remains strong. San Mateo's outreach to LTC Hancock's soldiers was received with love, honoring each one of his victorious warriors. God Bless You All. Honor and Country.
>
> *Linda Patterson*
> *Americans Serving Americans*

To say that the entire three days in San Mateo was emotional is a great understatement. Pen pals were united, Vietnam Veterans were honored, and the July 4th parade took on a new vibrancy. San Mateo, and its driving force, Linda Patterson, could not have been more gracious or supportive. Each of the soldiers would be awarded a badge that said, "Adopted Sons of San Mateo."

> Block Leave. One thing I want to bring up about my Combat Brothers. I have many friends from grade school/junior high/high school/sports. I'm still friends with most of these people today. When I was on block leave, I would think of my Combat Brothers from the Mortar Platoon. These men are my family. In the future, I would be at their weddings, many vacations, reunions, fishing trips and even trips to Fort Campbell.
>
> San Mateo, California (4th of July Parade) was one more great experience with 1-327 Infantry. We were invited to march in the San Mateo Parade by Linda Patterson. This woman lost her brother in Vietnam and adopted all of us in the 1-327 Infantry. I have met this great woman twice now and we have spoken to her over the phone. Linda loves all of us and we love her for her support. The parade was special for me because I got to spend time with my Uncle Sam Guidici, Aunt Lu, and Cousins Fred and Ross. They were very proud of me and the 101st Airborne. That was the last time I would see my uncle alive. He would pass away a few months later.
>
> When someone asks me about my Combat Infantryman Badge (CIB) or 101st Airborne combat patch when I was full time in the Army, I would tell the story of leadership. I bring up the old Army FM 22-100, BE KNOW DO. That was us! I talked about how proud we were as young soldiers in 1-327 Infantry. We had no fear, an unbelievable fighting spirit, and Love of Country. It was the best time to be alive.
>
> When I talk to my family and friends about the Gulf War, I thank them for their support. All the mail and packages we received. The support I received from family and friends was humbling. When Paulette Rak, a family friend, was hours from death, I drove to the house to see her. I sat next to her crying and said this, "Thank You from all of us in the Mortar Platoon/Gulf War Brothers for everything you did, and I will never forget it." Off the record, she sent us shampoo bottles of Southern Comfort in mid-January 1991. It was illegal in the Kingdom of Saudi Arabia to consume or have in our position. Miss Paulette Rak, she loved her Adopted Sons in the Mortar Platoon.
>
> When I talk to my kids and wife about the Gulf War, I tell them we worked hard/trained hard/fought hard. It's about the MAN next to you. We all wanted everyone to make it back home and have a

long great life. We have reunions and laugh about stupid shit. I tell my wife Joanna about people that are very important in my life, the men I served with in that God forsaken shithole. My wife understood completely about the Flag Folding Ceremony for MSG Thomas Levesque. She knows the love I have for the men I served with in the Gulf War…

PFC Rich Hagedorn
Mortar Platoon

As occurred after Vietnam, friends of ABU in San Mateo, California demanded that ABU come to San Mateo for a proper welcome home. Over the 1991 Independence Day holiday, ABU and other members of 1-327 Infantry flew to San Mateo and spent several days there with our friends. We participated in a parade and a military banquet among other events. I can't say enough good things about our hosts in San Mateo, but they will always have my undying gratitude and thankfulness for their friendship and loyalty to ABU.

CPT Ken Russell
A Company Commander

CHAPTER 18

JOINT READINESS TRAINING CENTER

Fort Chaffee, Arkansas
October 1991

"Once More into the Breach"

The Joint Readiness Training Center (JRTC) is one of the three Combat Training Centers that prepare Army units for combat. In 1991, JRTC was located at Fort Chaffee, Arkansas and provided a jungle and counter-insurgency scenario similar to Vietnam, mainly for light infantry forces. The rotations to JRTC were hard and rigorous, and a unit going through would have to train for and focus on the rotation for many months to do well. The division's rotation schedule was for three infantry battalions to go through JRTC, sequentially, in October 1991. The division plan was that each of the three infantry brigades would supply one of their battalions to participate. 2d Brigade drew the short straw and would be the controlling brigade headquarters for all the battalions going through.

In 1st Brigade, the battalion commanders of 2-327 Infantry, LTC Gary Thomas, and 3-327 Infantry, LTC Gary Bridges, were both turning over command in June of 1991. I would have only seven months left in command by the time the October rotation. I had just spent eight months in the desert, and I *assumed* that my battalion would not be selected and that one of the incoming commanders would be chosen to go. I was wrong. Upon asking COL Hill what the rationale was for 1-327 Infantry being selected, he said that division did not want it "screwed up."

In trying to figure out a train-up program for the rotation, I considered several facts: First, the soldiers had just been separated from their loved ones for eight months. Second, our level of training was pretty good. Third, our wheeled vehicles and most of our radios were still on ships sailing back to America.

The training plan we developed, I believed, was reasonable. The battalion would train—and train hard—but not to the point of being stupid. We would not train on weekends, and we would limit the amount of time we would be out in the field to two to three days at a time. Most importantly, we would not go to JRTC "tired." Before we went into "The Box," we would take some time off and go down as refreshed as we could. As the saying goes, "If not well-prepared, be well-rested." I believed the battalion could be both.

When the battalion arrived at Fort Chaffee, my first visit was to 2d Brigade headquarters, as their battalion had been the first to go through The Box. I went with MAJ Dempsey, who was now my XO, and MAJ Jesse Pugh, my new Battalion S3. When we arrived, the brigade headquarters was very much in disarray. Many of the staff officers and NCOs were sleeping on their desks and one staff officer remarked that the OPFOR was "everywhere." This was very much what the World Class OPFOR did to rotating units—it stretched them out and destroyed their morale by seeming to be invincible and ubiquitous.

Two days later, 1-327 Infantry went into "The Box" and, on the first day, we got "destroyed." The battalion did an air assault, and when it landed the naval gunfire that was supposed to be our indirect fire support never materialized. What a disaster. CPT Ken Russell, the Alpha Company Commander, famously said that his communications were so bad that "I can't even talk to myself."

When it was over and the battalion "re-keyed" its laser equipment, I had to face three "in your face" facts. First, the OPFOR squads, because of their training and their knowledge of the terrain and how the "game was played," were better than one of my platoons. Second, the scenario would always shortchange the battalion on fire support. Third, my battalion was still lethal, but it had to be used properly.

To make sure that there was not a repeat of Day 1, I implemented the rule that in the battalion every unit would be in a position to be mutually supported. No squad or platoon would be separated from its company and no company would be put in a position where it could not be supported rapidly by another company. This idea flew in the face of the counterinsurgency theory of saturating an area with squad elements to find the guerrillas and then piling on when they are found. For me, this was not going to work against this clever and lethal OPFOR.

Upon 2d Brigade headquarters receiving the disposition of my units for future operations, I received a visit from the Brigade S3. The S3 asked me why I was not spreading my forces out and saturating the area. I told him I was not going to get beat like on Day 1 and that I needed to make sure that when my units ran into the OPFOR, the OPFOR would have to tangle with a much larger unit than they expected. The Brigade S3 was not pleased. I next received a visit from the 2d Brigade commander, COL Ted Purdom. COL Purdom also asked why I was not spreading my forces out. I repeated my rationale to him, and, in the end, he allowed me to place my companies and platoons where I deemed fit, something for which I have always been grateful. For the following four days, the OPFOR would be treated very roughly by 1-327 Infantry.

Our lack of initiative went against everything I had ever learned, but for some reason the first night at JRTC just put us on our heels. I made some mistakes in combat and fortunately they did not cost us, but I was learning a good lesson right now without the high stakes of combat. At that exact moment, my PRC-77 came to life with the voice of LTC Frank Hancock who had been monitoring our company net and my futile efforts to raise any leadership on the radio. I remember it like it was yesterday over the entire battalion net: "Matt, this is your Senior Rater. Get out of that god**mn ditch and get your ass on top of that hill!!" That comment from Warlord was all I needed to stop feeling sorry for myself and pull myself back to reality and react the way the US Army had trained us—when lacking leadership, remember the commander's intent and take the initiative. After the "gentle nudge" from Warlord, we ultimately succeeded in taking Ham Slice Hill that night and that was the turning point for the rotation for my platoon—from that night forward we aggressively took the fight to the OPFOR and never failed to take the initiative.

This is a lesson I internalized for the rest of my career, which included many combat tours after 9-11 in both Afghanistan and again in Iraq; take the initiative, don't wait for guidance, know the commander's intent, and take the fight to the enemy. The Warlord's leadership style rubbed off on me and I applied that in my formations post 9-11 as a company commander, battalion operations officer, and battalion commander in combat.

2LT Matt Karres
2d Platoon Leader, C Company

Two incidents stand out to exemplify how the OPFOR was treated in those last four days of the battalion being in The Box. The first incident was the "Carnis Village" scenario. In this scenario, the "mayor" of the insurgent village requested support from the battalion. When the support was sent, it would be ambushed and killed by the OPFOR. This occurred and one of the battalion's soldiers was "killed."

The village then sent another request for a second soldier. When the emissary requested the second soldier I said, "No," and he said the mayor demanded it. I then said, in a coarse and vulgar manner, "Fuck Carnis Village. You tell the mayor he can suck my dick and die." Of course, this quote was being copied verbatim by the O/C standing behind me and would later be shown to the entire battalion at the end-of-exercise After-Action-Review, to much applause. This was the post-DESERT STORM Army—before Somalia, Haiti, Bosnia, Kosovo, Afghanistan, and Iraq II. No person from brigade came down and said I had to kowtow to the mayor of Carnis Village. In retrospect, this makes sense.

The last scenario was the final attack on the insurgents' base camp. The OPFOR had approximately 100 soldiers there and they were dug-in on a hillside. The battalion had about 500 soldiers available to attack and was given the mission to take down their position. Again, the OPFOR had done the same scenario innumerable times and assumed it had every contingency covered.

Because of the division's maneuver capability with our Black Hawk and Chinook helicopters, there was always a possibility of conducting a "false insertion" of troops, where empty helicopters are landed, and no troops get out. The only thing the enemy sees is helicopters landing and taking off again—they assume that a force has been landed. In my five years assigned to the 101st, which includes my time as a captain in 2-327 Infantry, I had never seen or heard of the false insertion being used. The usual rationale for not doing it was that such an operation was too risky and "used up too many resources." I believed that the limited visibility at Fort Chaffee, with its thick vegetation, the use of darkness, and the fact that false insertions had not been used before would make it successful.

When our operational plan was briefed to 2d Brigade, I received a visit from COL Purdom, the brigade commander. He told me he believed the false insertion would not work. I gave him my reasons for wanting to do it and he agreed to resource my plan with ten Black Hawk helicopters dedicated to this deception.

When the attack took place, my Delta Company had placed a section of TOWS (two vehicles) on the backside of the enemy-occupied hill, overwatching it with thermal night sites to detect if the OPFOR tried to escape. If the OPFOR believed the false insertion was, in fact, a genuine landing of troops, they would not come off the backside of the hill and would stay put. When CPT Gill, Delta Company Commander, passed the information, "They are not coming off," I turned to MAJ Pugh, the S3, and said, "They're fucked." And they were.

At the final outbrief, the slides with the statistics for the last few days' encounters were put up, including my "Carnis Village" quote. The OPFOR had started with 106 soldiers. At the end of the rotation the OPFOR only had three "fit for duty." Upon leaving the outbrief building, BG Jack Keane, our Assistant Division Commander for Operations, pulled me aside and talked to me. Before coming to the 101st in the summer of 1991, he had been the Commander of JRTC for two years and would later become the Vice-Chief of Staff of the Army. When he retired, he became the face of military analysis on Fox News. BG Keane said to me with a smile, "I have never seen the World Class OPFOR treated that way." I thought to myself, "I bet he hasn't."

Observations

While the JRTC rotation was not combat, it was stressful, rigorous, and as hard as it was designed to be. In retrospect, the fact that we did not over-train and did not "abuse" the soldiers to get ready worked to our advantage. Additionally, "Thinking Hard" after one day in The Box and adjusting our tactics to defeat the OPFOR as thoroughly as we did was also something to be proud of.

CHAPTER 19

"ALL'S WELL THAT ENDS WELL"

Lessons Learned

When I look back on the Army, the 101st Airborne, and 1-327 Infantry in DESERT STORM, there are three big ideas that I would pass on to posterity:

Focus on Lethality

If the US Army is ever again in need of getting its bearings and righting its direction, the 1980s roadmap to recovery is a great place to start. The 1973 post-Vietnam Army was, at best, a mediocre army. For a country that does not have enemies lurking about ready to destroy it, this is acceptable. For the United States, which is the leader of the Free World and has identifiable enemies, it is a dangerous place to be. The leaders of the post-Vietnam Army understood that a mediocre Army was not a luxury the United States could afford, especially after the carnage of the Yom Kippur War.

Everything that the Army did for the next seventeen years was focused on giving it the capability and the intellectual strength to win a high-intensity war against the Soviets. This focus on lethality became a reality when the Reagan Administration funded the equipment and training facilities that were needed for this type of force. Being lethal and destroying your enemy is what counts in war. That is what the 1980s Army leaders believed and why they made the US Army as lethal as possible. Every other whim and fad became superfluous to the goal of fielding a bone-shattering Army.

Train and Treat Your Soldiers as if They Were Your Own Sons and Daughters

The post-Vietnam Army was an Army of volunteers. It was a robust Army of 790,000 citizen-soldiers who had made the choice to serve. There was great emphasis on making the new volunteer Army a professional army. Training was focused, realistic, and rigorous. Meritocracy ruled. If you were good the Army was going to promote you. If not, the Army was not going to promote you.

From the individual to the division and corps staffs, training was meant to make the individual and the unit professional and combat ready. At the same time, efforts were directed to make the life of the soldier as amenable as possible. Pay raises, facilities upgrades, and non-abusive discipline were the rule, not the exception. If a soldier volunteers to defend his country, then at a minimum the soldier should be treated with respect and paid accordingly. Respect and fair and rational discipline were expected to be given to all soldiers. The 1980s was a GREAT time to be a soldier. "Be All You Can Be" became the culture of the 1980s Army.

Train Soldiers to be Hard...but also to Think

The last piece of advice I would pass to future leaders is to train your soldiers to be hard but to also be thinkers. I have always believed that there is a fine line between being really hard and being really stupid. So, if soldiers are trained to use their brains along with their muscles, then mission success is much more likely. When I think of CPT Jose Delgado and SGT Jesus Gonzalez, I just thank God that they had the moxie and pluck to solve a convoluted intelligence puzzle and the force of will to get their superiors to accept their analysis. It literally made a life and death difference for 1-327 soldiers.

In Retrospect

In June 1992, I would give up command of 1-327 Infantry to attend the US Army War College. From there, I would be assigned to the US Pacific Command in Hawaii for three years as their Strategy Officer. In 1996, I would return to the War College as an instructor in the Department of Military Strategy, Plans, and Operations (teaching how to make war at the Operational and Strategic levels) and eventually become the Department Chairman for four years. In 2002, I retired from the Army after thirty years of service. After I retired from the Army, I would stay active teaching high school Army Junior ROTC for sixteen years, refereeing high school basketball for twenty-two years, teaching ballroom dancing (a long story) for twenty-six years, and being a grandfather for six grandchildren.

The battalion, as all units do, eventually went to the four winds. Many stayed in the Army despite living as junior officers, NCOs, and soldiers in the "hellhole" of the Arabian Desert, and many would fight in the twenty-year War on Terror. Of the forty officers in the battalion, twenty would stay in the army and make it a career. It is very unusual to have so many junior leaders from one battalion stay in the service to become field grade officers. John Chappell, Tom Dempsey, Gerry Tertychny, Bill Simril, Darcy Brewer, George Glaze, Sean Reger, Matt Karres, Sung Lee, Bryan Blue, Jay Peterson, Bryan Bedell, and Chris Reed would all make colonel. Ken Russell, Al Gill, Mike Landers, John Santini, Erik Valentzas, and Jay White would make lieutenant colonel, and Tom Evans would retire as a major, also teaching high school Army Junior ROTC.

John Chappell would command 2-187 Infantry in the 101st and Tom Dempsey would command a battalion at Fort Knox, Kentucky. Bill Simril would command an OPFOR battalion, 2/11 Armored Cavalry Regiment, at the National Training Center and during a deployment to Iraq and George Glaze would command 1-18 Infantry in the 1st Infantry Division in Baghdad in 2007. Jay Peterson would go on to command 1-507 Infantry (Airborne), the jump school battalion, at Fort Benning, Georgia. Chris Reed would also command a training battalion there. Darcy Brewer would become the Garrison Commander of the Presidio in Monterey, California. Sean Reger would leave the active army and serve in the National Guard, where he commanded 2-104 Cavalry in Pennsylvania.

Ken Russell served as an instructor at the US Army Command and General Staff College in Fort Leavenworth, Kansas, and would continue in that position as a civilian after he retired from the Army. Al Gill would serve as a speechwriter for the Chief of Staff of the Army and would retire as the Professor of Military Science at Georgetown University.

Sung Lee, Gerry Tertychny, Bryan Blue, Matt Karres, and Erik Valentzas would transfer to Army Special Forces in the early 1990s. Sung would eventually become the Deputy Commander of the 1st Special Forces Group at Fort Lewis, Washington. Gerry would serve as Professor of Military Science at Valley Forge Military College, command a Division Stability-Transition Team in Baghdad in 2010, and retire as the Director, Special Operations Forces, at the US Army War College, where I would preside over his retirement ceremony. His son, Jake, is an Army officer and an AH64 Apache pilot. Erik Valentzas spent the majority of his service as a Special Forces officer in Central and South America. Matt Karres would serve as the commander of the Special Troops Battalion, 1st Cavalry Division and as the Deputy Commander of the 3d Special Forces Group at Fort Bragg, North Carolina before retiring as the Chief of Staff, 1st Special Forces Command. Matt, as a retiree, would help Afghani interpreters escape the Taliban after the fall of Kabul in 2021.

My adjutant, Tom Guleff, would leave the Army and enter politics and the manufacturing business. Tom's son, Logan, won the American reality cooking competition, Master Chef Junior. Dave Esposito would become a leadership expert, founding the company Harvest Time Partners, which provides resources to support and encourage individuals, families, and organizations to reach their full potential in an increasingly complex world. Mike Huebner would also leave the Army and is now serving as a postman. Linda Patterson, from San Mateo, would found the non-profit organization Americans Supporting America (ASA). ASA has facilitated the adoption of many Army units by towns and cities across the country.

CSM Riley would retire right after DESERT STORM after thirty years of service and become a postman and eventually retire from that position. Rich Hagedorn, one of my mortar men, would retire as a Senior NCO/AGR with the Nebraska Army National Guard and would earn a place in their Hall of Fame. He spends his time taking service-disabled veterans waterfowl hunting and fishing. Stan Banach, another mortarman, put himself through college, earning a BA in Electronics Engineering. Stan became a Systems Engineer and helped develop the first internet-based Live Orthopedic Surgical Training Center.

Larry Maroto, a TOW gunner, lives in Florida and is currently working in his twenty-seventh year in law enforcement. My driver, Bruce Dittfield, became a manager in the automobile industry, while Bill Reister, my intrepid Air Force Liaison Officer, left the Air Force and became an IT consultant. LTC Dick Cody, the Apache battalion commander, would stay in the Army and eventually become a 4-star general and the Vice-Chief of Staff of the Army.

Frank Bills would make his home in Nashville, Tennessee. After DESERT STORM, Frank would receive a commendation from President George H.W. Bush for his actions concerning the nerve agent incident on 28 January 1991, along with a photo signed by both President and Barbara Bush that states, "Job Well Done." In December 2006, Frank's younger brother SSG Joseph Bills, was serving as a Chaplain's Assistant in the U.S. Army in Iraq and was hand-selected to escort the remains of Saddam Hussein to his final resting place in Tikrit. This action is detailed in the book, *Battlefields & Blessings*.

Finally, CPT Jose Delgado and SGT Jesus Gonzalez, my two hard-thinking intelligence analysts, would continue in the intelligence business, but not with the Army. Jose currently serves in the Department of Justice as the Director of the Organized Crime and Drug Enforcement Task Force Fusion Center, while Jesus is hunting down spies and other bad guys for a federal agency.

What Could Have Been—But Was Not

Trying to project what would have happened if CPT Delgado and SGT Gonzalez had not solved the trench line puzzle is difficult, but not impossible. The original plan had approximately sixty soldiers from A Company, and other support troops, landing 500 meters from the trench line. The landing time was 0600 hours, which meant it would have been in darkness. The Iraqis may or may not have been alert or awake upon the arrival of the first lift.

There was no artillery fire or close air support on the landing zone. Nor was there any artillery in range of the objective—it wasn't due in for another hour. Again, the intelligence assessment was that the trench line was unoccupied. The fact that there were 344 Iraqis in the trench line had escaped everybody, and that includes Delgado, Gonzalez, and me. Nobody had anticipated that the battalion was landing on the only large Iraqi unit within 400 square miles. The only immediate indirect fire available was the Apaches and the follow-on Cobras. Because it was dark, the Iraqis probably would not have seen the Apaches circling the landing zone. They would, however, have seen and heard the Black Hawks land.

The Iraqis had four ZPU4 anti-aircraft weapons, along with numerous other types of machine guns and automatic rifles. The ZPU4s had a maximum effective range of 1.4 kilometers, which means the landing Black Hawks were well within range. When the A Company soldiers exited the helicopters, they were loaded down with 120-pound packs, chemical protective suits, and materiel to build bunkers. There was no cover or concealment for the troops exiting the helicopters. Alpha Company had its 60mm mortars, but they were in the open and the mortar ammunition was scattered around the LZ in the men's rucksacks. The 81mm mortar platoon was just arriving and not set up. The 105mm artillery battery wouldn't arrive for another hour. Because A Company was so close to the trench line and the Iraqis, any close air support and artillery support, when it became available, would be difficult to employ and would just as likely land on A Company. My conclusion is if the Iraqis opened fire on the helicopters as they were landing, it would have been a very hard day for that lift.

The closest unit to the landing zone was my B Company, commanded by CPT Bill Simril. B Company was 5 kilometers away from the fight and initially had only half of its company, until the second lift arrived. Moving B Company or CPT Darcy Brewer's C Company, which was 10 kilometers away, would take time and be hard to accomplish. They were too far away and had to secure the FOB perimeter against a potential Iraqi threat from the west. Additionally, the assumption that, at most, there were thirty to fifty Iraqi soldiers in the trench line could have led to some tragic courses of action being taken.

A Company's 2d Platoon, arriving on the second lift, would have had to be diverted so they didn't fly into an ongoing firefight against the dug-in Iraqis. But diverted to where? And how would the casualties have been treated and evacuated? Until that Iraqi position had been destroyed, or at least reduced, the setup of FOB COBRA was on hold. This would have thrown off the whole 101st timetable for the follow-on air assaults by the 2d and 3d Brigades, and that would have thrown off the entire XVIII Airborne Corps plan.

How long would it have taken to subdue that battalion without close air support and artillery? My guess is quite a while, and it would certainly have required the assistance of more troops than I had in my battalion. The closest units were 2-327 Infantry and 3-327 Infantry, and both battalions were over 20 kilometers from this fight.

How would the division have reacted to this? I don't know, but the planners would definitely have had to find another place for their refuel point and would also have had to figure out how to extricate my battalion. The resupply units that were coming on TF CITADEL would also have to be redirected to another part of the FOB.

What would be history's assessment of the 101st Airborne's air assault into Iraq during DESERT STORM? Now, the operation is used in army field manuals as an example of how to execute an effective operational maneuver. Without Delgado and Gonzalez, I doubt this would be the case. In fact, the whole air assault concept, and the future of the air assault division, would probably have been in jeopardy.

The good news in all of this is that the situation, as described above, didn't happen. CPT Delgado and SGT Gonzalez did what they knew had to be done, my staff listened to them, I believed in all of them, and, finally, COL Hill believed in them and altered the plan. From top to bottom, the training and preparation that dominated the US Army in the 1980s came into play. We were able to leverage the mobility and flexibility that our helicopters gave us and shift the LZ. Once on the ground, we were able to mass the fires of our infantry, artillery, attack helicopters, and close air support to compel the Iraqis to surrender.

There is a misconception about DESERT STORM that Iraqi units immediately surrendered once confronted by American forces. This unit did not. Despite the weight of fire raining down on them, they did not quit until the F16s and A10s dropped bombs on their position. In the end, it took my whole battalion to defeat Major Khadir's force. A Company, D Company, the Scout Platoon, the Mortar Platoon, and the Battalion Headquarters were on the objective. B and C Companies were guarding against an Iraqi threat from the west, and a significant number of troops were on the ground convoy. What could have been a tragedy did not occur. What could have been an infamous battle was not. As Shakespeare said, "All's well that ends well."

WORKS CITED

101st Airborne Division (Air Assault). *Lessons Learned from Operations Desert Shield and Desert Storm.* July 1991.

101st Airborne Division (Air Assault). *Reproduction Briefing Charts/Slides on Desert Shield/Storm.* July 1991.

"Air Assault in the Gulf." *Https://History.army.mil/Documents/SWA/DSIT/Peay.htm*, US Army Center of Military History. Accessed 23 Apr. 2024.

Bolger, Daniel P. *Death Ground.* Presidio Press, 2 Dec. 2003.

Broderick, John, LTC. *Air Assault Logistics during Desert Storm: A Personal Experience Monograph.* 1993, apps.dtic.mil/sti/pdfs/ADA264203.pdf.

Charles Lane Toomey. *XVIII Airborne Corps in Desert Storm*. Hellgate Press, 2004.

Citino, Robert Michael. *Blitzkrieg to Desert Storm : The Evolution of Operational Warfare*. Lawrence, Kan., University Press Of Kansas, 2004.

"Department of the Army Historical Summary: FY 1988." *Chapter 3: Training – DAHSUM FY 1988 (Army.mil)*, 1988, history.army.mil/books/DAHSUM/1988/ch03.htm#:~:text=Begun%20in%201975%20and%20now%20in%20its%20fourth,different%20tasks%20and%20standards%20for%20each%20unit%20echelon.

Flanagan, E.M. *Lightning*. Simon & Schuster Books for Young Readers, 1994.

Gifford, Robert. "Stress and Stressors of the Early Phases of the Persian Gulf War." *PMC PubMed Central*, National Library of Medicine, 26 Apr. 2006.

Houlahan, Thomas. *Gulf War : The Complete History*. New London, Schrenker Military Publishing, 1999.

Jones, Robert E. *The History of the 101st Airborne Division Screaming Eagles*. Turner Publishing Company, 2005.

McManus, John C. *Grunts*. Penguin, 3 Aug. 2010.

Moore, Hal, LTC. "After Action Report, IA DRANG Valley Operation 1st Battalion, 7th Cavalry 14-16 November 1965." *Colonel Hieu and LTC Hal Moore Re: LZ X-Ray after Action Report (M) (Archive.org)*, 1965.

Navy CyberSpace. "U.S. Military Pay Raise History (1794 to Present Day)." *Www.navycs.com*, www.navycs.com/charts/.

Priest, Dana. "Chemical Alarms Rang, but Desert Location Is Lost." *Washington Post*, 14 Nov. 1996.

Rostker, Bernard D. "The Evolution of the All-Volunteer Force": *Rand.org*, RAND Corporation, 2019, www.rand.org/pubs/research_briefs/RB9195.html.

Scales, Robert H. *CERTAIN VICTORY: The Us Army in the Gulf.* U.S. Army General Command and General Staff College Press, 1994.

Steele, Dennis. "155 Miles into Iraq: The 101st Strikes Deep." *Army*, Aug. 1991.

United States. Army. *U. S. Army Tactics Field Manual*. Lyons Press, 2013.